The works of Robert G. Ingersoll

Robert Green Ingersoll, Clinton P Farrell

Nabu Public Domain Reprints:

You are holding a reproduction of an original work published before 1923 that is in the public domain in the United States of America, and possibly other countries. You may freely copy and distribute this work as no entity (individual or corporate) has a copyright on the body of the work. This book may contain prior copyright references, and library stamps (as most of these works were scanned from library copies). These have been scanned and retained as part of the historical artifact.

This book may have occasional imperfections such as missing or blurred pages, poor pictures, errant marks, etc. that were either part of the original artifact, or were introduced by the scanning process. We believe this work is culturally important, and despite the imperfections, have elected to bring it back into print as part of our continuing commitment to the preservation of printed works worldwide. We appreciate your understanding of the imperfections in the preservation process, and hope you enjoy this valuable book.

THE WORKS

OF

ROBERT G. INGERSOLL.

New Dresden Edition.

There can be but little liberty on earth while men worship a tyrant in heaven.

IN TWELVE VOLUMES.

VOLUME FIVE.

DISCUSSIONS.

C. P. FARRELL.

THE INGERSOLL PUBLISHERS, Inc.
NEW YORK CITY.

COPYRIGHTED,
1900,
C. P. FARRELL.

CONTENTS OF VOLUME V.

SIX INTERVIEWS ON TALMAGE.
(1882)

Preface—First Interview: Great Men as Witnesses to the Truth of the Gospel—No man should quote the Words of Another unless he is willing to Accept all the Opinions of that Man—Reasons of more Weight than Reputations—Would a general Acceptance of Unbelief fill the Penitentiaries?—My Creed—Most Criminals Orthodox—Religion and Morality not Necessarily Associates—On the Creation of the Universe out of Omnipotence—Mr. Talmage's Theory about the Production of Light prior to the Creation of the Sun—The Deluge and the Ark—Mr. Talmage's tendency to Belittle the Bible Miracles—His Chemical, Geological, and Agricultural Views—His Disregard of Good Manners—Second Interview: An Insulting Text—God's Design in Creating Guiteau to be the Assassin of Garfield—Mr. Talmage brings the Charge of Blasphemy—Some Real Blasphemers—The Tabernacle Pastor tells the exact Opposite of the Truth about Col. Ingersoll's Attitude toward the Circulation of Immoral Books—"Assassinating" God—Mr. Talmage finds Nearly All the Invention of Modern Times Mentioned in the Bible—The Reverend Gentleman corrects the Translators of the Bible in the Matter of the Rib Story—Denies that Polygamy is permitted by the Old Testament—His Defence of Queen Victoria and Violation of the Grave of George Eliot—Exhibits a Christian Spirit—Third Interview: Mr. Talmage's Partiality in the Bestowal of his Love—Denies the Right of Laymen to Examine the Scriptures—Thinks the Infidels Victims of Bibliophobia—He explains the Stopping of the Sun and Moon at the Command of Joshua—Instances a Dark Day in the Early Part of the Century—Charges that Holy Things are Made Light of—Reaffirms his Confidence in the Whale and Jonah Story—The Commandment which Forbids the making of Graven Images—Affirmation that the Bible is the Friend of Woman—The Present Condition of Woman—Fourth Interview: Colonel Ingersoll Compared by Mr. Talmage to Jehoiakim, who Consigned Writings of Jeremiah to the Flames—An Intimation that Infidels wish to have all copies of the Bible Destroyed by Fire—Laughter Deprecated—Col. Ingersoll Accused of Denouncing his Father—Mr. Talmage holds that a Man may be Perfectly Happy in Heaven with His Mother in Hell—Challenges the Infidel to Read a Chapter from St. John—On the "Chief Solace of the World"—Discovers an Attempt is being made to Put Out the Light-houses of the Farther Shore—Affirms our Debt to Christianity for Schools, Hospitals, etc.—Denies that Infidels have ever Done any Good—Fifth

CONTENTS.

Interview: Inquiries if Men gather Grapes of Thorns, or Figs of Thistles, and is Answered in the Negative—Resents the Charge that the Bible is a Cruel Book—Demands to Know where the Cruelty of the Bible Crops out in the Lives of Christians—Col. Ingersoll Accused of saying that the Bible is a Collection of Polluted Writings—Mr. Talmage Asserts the Orchestral Harmony of the Scriptures from Genesis to Revelation, and Repudiates the Theory of Contradictions—His View of Mankind Indicated in Quotations from his Confession of Faith—He Insists that the Bible is Scientific—Traces the New Testament to its Source with St. John—Pledges his Word that no Man ever Died for a Lie Cheerfully and Triumphantly—As to Prophecies and Predictions—Alleged "Prophetic" Fate of the Jewish People—Sixth Interview: Dr. Talmage takes the Ground that the Unrivalled Circulation of the Bible Proves that it is Inspired—Forgets that a Scientific Fact does not depend on the Vote of Numbers—Names some Christian Millions—His Arguments Characterized as the Poorest, Weakest, and Best Possible in Support of the Doctrine of Inspiration—Will God, in Judging a Man, take into Consideration the Circumstances of that Man's Life?—Satisfactory Reasons for Not Believing that the Bible is inspired, ... 7–359

THE TALMAGIAN CATECHISM.

The Pith and Marrow of what Mr. Talmage has been Pleased to Say, set forth in the form of a Shorter Catechism, . . 363–443

A VINDICATION OF THOMAS PAINE.
(1877)

Letter to the New York *Observer*—An Offer to Pay One Thousand Dollars in Gold for Proof that Thomas Paine or Voltaire Died in Terror because of any Religious Opinions Either had Expressed—Proposition to Create a Tribunal to Hear the Evidence—The *Observer*, after having Called upon Col. Ingersoll to Deposit the Money, and Characterized his Talk as " Infidel 'Buncombe,' " Denies its Own Words, but attempts to Prove them—Its Memory Refreshed by Col. Ingersoll and the Slander Refuted—Proof that Paine did Not Recant—Testimony of Thomas Nixon, Daniel Pelton, Mr. Jarvis, B. F. Haskin, Dr Manley, Amasa Woodsworth, Gilbert Vale, Philip Graves, M. D, Willet Hicks, A. C. Hankinson, John Hogeboom, W. J. Hilton, James Cheetham, Revs. Milledollar and Cunningham, Mrs. Hedden, Andrew A. Dean, William Carver,—The Statements of Mary Roscoe and Mary Hindsdale Examined—William Cobbett's Account of a Call upon Mary Hinsdale—Did Thomas Paine live the Life of a Drunken Beast, and did he Die a Drunken, Cowardly, and Beastly Death?—Grant Thorburn's Charges Examined—Statement of the Rev. J. D. Wickham, D.D., shown to be Utterly False—False Witness of the Rev. Charles Hawley, D.D.—W. H. Ladd, James Cheetham, and Mary Hinsdale—Paine's Note to Cheetham—Mr. Staple, Mr. Purdy, Col. John Fellows, James Wilburn, Walter Morton, Clio Rickman, Judge Herttell, H. Margary, Elihu Palmer, Mr.

PREFACE.

SEVERAL people, having read the sermons of Mr. Talmage in which he reviews some of my lectures, have advised me not to pay the slightest attention to the Brooklyn divine. They think that no new arguments have been brought forward, and they have even gone so far as to say that some of the best of the old ones have been left out.

After thinking the matter over, I became satisfied that my friends were mistaken, that they had been carried away by the general current of modern thought, and were not in a frame of mind to feel the force of the arguments of Mr. Talmage, or to clearly see the candor that characterizes his utterances.

At the first reading, the logic of these sermons does not impress you. The style is of a character calculated to throw the searcher after facts and arguments off his guard. The imagination of the preacher is so lurid; he is so free from the ordinary forms of expression; his statements are so much stranger than truth, and his conclusions so utterly independent of his premises, that the reader is too astonished to be convinced. Not until I had read with great care the six discourses delivered for my benefit had I any clear and well-defined idea of the logical force of Mr. Talmage. I had but little conception of his candor, was almost totally ignorant of his power to render the simple complex and the plain obscure by the mutilation of metaphor and the incoherence of inspired declamation. Neither did I know the generous accuracy with which he states the position of an opponent, and the fairness he exhibits in a religious discussion.

He has without doubt studied the Bible as closely and critically as he has the works of Buckle and Darwin, and he seems to have paid as much attention to scientific subjects as most theologians. His theory of light and his views upon geology are strikingly original, and his astronomical theories are certainly as profound as practical. If his statements can be relied upon, he has successfully refuted the teachings of

Humboldt and Haeckel, and exploded the blunders of Spencer and Tyndall. Besides all this, he has the courage of his convictions—he does not quail before a fact, and he does not strike his colors even to a demonstration. He cares nothing for human experience. He cannot be put down with statistics, nor driven from his position by the certainties of science. He cares neither for the persistence of force, nor the indestructibility of matter.

He believes in the Bible, and he has the bravery to defend his belief. In this, he proudly stands almost alone. He knows that the salvation of the world depends upon a belief in his creed. He knows that what are called "the sciences" are of no importance in the other world. He clearly sees that it is better to live and die ignorant here, if you can wear a crown of glory hereafter. He knows it is useless to be perfectly familiar with all the sciences in this world, and then in the next "lift up your eyes, " being in torment." He knows, too, that God will not punish any man for denying a fact in science. A man can deny the rotundity of the earth, the attraction of gravitation, the form of the earth's orbit, or the nebular hypothesis, with perfect impunity. He is not bound to be correct upon any philosophical subject. He is at liberty to deny and ridicule the rule of three, conic sections, and even the multiplication table. God permits every human being to be mistaken upon every subject but one. No man can lose his soul by denying physical facts. Jehovah does not take the slightest pride in his geology, or in his astronomy, or in mathematics, or in any school of philosophy—he is jealous only of his reputation as the author of the Bible. You may deny everything else in the universe except that book. This being so, Mr. Talmage takes the safe side, and insists that the Bible is inspired. He knows that at the day of judgment, not a scientific question will be asked. He knows that the Hæckels and Huxleys will, on that terrible day, regret that they ever learned to read. He knows that there is no "saving "grace" in any department of human knowledge; that mathematics and all the exact sciences and all the philosophies will be worse than useless. He knows that inventors, discoverers, thinkers and investigators, have no claim upon the mercy of Jehovah; that the educated will envy the ignorant, and that the writers and thinkers will curse their books.

He knows that man cannot be saved through what he knows—but only by means of what he believes. Theology is not a science. If it were, God would forgive his children for being mistaken about it. If it could be proved like geology, or astronomy, there would be no merit in believing it. From a belief in the Bible, Mr. Talmage is not to be driven by uninspired evidence. He knows that his logic is liable to lead him astray, and that his reason cannot be depended upon. He believes that scientific men are no authority in matters concerning which nothing can be known, and he does not wish to put his soul in peril, by examining by the light of reason, the evidences of the supernatural.

He is perfectly consistent with his creed. What happens to us here is of no consequence compared with eternal joy or pain. The ambitions, honors, glories and triumphs of this world, compared with eternal things, are less than naught.

Better a cross here and a crown there, than a feast here and a fire there.

Lazarus was far more fortunate than Dives. The purple and fine linen of this short life are as nothing compared with the robes of the redeemed.

Mr. Talmage knows that philosophy is unsafe—that the sciences are sirens luring souls to eternal wreck. He knows that the deluded searchers after facts are planting thorns in their own pillows—that the geologists are digging pits for themselves, and that the astronomers are robbing their souls of the heaven they explore. He knows that thought, capacity, and intellectual courage are dangerous, and this belief gives him a feeling of personal security.

The Bible is adapted to the world as it is. Most people are ignorant, and but few have the capacity to comprehend philosophical and scientific subjects, and if salvation depended upon understanding even one of the sciences, nearly everybody would be lost. Mr. Talmage sees that it was exceedingly merciful in God to base salvation on belief instead of on brain. Millions can believe, while only a few can understand. Even the effort to understand is a kind of treason born of pride and ingratitude. This being so, it is far safer, far better, to be credulous than critical. You are offered an infinite reward for believing the Bible. If you examine it you may find it impossible for you to believe it. Consequently, examination is dangerous. Mr. Talmage knows that it is not necessary to understand the Bible in order to believe it. You must believe it first. Then, if on reading it you find anything that appears false, absurd, or impossible, you may be sure that it is only an appearance, and that the real fault is in yourself. It is certain that persons wholly incapable of reasoning are absolutely safe, and that to be born brainless is to be saved in advance.

Mr. Talmage takes the ground,—and certainly from his point of view nothing can be more reasonable—that thought should be avoided, after one has "experienced religion" and has been the subject of "regeneration." Every sinner should listen to sermons, read religious books, and keep thinking, until he becomes a Christian. Then he should stop. After that, thinking is not the road to heaven. The real point and the real difficulty is to stop thinking just at the right time. Young Christians, who have no idea of what they are doing, often go on thinking after joining the church, and in this way heresy is born, and heresy is often the father of infidelity. If Christians would follow the advice and example of Mr. Talmage all disagreements about doctrine would be avoided. In this way the church could secure absolute intellectual peace and all the disputes, heartburnings, jealousies and hatreds born of thought, discussion and reasoning, would be impossible.

In the estimation of Mr. Talmage, the man who doubts and examines is not fit for the society of angels. There are no disputes, no discussions in heaven. The angels do not think; they believe, they enjoy. The highest form of religion is repression. We should conquer the passions and destroy desire. We should control the mind and stop thinking. In this way we " offer ourselves a "living sacrifice, holy, acceptable unto God." When desire dies, when thought ceases, we shall be pure. —This is heaven.

ROBERT G. INGERSOLL.

WASHINGTON, D. C.,
    April, 1882.

INGERSOLL'S INTERVIEWS
ON TALMAGE.

INGERSOLL'S INTERVIEWS.

FIRST INTERVIEW.

POLONIUS. *My lord, I will use them according to their desert.*
HAMLET. *God's bodikins, man, much better: use every man after his desert, and who should 'scape whipping? Use them after your own honor and dignity: the less they deserve, the more merit is in your bounty.*

Question. Have you read the sermon of Mr. Talmage, in which he exposes your misrepresentations?

Answer. I have read such reports as appeared in some of the New York papers.

Question. What do you think of what he has to say?

Answer. Some time ago I gave it as my opinion of Mr. Talmage that, while he was a man of most excellent judgment, he was somewhat deficient in imagination. I find that he has the disease that seems to afflict most theologians, and that is, a kind of intellectual toadyism, that uses the names of supposed great men instead of arguments. It is perfectly astonishing to the average preacher that any one should have the temerity to differ, on the subject of theology, with Andrew Jackson, Daniel Webster, and other gentlemen eminent for piety during their lives, but who, as a rule, expressed their theological opinions a few minutes before dissolution. These ministers are perfectly delighted to have some great politician, some judge, soldier, or president, certify to the truth of the Bible and to the moral character of Jesus Christ.

Mr. Talmage insists that if a witness is false in one particular, his entire testimony must be thrown away. Daniel Webster was in favor of the Fugitive Slave Law, and thought it the duty of the North to capture the poor slave-mother. He was willing to stand between a human being and his freedom. He was willing to assist in compelling persons to work without any pay except such marks of the lash as they might receive. Yet this man is brought forward as a witness for the truth of the gospel. If he was false in his testimony as to liberty, what is his affidavit worth as to the value of Christianity? Andrew Jackson was a brave man, a good general, a patriot second to none, an excellent judge of horses, and a brave duelist. I admit that in his old age he relied considerably upon the atonement. I think Jackson was really a very great man, and probably no President impressed himself more deeply upon the American people than the hero of New Orleans, but as a theologian he was, in my judgment, a most decided failure, and his opinion as to the authenticity of the Scriptures is of no earthly value. It was a subject upon which he knew probably as little as Mr. Talmage does about modern infidelity. Thousands of people will quote Jackson in favor of religion, about which he knew nothing, and yet have no confidence in his political opinions, although he devoted the best part of his life to politics.

No man should quote the words of another, in place of an argument, unless he is willing to accept all the opinions of that man. Lord Bacon denied the Copernican system of astronomy, and, according to Mr. Talmage, having made that mistake, his opinions upon other subjects are equally worthless. Mr. Wesley believed in ghosts, witches, and personal devils, yet upon many subjects I have no doubt his opinions were correct. The truth is, that nearly everybody is right about some things and wrong about most things; and if a man's testimony is not to be taken until he is right on every subject, witnesses will be extremely scarce.

Personally, I care nothing about names. It makes no difference to me what the supposed great men of the past have said, except as what they have said contains an argument; and that argument is worth to me the force it naturally has upon my mind. Christians forget that in the realm of reason there are no serfs and no monarchs. When you submit to an argument, you do not submit to the man who made it. Christianity demands a certain obedience, a certain blind, unreasoning faith, and parades before the eyes of the ignorant, with great pomp and pride, the names of kings, soldiers, and statesmen who have admitted the truth of the Bible. Mr. Talmage introduces as a witness the Rev. Theodore Parker. This same Theodore Parker denounced the Presbyterian creed as the most infamous of all creeds, and said that the worst heathen god, wearing a necklace of live snakes, was a representation of mercy when compared with the God of John Calvin. Now, if this witness is false in any particular, of course he cannot be believed, according to Mr. Talmage, upon any subject, and yet Mr. Talmage introduces him upon the stand as a good witness.

Although I care but little for names, still I will suggest that, in all probability, Humboldt knew more upon this subject than all the pastors in the world. I certainly would have as much confidence in the opinion of Goethe as in that of William H. Seward; and as between Seward and Lincoln, I should take Lincoln; and when you come to Presidents, for my part, if I were compelled to pin my faith on the sleeve of anybody, I should take Jefferson's coat in preference to Jackson's. I believe that Haeckel is, to say the least, the equal of any theologian we have in this country, and the late John W. Draper certainly knew as much upon these great questions as the average parson. I believe that Darwin has investigated some of these things, that Tyndall and Huxley have turned their minds somewhat in the same direction, that Helmholtz has a few opinions, and that, in fact, thousands of able, intelligent and honest men differ almost entirely with Webster and Jackson.

So far as I am concerned, I think more of reasons than of reputations, more of principles than of persons, more of nature than of names, more of facts, than of faiths.

It is the same with books as with persons. Probably there is not a book in the world entirely destitute of truth, and not one entirely exempt from error. The Bible is like other books. There are mistakes in it, side by side with truths,—passages inculcating murder, and others exalting mercy; laws devilish and tyrannical, and others filled with wisdom and justice. It is foolish to say that if you accept a part, you must accept the whole. You must accept that which commends itself to your heart and brain. There never was a doctrine that a witness, or a book, should be thrown entirely away, because false in one particular. If in any particular the book, or the man, tells the truth, to that extent the truth should be accepted.

Truth is made no worse by the one who tells it, and a lie gets no real benefit from the reputation of its author.

Question. What do you think of the statement that a general belief in your teachings would fill all the penitentiaries, and that in twenty years there would be a hell in this world worse than the one expected in the other?

Answer. My creed is this:

1. Happiness is the only good.
2. The way to be happy, is to make others happy.

Other things being equal, that man is happiest who is nearest just—who is truthful, merciful and intelligent—in other words, the one who lives in accordance with the conditions of life.

3. The time to be happy is now, and the place to be happy, is here.

4. Reason is the lamp of the mind—the only torch of progress; and instead of blowing that out and depending upon darkness and dogma, it is far better to increase that sacred light.

5. Every man should be the intellectual proprietor of himself, honest with himself, and intellectually hospitable; and upon every brain reason should be enthroned as king.

6. Every man must bear the consequences, at least of his own actions. If he puts his hands in the fire, *his* hands must smart, and not the hands of another. In other words: each man must eat the fruit of the tree he plants.

I can not conceive that the teaching of these doctrines would fill penitentiaries, or crowd the gallows. The doctrine of forgiveness—the idea that somebody else can suffer in place of the guilty—the notion that just at the last the whole account can be settled—these ideas, doctrines, and notions are calculated to fill penitentiaries. Nothing breeds extravagance like the credit system.

Most criminals of the present day are orthodox believers, and the gallows seems to be the last round of the ladder reaching from earth to heaven. The Rev. Dr. Sunderland, of this city, in his sermon on the assassination of Garfield, takes the ground that God permitted the murder for the purpose of opening the eyes of the people to the evil effects of infidelity. According to this minister, God, in order to show his hatred of infidelity, " inspired," or allowed, one Christian to assassinate another.

Religion and morality do not necessarily go together. Mr. Talmage will insist to-day that morality is not sufficient to save any man from eternal punishment. As a matter of fact, religion has often been the enemy of morality. The moralist has been denounced by the theologians. He sustains the same relation to Christianity that the moderate drinker does to the total-abstinence society. The total-abstinence people say that the example of the moderate drinker is far worse upon the young than that of the drunkard—that the drunkard is a warning, while the moderate drinker is a perpetual temptation. So Christians say of moralists. According to them, the moralist sets a worse example than the criminal. The moralist not only insists that a man can be a good citizen, a kind husband, an affectionate father, without religion, but demonstrates the truth of his doctrine by his own life; whereas the criminal admits that in and of himself he is nothing, and can do nothing, but that he needs assistance from the church and its ministers.

The worst criminals of the modern world have been Christians—I mean by that, believers in Christianity—and the most monstrous crimes of the modern world have been committed by the most zealous believers. There is nothing in orthodox religion, apart from the morality it teaches, to prevent the commission of crime. On the other hand, the perpetual proffer of forgiveness is a direct premium upon what Christians are pleased to call the commission of sin.

Christianity has produced no greater character than Epictetus, no greater sovereign than Marcus Aurelius. The wickedness of the past was a good deal like that of the present. As a rule, kings have been wicked in direct proportion to their power—their power having been lessened, their crimes have decreased. As a matter of fact, paganism, of itself, did not produce any great men; neither has Christianity. Millions of influences determine individual character, and the religion of the country in which a man happens to be born may determine many of his opinions, without influencing, to any great extent, his real character.

There have been brave, honest, and intelligent men in and out of every church.

Question. Mr. Talmage says that you insist that, according to the Bible, the universe was made out of nothing, and he denounces your statement as a gross misrepresentation. What have you stated upon that subject?

Answer. What I said was substantially this: "We "are told in the first chapter of Genesis, that in the "beginning God created the heaven and the earth. "If this means anything, it means that God pro- "duced—caused to exist, called into being—the "heaven and the earth. It will not do to say that "God formed the heaven and the earth of previously "existing matter. Moses conveys, and intended to "convey, the idea that the matter of which the "universe is composed was created."

This has always been my position. I did **not** suppose that *nothing* was used as the raw material; but if the Mosaic account means anything, it means that whereas there was *nothing*, God caused something to exist—created what we know as matter. I can not conceive of something being made, created, without anything to make anything with. I have no more confidence in fiat worlds than I have in fiat money. Mr. Talmage tells us that God did not make the universe out of *nothing*, but out of "omnipotence." Exactly how God changed "omnipotence" into matter is not stated. If there was *nothing* in the universe, *omnipotence* could do you no good. The weakest man in the world can lift as much *nothing* as God.

Mr. Talmage seems to think that to create something from *nothing* is simply a question of strength — that it requires infinite muscle — that it is only a question of biceps. Of course, omnipotence is an attribute, not an entity, not a raw material; and the idea that something can be made out of omnipotence — using that as the raw material — is infinitely absurd. It would have been equally logical to say that God made the universe out of his omniscience, or his omnipresence, or his unchangeableness, or out of his honesty, his holiness, or his incapacity to do evil. I confess my utter inability to understand, or even to suspect, what the reverend gentleman means, when he says that God created the universe out of his "omnipotence."

I admit that the Bible does not tell *when* God created

the universe. It is simply said that he did this " in the
" beginning." We are left, however, to infer that " the
" beginning " was Monday morning, and that on the
first Monday God created the matter in an exceedingly
chaotic state ; that on Tuesday he made a firmament
to divide the waters from the waters ; that on Wednesday he gathered the waters together in seas and
allowed the dry land to appear. We are also told that
on that day " the earth brought forth grass and herb
" yielding seed after his kind, and the tree yielding
" fruit, whose seed was in itself, after his kind." This
was before the creation of the sun, but Mr. Talmage
takes the ground that there are many other sources of
light ; that " there may have been volcanoes in active
" operation on other planets." I have my doubts,
however, about the light of volcanoes being sufficient
to produce or sustain vegetable life, and think it a
little doubtful about trees growing only by " volcanic
" glare." Neither do I think one could depend upon
" three thousand miles of liquid granite " for the production of grass and trees, nor upon " light that rocks
" might emit in the process of crystallization." I doubt
whether trees would succeed simply with the assistance
of the " Aurora Borealis or the Aurora Australis."
There are other sources of light, not mentioned by

Mr. Talmage—lightning-bugs, phosphorescent beetles, and fox-fire. I should think that it would be humiliating, in this age, for an orthodox preacher to insist that vegetation could exist upon this planet without the light of the sun — that trees could grow, blossom and bear fruit, having no light but the flames of volcanoes, or that emitted by liquid granite, or thrown off by the crystallization of rocks.

There is another thing, also, that should not be forgotten, and that is, that there is an even balance forever kept between the totals of animal and vegetable life — that certain forms of animal life go with certain forms of vegetable life. Mr. Haeckel has shown that " in the first epoch, algæ and skull-less vertebrates " were found together; in the second, ferns and fishes; " in the third, pines and reptiles; in the fourth, foliace- " ous forests and mammals." Vegetable and animal life sustain a necessary relation; they exist together; they act and interact, and each depends upon the other. The real point of difference between Mr. Talmage and myself is this: He says that God made the universe out of his "omnipotence," and I say that, although I *know* nothing whatever upon the subject, my opinion is, that the universe has existed from eternity — that it continually changes in form, but that it never was created or called into being by any power. I think that all that is, is all the God there is.

Question. Mr. Talmage charges you with having misrepresented the Bible story of the deluge. Has he correctly stated your position?

Answer. Mr. Talmage takes the ground that the flood was only partial, and was, after all, not much of a flood. The Bible tells us that God said he would " destroy all flesh wherein is the breath of life from " under heaven, and that everything that is in the " earth shall die;" that God also said: "I will destroy " man, whom I have created, from the face of the " earth; both man and beast and the creeping thing " and the fowls of the air, and every living substance " that I have made will I destroy from off the face of " the earth."

I did not suppose that there was any miracle in the Bible larger than the credulity of Mr. Talmage. The flood story, however, seems to be a little more than he can bear. He is like the witness who stated that he had read *Gulliver's Travels*, the *Stories of Munchausen*, and the *Flying Wife*, including *Robinson Crusoe*, and believed them all; but that Wirt's *Life of Patrick Henry* was a little more than he could stand.

It is strange that a man who believes that God created the universe out of "omnipotence" should believe that he had not enough omnipotence left to drown a world the size of this. Mr. Talmage seeks to make the story of the flood reasonable. The moment it is reasonable, it ceases to be miraculous. Certainly God cannot afford to reward a man with eternal joy for believing a reasonable story. Faith is only necessary when the story is unreasonable, and if the flood only gets small enough, I can believe it myself. I ask for evidence, and Mr. Talmage seeks to make the story so little that it can be believed without evidence. He tells us that it was a kind of "local option" flood—a little wet for that part of the country.

Why was it necessary to save the birds? They certainly could have gotten out of the way of a real small flood. Of the birds, Noah took fourteen of each species. He was commanded to take of the fowls of the air by sevens—seven of each sex—and, as there are at least 12,500 species, Noah collected an aviary of about 175,000 birds, provided the flood was general. If it was local, there are no means of determining the number. But why, if the flood was local, should he have taken any of the fowls of the air into his ark?

All they had to do was to fly away, or "roost high;" and it would have been just as easy for God to have implanted in them, for the moment, the instinct of getting out of the way as the instinct of hunting the ark. It would have been quite a saving of room and provisions, and would have materially lessened the labor and anxiety of Noah and his sons.

Besides, if it had been a partial flood, and great enough to cover the highest mountains in that country, the highest mountain being about seventeen thousand feet, the flood would have been covered with a sheet of ice several thousand feet in thickness. If a column of water could have been thrown seventeen thousand feet high and kept stationary, several thousand feet of the upper end would have frozen. If, however, the deluge was general, then the atmosphere would have been forced out the same on all sides, and the climate remained substantially normal.

Nothing can be more absurd than to attempt to explain the flood by calling it partial.

Mr. Talmage also says that the window ran clear round the ark, and that if I had only known as much Hebrew as a man could put on his little finger, I would have known that the window went clear round. To this I reply that, if his position is correct, then the original translators of King James' edition did not know as much Hebrew as they could have put on their little fingers; and yet I am obliged to believe their translation or be eternally damned. If the window went clear round, the inspired writer should have said so, and the learned translators should have given us the truth. No one pretends that there was more than one door, and yet the same language is used about the door, except this—that the exact size of the window is given, and the only peculiarity mentioned as to the door is that it shut from the outside. For any one to see that Mr. Talmage is wrong on the window question, it is only necessary to read the story of the deluge.

Mr. Talmage also endeavors to decrease the depth of the flood. If the flood did not cover the highest hills, many people might have been saved. He also insists that all the water did not come from the rains, but that "the fountains of the great deep were broken "up." What are "the fountains of the great deep"? How would their being "broken up" increase the depth of the water? He seems to imagine that these "fountains" were in some way imprisoned—anxious to get to the surface, and that, at that time, an opportunity was given for water to run up hill, or in some mysterious way to rise above its level. According to the account, the ark was at the mercy of the waves for at least seven months. If this flood was only partial, it seems a little curious that the water did not seek its level in less than seven months. With anything like a fair chance, by that time most of it would have found its way to the sea again.

There is in the literature of ignorance no more perfectly absurd and cruel story than that of the deluge.

I am very sorry that Mr. Talmage should disagree with some of the great commentators. Dr. Scott tells us that, in all probability, the angels assisted in getting the animals into the ark. Dr. Henry insists that the waters in the bowels of the earth, at God's command, sprung up and flooded the earth. Dr. Clark tells us that it would have been much easier for God to have destroyed all the people and made some new ones, but that he did not want to waste anything. Dr. Henry also tells us that the lions, while in the ark, ate straw like oxen. Nothing could be more amusing than to see a few lions eating good, dry straw. This commentator assures us that the waters rose so high that the loftiest mountains were overflowed fifteen cubits, so that salvation was not hoped for from any hills or mountains. He tells us that some of the people got on top of the ark, and hoped to shift for themselves, but that, in all probability, they were washed off by the rain. When we consider that the rain must have fallen at the rate of about eight hundred feet a day, I am inclined to think that they were washed off.

Mr. Talmage has clearly misrepresented the Bible. He is not prepared to believe the story as it is told. The seeds of infidelity seem to be germinating in his mind. His position no doubt will be a great relief to most of his hearers. After this, their credulity will not be strained. They can say that there was probably quite a storm, some rain, to an extent that rendered it necessary for Noah and his family—his dogs, cats, and chickens—to get in a boat. This would not be unreasonable. The same thing happens almost every year on the shores of great rivers, and consequently the story of the flood is an exceedingly reasonable one.

Mr. Talmage also endeavors to account for the miraculous collection of the animals in the ark by the universal instinct to get out of the rain. There are at least two objections to this: 1. The animals went into the ark before the rain commenced; 2. I have never noticed any great desire on the part of ducks, geese, and loons to get out of the water. Mr. Talmage must have been misled by a line from an old nursery book that says: "And the little fishes got "under the bridge to keep out of the rain." He tells us that Noah described what he saw. He is the first theologian who claims that Genesis was written by Noah, or that Noah wrote any account of the flood. Most Christians insist that the account of the flood was written by Moses, and that he was inspired to write it. Of course, it will not do for me to say that Mr. Talmage has misrepresented the facts.

Question. You are also charged with misrepresentation in your statement as to where the ark at last rested. It is claimed by Mr. Talmage that there is nothing in the Bible to show that the ark rested on the highest mountains.

Answer. Of course I have no knowledge as to where the ark really came to anchor, but after it struck bottom, we are told that a dove was sent out, and that the dove found no place whereon to rest her foot. If the ark touched ground in the low country, surely the mountains were out of water, and an ordinary mountain furnishes, as a rule, space enough for a dove's foot. We must infer that the ark rested on the only land then above water, or near enough above water to strike the keel of Noah's boat. Mount Ararat is about seventeen thousand feet high; so I take it that the top of that mountain was where Noah ran aground—otherwise, the account means nothing.

Here Mr. Talmage again shows his tendency to belittle the miracles of the Bible. I am astonished that he should doubt the power of God to keep an ark on a mountain seventeen thousand feet high. He could have changed the climate for that occasion. He could have made all the rocks and glaciers produce wheat and corn in abundance. Certainly God, who could overwhelm a world with a flood, had the power to change every law and fact in nature.

I am surprised that Mr. Talmage is not willing to believe the story as it is told. What right has he to question the statements of an inspired writer? Why should he set up his judgment against the Websters and Jacksons? Is it not infinitely impudent in him to contrast his penny-dip with the sun of inspiration? What right has he to any opinion upon the subject? He must take the Bible as it reads. He should remember that the greater the miracle the greater should be his faith.

Question. You do not seem to have any great opinion of the chemical, geological, and agricultural views expressed by Mr. Talmage?

Answer. You must remember that Mr. Talmage has a certain thing to defend. He takes the Bible as actually true, and with the Bible as his standard, he compares and measures all sciences. He does not study geology to find whether the Mosaic account is true, but he reads the Mosaic account for the purpose of showing that geology can not be depended upon. His idea that "one day is as a thousand years with "God," and that therefore the "days" mentioned in the Mosaic account are not days of twenty-four hours, but long periods, is contradicted by the Bible itself. The great reason given for keeping the Sabbath day is, that "God rested on the seventh day and was refreshed." Now, it does not say that he rested on the "seventh "period," or the "seventh good-while," or the "seventh long-time," but on the "seventh day." In imitation of this example we are also to rest—not on the seventh good-while, but on the seventh day. Nothing delights the average minister more than to find that a passage of Scripture is capable of several interpretations. Nothing in the inspired book is so dangerous as accuracy. If the holy writer uses general terms, an ingenious theologian can harmonize a seemingly preposterous statement with the most obdurate fact. An "inspired" book should contain neither statistics nor dates—as few names as possible, and not one word about geology or astronomy. Mr. Talmage is doing the best he can to uphold the fables of the Jews. They are the foundation of his faith. He believes in the water of the past and the fire of the future—in the God of flood and flame—the eternal torturer of his helpless children.

It is exceedingly unfortunate that Mr. Talmage does not appreciate the importance of good manners, that he does not rightly estimate the convincing power of kindness and good nature. It is unfortunate that a Christian, believing in universal forgiveness, should exhibit so much of the spirit of detraction, that he should run so easily and naturally into epithets, and that he should mistake vituperation for logic. Thousands of people, knowing but little of the mysteries of Christianity—never having studied theology,—may become prejudiced against the church, and doubt the divine origin of a religion whose defenders seem to rely, at least to a great degree, upon malignant personalities. Mr. Talmage should remember that in a discussion of this kind, he is supposed to represent a being of infinite wisdom and goodness. Surely, the representative of the infinite can afford to be candid, can afford to be kind. When he contemplates the condition of a fellow-being destitute of religion, a fellow-being now travelling the thorny path to eternal fire, he should be filled with pity instead of hate. Instead of deforming his mouth with scorn, his eyes should be filled with tears. He should take into consideration the vast difference between an infidel and a minister of the gospel,—knowing, as he does, that a crown of glory has been prepared for the minister, and that flames are waiting for the soul of the unbeliever. He should bear with philosophic fortitude the apparent success of the skeptic, for a few days in this brief life, since he knows that in a little while the question will be eternally settled in his favor, and that the humiliation of a day is as nothing compared with the victory of eternity. In this world, the skeptic appears to have the best of the argument; logic seems to be on the side of blasphemy; common sense apparently goes hand in hand with infidelity, and the few things we are absolutely certain of, seem inconsistent with the Christian creeds.

This, however, as Mr. Talmage well knows, is but apparent. God has arranged the world in this way for the purpose of testing the Christian's faith. Beyond all these facts, beyond logic, beyond reason, Mr. Talmage, by the light of faith, clearly sees the eternal truth. This clearness of vision should give him the serenity of candor and the kindness born of absolute knowledge. He, being a child of the light, should not expect the perfect from the children of darkness. He should not judge Humboldt and Wesley by the same standard. He should remember that Wesley was especially set apart and illuminated by divine wisdom, while Humboldt was left to grope in the shadows of nature. He should also remember that ministers are not like other people. They have been "called." They have been "chosen" by infinite wisdom. They have been "set apart," and they have bread to eat that we know not of. While other people are forced to pursue the difficult paths of investigation, they fly with the wings of faith.

Mr. Talmage is perfectly aware of the advantages he enjoys, and yet he deems it dangerous to be fair. This, in my judgment, is his mistake. If he cannot easily point out the absurdities and contradictions in infidel lectures, surely God would never have selected him for that task. We cannot believe that imperfect instruments would be chosen by infinite wisdom. Certain lambs have been entrusted to the care of Mr. Talmage, the shepherd. Certainly God would not select a shepherd unable to cope with an average wolf. Such a shepherd is only the appearance of protection. When the wolf is not there, he is a useless expense, and when the wolf comes, he goes. I cannot believe that God would select a shepherd of that kind. Neither can the shepherd justify his selection by abusing the wolf when out of sight. The fear ought to be on the other side. A divinely appointed shepherd ought to be able to convince his sheep that a wolf is a dangerous animal, and ought to be able to give his reasons. It may be that the shepherd has a certain interest in exaggerating the cruelty and ferocity of the wolf, and even the number of the wolves. Should it turn out that the wolves exist only in the imagination of the shepherd, the sheep might refuse to pay the salary of their protector. It will, however, be hard to calculate the extent to which the sheep will lose confidence in a shepherd who has not even the courage to state the facts about the wolf. But what must be the result when the sheep find that the supposed wolf is, in fact, their friend, and that he is endeavoring to rescue them from the exactions of the pretended shepherd, who creates, by falsehood, the fear on which he lives?

SECOND INTERVIEW.

SECOND INTERVIEW.

Por. *Why, man, what's the matter? Don't tear your hair.*
Sir Hugh. *I have been beaten in a discussion, overwhelmed and humiliated.*
Por. *Why didn't you call your adversary a fool?*
Sir Hugh. *My God! I forgot it!*

QUESTION. I want to ask you a few questions about the second sermon of Mr. Talmage; have you read it, and what do you think of it?

Answer. The text taken by the reverend gentleman is an insult, and was probably intended as such: "The fool hath said in his heart, there is no God." Mr. Talmage seeks to apply this text to any one who denies that the Jehovah of the Jews was and is the infinite and eternal Creator of all. He is perfectly satisfied that any man who differs with him on this question is a "fool," and he has the Christian forbearance and kindness to say so. I presume he is honest in this opinion, and no doubt regards Bruno, Spinoza and Humboldt as driveling imbeciles. He entertains the same opinion of some of the greatest, wisest and best of Greece and Rome.

No man is fitted to reason upon this question who has not the intelligence to see the difficulties in all theories. No man has yet evolved a theory that satisfactorily accounts for all that is. No matter what his opinion may be, he is beset by a thousand difficulties, and innumerable things insist upon an explanation. The best that any man can do is to take that theory which to his mind presents the fewest difficulties. Mr. Talmage has been educated in a certain way—has a brain of a certain quantity, quality and form—and accepts, in spite it may be, of himself, a certain theory. Others, formed differently, having lived under different circumstances, cannot accept the Talmagian view, and thereupon he denounces them as fools. In this he follows the example of David the murderer; of David, who advised one of his children to assassinate another; of David, whose last words were those of hate and crime. Mr. Talmage insists that it takes no especial brain to reason out a "design" in Nature, and in a moment afterward says that "when the world slew

"Jesus, it showed what it would do with the eternal
"God, if once it could get its hands on Him." Why
should a God of infinite wisdom create people who
would gladly murder their Creator? Was there any
particular "design" in that? Does the existence
of such people conclusively prove the existence of a
good Designer? It seems to me—and I take it that
my thought is natural, as I have only been born
once—that an infinitely wise and good God would
naturally create good people, and if he has not, certainly the fault is his. The God of Mr. Talmage
knew, when he created Guiteau, that he would
assassinate Garfield. Why did he create him? Did
he want Garfield assassinated? Will somebody be
kind enough to show the "design" in this transaction? Is it possible to see "design" in earthquakes, in volcanoes, in pestilence, in famine, in
ruthless and relentless war? Can we find "design" in
the fact that every animal lives upon some other—
that every drop of every sea is a battlefield where
the strong devour the weak? Over the precipice
of cruelty rolls a perpetual Niagara of blood. Is
there "design" in this? Why should a good God
people a world with men capable of burning their
fellow-men—and capable of burning the greatest and

best? Why does a good God permit these things? It is said of Christ that he was infinitely kind and generous, infinitely merciful, because when on earth he cured the sick, the lame and blind. Has he not as much power now as he had then? If he was and is the God of all worlds, why does he not now give back to the widow her son? Why does he withhold light from the eyes of the blind? And why does one who had the power miraculously to feed thousands, allow millions to die for want of food? Did Christ only have pity when he was part human? Are we indebted for his kindness to the flesh that clothed his spirit? Where is he now? Where has he been through all the centuries of slavery and crime? If this universe was "designed," then all that happens was "designed." If a man constructs an engine, the boiler of which explodes, we say either that he did not know the strength of his materials, or that he was reckless of human life. If an infinite being should construct a weak or imperfect machine, he must be held accountable for all that happens. He cannot be permitted to say that he did not know the strength of the materials. He is directly and absolutely responsible. So, if this world was designed by a being of infinite power and wisdom, he is responsible for the result of that design. My position is this : **I do not know.** But there are so many objections to the personal-God theory, that it is impossible for me to accept it. I prefer to say that the universe is all the God there is. I prefer to make no being responsible. I prefer to say : If the naked are clothed, man must clothe them ; if the hungry are fed, man must feed them. I prefer to rely upon human endeavor, upon human intelligence, upon the heart and brain of man. There is no evidence that God has ever interfered in the affairs of man. The hand of earth is stretched uselessly toward heaven. From the clouds there comes no help. In vain the shipwrecked cry to God. In vain the imprisoned ask for liberty and light—the world moves on, and the heavens are deaf and dumb and blind. The frost freezes, the fire burns, slander smites, the wrong triumphs, the good suffer, and prayer dies upon the lips of faith.

Question. Mr. Talmage charges you with being "the champion blasphemer of America"—what do you understand blasphemy to be ?

Answer. Blasphemy is an epithet bestowed by superstition upon common sense. Whoever investigates a religion as he would any department of science, is called a blasphemer. Whoever contradicts a priest, whoever has the impudence to use his own reason, whoever is brave enough to express his honest thought, is a blasphemer in the eyes of the religionist. When a missionary speaks slightingly of the wooden god of a savage, the savage regards him as a blasphemer. To laugh at the pretensions of Mohammed in Constantinople is blasphemy. To say in St. Petersburg that Mohammed was a prophet of God is also blasphemy. There was a time when to acknowledge the divinity of Christ in Jerusalem was blasphemy. To deny his divinity is now blasphemy in New York. Blasphemy is to a considerable extent a geographical question. It depends not only on what you say, but where you are when you say it. Blasphemy is what the old calls the new,—what last year's leaf says to this year's bud. The founder of every religion was a blasphemer. The Jews so regarded Christ, and the Athenians had the same opinion of Socrates. Catholics have always looked upon Protestants as blasphemers, and Protestants have always held the same generous opinion of Catholics. To deny that Mary is the Mother of God is blasphemy. To say that she is the Mother of God is blasphemy. Some savages think that a dried snake skin stuffed with leaves is sacred, and he who thinks otherwise is a blasphemer. It was once blasphemy to laugh at Diana, of the Ephesians. Many people think that it is blasphemous to tell your real opinion of the Jewish Jehovah. Others imagine that words can be printed upon paper, and the paper bound into a book covered with sheepskin, and that the book is sacred, and that to question its sacredness is blasphemy. Blasphemy is also a crime against God, but nothing can be more absurd than a crime against God. If God is infinite, you cannot injure him. You cannot commit a crime against any being that you cannot injure. Of course, the infinite cannot be injured. Man is a conditioned being. By changing his conditions, his surroundings, you can injure him; but if God is infinite, he is conditionless. If he is conditionless, he cannot by any possibility be injured. You can neither increase, nor decrease, the well-being of the infinite. Consequently, a crime against God is a demonstrated impossibility. The cry of blasphemy means only that the argument of the blasphemer cannot be answered. The sleight-of-hand performer, when some one tries to raise the curtain behind which he operates, cries "blasphemer!" The priest, finding that he has been attacked by common sense,—

by a fact,—resorts to the same cry. Blasphemy is the black flag of theology, and it means: No argument and no quarter! It is an appeal to prejudice, to passions, to ignorance. It is the last resort of a defeated priest. Blasphemy marks the point where argument stops and slander begins. In old times, it was the signal for throwing stones, for gathering fagots and for tearing flesh; now it means falsehood and calumny.

Question. Then you think that there is no such thing as the crime of blasphemy, and that no such offence can be committed?

Answer. Any one who knowingly speaks in favor of injustice is a blasphemer. Whoever wishes to destroy liberty of thought,—the honest expression of ideas,—is a blasphemer. Whoever is willing to malign his neighbor, simply because he differs with him upon a subject about which neither of them knows anything for certain, is a blasphemer. If a crime can be committed against God, he commits it who imputes to God the commission of crime. The man who says that God ordered the assassination of women and babes, that he gave maidens to satisfy the lust of soldiers, that he enslaved his own children,—that man is a blasphemer. In my judgment, it would be far better to deny the existence of God entirely. It seems to me that every man ought to give his honest opinion. No man should suppose that any infinite God requires him to tell as truth that which he knows nothing about.

Mr. Talmage, in order to make a point against infidelity, states from his pulpit that I am in favor of poisoning the minds of children by the circulation of immoral books. The statement is entirely false. He ought to have known that I withdrew from the Liberal League upon the very question whether the law should be repealed or modified. I favored a modification of that law, so that books and papers could not be thrown from the mails simply because they were "infidel."

I was and am in favor of the destruction of every immoral book in the world. I was and am in favor, not only of the law against the circulation of such filth, but want it executed to the letter in every State of this Union. Long before he made that statement, I had introduced a resolution to that effect, and supported the resolution in a speech. Notwithstanding these facts, hundreds of clergymen have made haste to tell the exact opposite of the truth. This they have done in the name of Christianity, under the pretence of pleasing their God. In my judgment, it is far better to tell your honest opinions, even upon the subject of theology, than to knowingly tell a falsehood about a fellow-man. Mr. Talmage may have been ignorant of the truth. He may have been misled by other ministers, and for his benefit I make this explanation. I wanted the laws modified so that bigotry could not interfere with the literature of intelligence; but I did not want, in any way, to shield the writers or publishers of immoral books. Upon this subject I used, at the last meeting of the Liberal League that I attended, the following language:

"But there is a distinction wide as the Mississippi, "yes, wider than the Atlantic, wider than all oceans, "between the literature of immorality and the litera- "ture of free thought. One is a crawling, slimy lizard, "and the other an angel with wings of light. Let us "draw this distinction. Let us understand ourselves. "Do not make the wholesale statement that all these "laws ought to be repealed. They ought not to be "repealed. Some of them are good, and the law "against sending instruments of vice through the "mails is good. The law against sending obscene "pictures and books is good. The law against send-

"ing bogus diplomas through the mails, to allow a
"lot of ignorant hyenas to prey upon the sick people
"of the world, is a good law. The law against rascals
"who are getting up bogus lotteries, and sending their
"circulars in the mails is a good law. You know, as
"well as I, that there are certain books not fit to go
"through the mails. You know that. You know there
"are certain pictures not fit to be transmitted, not fit
"to be delivered to any human being. When these
"books and pictures come into the control of the
"United States, I say, burn them up! And when any
"man has been indicted who has been trying to make
"money by pandering to the lowest passions in the
"human breast, then I say, prosecute him! let the
"law take its course."

I can hardly convince myself that when Mr. Talmage made the charge, he was acquainted with the facts. It seems incredible that any man, pretending to be governed by the law of common honesty, could make a charge like this knowing it to be untrue. Under no circumstances, would I charge Mr. Talmage with being an infamous man, unless the evidence was complete and overwhelming. Even then, I should hesitate long before making the charge. The side I take on theological questions does not render a resort to slander or calumny a necessity. If Mr. Talmage is an honorable man, he will take back the statement he has made. Even if there is a God, I hardly think that he will reward one of his children for maligning another; and to one who has told falsehoods about " infidels," that having been his only virtue, I doubt whether he will say : " Well done good and faithful " servant."

Question. What have you to say to the charge that you are endeavoring to "assassinate God," and that you are " far worse than the man who at- " tempts to kill his father, or his mother, or his sister, " or his brother"?

Answer. Well, I think that is about as reasonable as anything he says. No one wishes, so far as I know, to assassinate God. The idea of assassinating an infinite being is of course infinitely absurd. One would think Mr. Talmage had lost his reason! And yet this man stands at the head of the Presbyterian clergy. It is for this reason that I answer him. He is the only Presbyterian minister in the United States, so far as I know, able to draw an audience. He is, without doubt, the leader of that denomination.

He is orthodox and conservative. He believes implicitly in the "Five Points" of Calvin, and says nothing simply for the purpose of attracting attention. He believes that God damns a man for his own glory; that he sends babes to hell to establish his mercy, and that he filled the world with disease and crime simply to demonstrate his wisdom. He believes that billions of years before the earth was, God had made up his mind as to the exact number that he would eternally damn, and had counted his saints. This doctrine he calls "glad tidings of great joy." He really believes that every man who is true to himself is waging war against God; that every infidel is a rebel; that every Freethinker is a traitor, and that only those are good subjects who have joined the Presbyterian Church, know the Shorter Catechism by heart, and subscribe liberally toward lifting the mortgage on the Brooklyn Tabernacle. All the rest are endeavoring to assassinate God, plotting the murder of the Holy Ghost, and applauding the Jews for the crucifixion of Christ. If Mr. Talmage is correct in his views as to the power and wisdom of God, I imagine that his enemies at last will be overthrown, that the assassins and murderers will not succeed, and that the Infinite, with Mr. Talmage's assistance, will finally triumph. If there is an infinite God, certainly he ought to have made man grand enough to have and express an opinion of his own. Is it possible that God can be gratified with the applause of moral cowards? Does he seek to enhance his glory by receiving the adulation of cringing slaves? Is God satisfied with the adoration of the frightened?

Question. You notice that Mr. Talmage finds nearly all the inventions of modern times mentioned in the Bible?

Answer. Yes; Mr. Talmage has made an exceedingly important discovery. I admit that I am somewhat amazed at the wisdom of the ancients. This discovery has been made just in the nick of time. Millions of people were losing their respect for the Old Testament. They were beginning to think that there was some discrepancy between the prophecies of Ezekiel and Daniel and the latest developments in physical science. Thousands of preachers were telling their flocks that the Bible is not a scientific book; that Joshua was not an inspired astronomer, that God never enlightened Moses about geology, and that Ezekiel did not understand the entire art of cookery. These admissions caused some young people to suspect that the Bible, after all, was not inspired ; that the prophets of antiquity did not know as much as the discoverers of to-day. The Bible was falling into disrepute. Mr. Talmage has rushed to the rescue. He shows, and shows conclusively as anything can be shown from the Bible, that Job understood all the laws of light thousands of years before Newton lived ; that he anticipated the discoveries of Descartes, Huxley and Tyndall ; that he was familiar with the telegraph and telephone ; that Morse, Bell and Edison simply put his discoveries in successful operation ; that Nahum was, in fact, a master-mechanic ; that he understood perfectly the modern railway and described it so accurately that Trevethick, Foster and Stephenson had no difficulty in constructing a locomotive. He also has discovered that Job was well acquainted with the trade winds, and understood the mysterious currents, tides and pulses of the sea ; that Lieutenant Maury was a plagiarist ; that Humboldt was simply a biblical student. He finds that Isaiah and Solomon were far in advance of Galileo, Morse, Meyer and Watt. This is a discovery wholly unexpected to me. If Mr. Talmage is right, I am satisfied the Bible is an inspired book. If it shall turn out that Joshua was superior to Laplace, that Moses knew more about geology than Humboldt, that Job as a scientist was the superior of Kepler, that Isaiah knew more than Copernicus, and that even the minor prophets excelled the inventors and discoverers of our time—then I will admit that infidelity must become speechless forever. Until I read this sermon, I had never even suspected that the inventions of modern times were known to the ancient Jews. I never supposed that Nahum knew the least thing about railroads, or that Job would have known a telegraph if he had seen it. I never supposed that Joshua comprehended the three laws of Kepler. Of course I have not read the Old Testament with as much care as some other people have, and when I did read it, I was not looking for inventions and discoveries. I had been told so often that the Bible was no authority upon scientific questions, that I was lulled into a state of lethargy. What is amazing to me is, that so many men did read it without getting the slightest hint of the smallest invention. To think that the Jews read that book for hundreds and hundreds of years, and yet went to their graves without the slightest notion of astronomy, or geology, of railroads, telegraphs, or steamboats! And then to think that the early fathers made it the study of their lives and died without inventing anything! I am astonished that Mr. Talmage himself does not figure in the records of the Patent Office. I cannot account for this, except upon the supposition that he is too honest to infringe on the patents of the patriarchs. After this, I shall read the Old Testament with more care.

Question. Do you see that Mr. Talmage endeavors to convict you of great ignorance in not knowing that the word translated "rib" should have been translated "side," and that Eve, after all, was not made out of a rib, but out of Adam's side?

Answer. I may have been misled by taking the Bible as it is translated. The Bible account is simply this: "And the Lord God caused a deep sleep to fall
" upon Adam, and he slept. And he took one of
" his ribs and closed up the flesh instead thereof;
" and the rib which the Lord God had taken from
" man made he a woman, and brought her unto the
" man. And Adam said: This is now bone of my
" bones, and flesh of my flesh: she shall be called
" woman, because she was taken out of man." If Mr. Talmage is right, then the account should be as follows: " And the Lord God caused a deep sleep

"to fall upon Adam, and he slept; and he took one
"of his sides, and closed up the flesh instead thereof;
"and the side which the Lord God had taken from
"man made he a woman, and brought her unto the
"man. And Adam said: This is now side of my
"side, and flesh of my flesh." I do not see that the
story is made any better by using the word "side"
instead of "rib." It would be just as hard for God
to make a woman out of a man's side as out of a
rib. Mr. Talmage ought not to question the power
of God to make a woman out of a bone, and he must
recollect that the less the material the greater the
miracle.

There are two accounts of the creation of man,
in Genesis, the first being in the twenty-first verse
of the first chapter and the second being in the
twenty-first and twenty-second verses of the second chapter.

According to the second account, "God formed
"man of the dust of the ground, and breathed into
"his nostrils the breath of life." And after this,
"God planted a garden eastward in Eden and put
"the man" in this garden. After this, "He made
"every tree to grow that was good for food and
"pleasant to the sight," and, in addition, "the tree

" of life in the midst of the garden," beside "the tree
" of the knowledge of good and evil." And he "put
" the man in the garden to dress it and keep it,"
telling him that he might eat of everything he saw
except of "the tree of the knowledge of good and
" evil."

After this, God having noticed that it " was not
" good for man to be alone, formed out of the ground
" every beast of the field, every fowl of the air, and
" brought them to Adam to see what he would call
" them, and Adam gave names to all cattle, and to
" the fowl of the air, and to every beast of the field.
" But for Adam there was not found an helpmeet for
" him."

We are not told how Adam learned the language, or how he understood what God said. I can hardly believe that any man can be created with the knowledge of a language. Education cannot be ready made and stuffed into a brain. Each person must learn a language for himself. Yet in this account we find a language ready made for man's use. And not only man was enabled to speak, but a serpent also has the power of speech, and the woman holds a conversation with this animal and with her husband; and yet no account is given of how any language was learned. God is described as walking in the garden in the cool of the day, speaking like a man—holding conversations with the man and woman, and occasionally addressing the serpent.

In the nursery rhymes of the world there is nothing more childish than this "inspired" account of the creation of man and woman.

The early fathers of the church held that woman was inferior to man, because man was not made for woman, but woman for man; because Adam was made first and Eve afterward. They had not the gallantry of Robert Burns, who accounted for the beauty of woman from the fact that God practiced on man first, and then gave woman the benefit of his experience. Think, in this age of the world, of a well-educated, intelligent gentleman telling his little child that about six thousand years ago a mysterious being called God made the world out of his "omnipotence;" then made a man out of some dust which he is supposed to have moulded into form; that he put this man in a garden for the purpose of keeping the trees trimmed; that after a little while he noticed that the man seemed lonesome, not particularly happy, almost homesick; that then it occurred to this God, that it would be a good thing for the man to have some company, somebody to help him trim the trees, to talk to him and cheer him up on rainy days; that, thereupon, this God caused a deep sleep to fall on the man, took a knife, or a long, sharp piece of "omnipotence," and took out one of the man's sides, or a rib, and of that made a woman; that then this man and woman got along real well till a snake got into the garden and induced the woman to eat of the tree of the knowledge of good and evil; that the woman got the man to take a bite; that afterwards both of them were detected by God, who was walking around in the cool of the evening, and thereupon they were turned out of the garden, lest they should put forth their hands and eat of the tree of life, and live forever.

This foolish story has been regarded as the sacred, inspired truth; as an account substantially written by God himself; and thousands and millions of people have supposed it necessary to believe this childish falsehood, in order to save their souls. Nothing more laughable can be found in the fairy tales and folk-lore of savages. Yet this is defended by the leading Presbyterian divine, and those who fail to believe in the truth of this story are called "brazen "faced fools," "deicides," and "blasphemers."

By this story woman in all Christian countries was degraded. She was considered too impure to preach the gospel, too impure to distribute the sacramental bread, too impure to hand about the sacred wine, too impure to step within the "holy of holies," in the Catholic Churches, too impure to be touched by a priest. Unmarried men were considered purer than husbands and fathers. Nuns were regarded as superior to mothers, a monastery holier than a home, a nunnery nearer sacred than the cradle. And through all these years it has been thought better to love God than to love man, better to love God than to love your wife and children, better to worship an imaginary deity than to help your fellow-men.

I regard the rights of men and women equal. In Love's fair realm, husband and wife are king and queen, sceptered and crowned alike, and seated on the self-same throne.

Question. Do you still insist that the Old Testament upholds polygamy? Mr. Talmage denies this charge, and shows how terribly God punished those who were not satisfied with one wife.

Answer. I see nothing in what Mr. Talmage has said calculated to change my opinion. It has been admitted by thousands of theologians that the Old Testament upholds polygamy. Mr. Talmage is among the first to deny it. It will not do to say that David was punished for the crime of polygamy or concubinage. He was "a man after God's own "heart." He was made a king. He was a successful general, and his blood is said to have flowed in the veins of God. Solomon was, according to the account, enriched with wisdom above all human beings. Was that a punishment for having had so many wives? Was Abraham pursued by the justice of God because of the crime against Hagar, or for the crime against his own wife? The verse quoted by Mr. Talmage to show that God was opposed to polygamy, namely, the eighteenth verse of the eighteenth chapter of Leviticus, cannot by any ingenuity be tortured into a command against polygamy. The most that can be possibly said of it is, that you shall not marry the sister of your wife, while your wife is living. Yet this passage is quoted by Mr. Talmage as "a thunder of prohibition against having more " than one wife." In the twentieth chapter of Leviticus it is enacted: "That if a man take a wife " and her mother they shall be burned with fire." A commandment like this shows that he might take his wife and somebody else's mother. These passages have nothing to do with polygamy. They show whom you may marry, not how many; and there is not in Leviticus a solitary word against polygamy—not one. Nor is there such a word in Genesis, nor Exodus, nor in the entire Pentateuch—not one word. These books are filled with the most minute directions about killing sheep, and goats and doves; about making clothes for priests, about fashioning tongs and snuffers; and yet, they contain not one word against polygamy. It never occurred to the inspired writers that polygamy was a crime. Polygamy was accepted as a matter of course. Women were simple property.

Mr. Talmage, however, insists that, although God was against polygamy, he permitted it, and at the same time threw his moral influence against it. Upon this subject he says: " No doubt God per-
" mitted polygamy to continue for sometime, just
" as he permits murder and arson, theft and gam-
" bling to-day to continue, although he is against
" them." If God is the author of the Ten Commandments, he prohibited murder and theft, but he said nothing about polygamy. If he was so terribly against that crime, why did he forget to

mention it? Was there not room enough on the tables of stone for just one word on this subject? Had he no time to give a commandment against slavery? Mr. Talmage of course insists that God had to deal with these things gradually, his idea being that if God had made a commandment against them all at once, the Jews would have had nothing more to do with him.

For instance: if we wanted to break cannibals of eating missionaries, we should not tell them all at once that it was wrong, that it was wicked, to eat missionaries raw; we should induce them first to cook the missionaries, and gradually wean them from raw flesh. This would be the first great step. We would stew the missionaries, and after a time put a little mutton in the stew, not enough to excite the suspicion of the cannibal, but just enough to get him in the habit of eating mutton without knowing it. Day after day we would put in more mutton and less missionary, until finally, the cannibal would be perfectly satisfied with clear mutton. Then we would tell him that it was wrong to eat missionary. After the cannibal got so that he liked mutton, and cared nothing for missionary, then it would be safe to have a law upon the subject.

Mr. Talmage insists that polygamy cannot exist among people who believe the Bible. In this he is mistaken. The Mormons all believe the Bible. There is not a single polygamist in Utah who does not insist upon the inspiration of the Old and New Testaments.

The Rev. Mr. Newman, a kind of peripatetic consular theologian, once had a discussion, I believe, with Elder Orson Pratt, at Salt Lake City, upon the question of polygamy. It is sufficient to say of this discussion that it is now circulated by the Mormons as a campaign document. The elder overwhelmed the parson. Passages of Scripture in favor of polygamy were quoted by the hundred. The lives of all the patriarchs were brought forward, and poor parson Newman was driven from the field. The truth is, the Jews at that time were much like our forefathers. They were barbarians, and many of their laws were unjust and cruel. Polygamy was the right of all; practiced, as a matter of fact, by the rich and powerful, and the rich and powerful were envied by the poor. In such esteem did the ancient Jews hold polygamy, that the number of Solomon's wives was given, simply to enhance his glory. My own opinion is, that Solomon had very few wives, and that polygamy was not general in Palestine. The country was too poor, and

Solomon, in all his glory was hardly able to support one wife. He was a poor barbarian king with a limited revenue, with a poor soil, with a sparse population, without art, without science and without power. He sustained about the same relation to other kings that Delaware does to other States. Mr. Talmage says that God persecuted Solomon, and yet, if he will turn to the twenty-second chapter of First Chronicles, he will find what God promised to Solomon. God, speaking to David, says : " Behold a son shall be born " to thee, who shall be a man of rest, and I will give him " rest from his enemies around about; for his name shall " be Solomon, and I will give peace and quietness " unto Israel in his days. He shall build a house in my " name, and he shall be my son and I will be his father, " and I will establish the throne of his kingdom over " Israel forever." Did God keep his promise ?

So he tells us that David was persecuted by God, on account of his offences, and yet I find in the twenty-eighth verse of the twenty-ninth chapter of First Chronicles, the following account of the death of David: "And he died in a good old age, full of " days, riches and honor." Is this true?

Question. What have you to say to the charge that you were mistaken in the number of years that the Hebrews were in Egypt? Mr. Talmage says that they were there 430 years, instead of 215 years.

Answer. If you will read the third chapter of Galatians, sixteenth and seventeenth verses, you will find that it was 430 years from the time God made the promise to Abraham to the giving of the law from Mount Sinai. The Hebrews did not go to Egypt for 215 years after the promise was made to Abraham, and consequently did not remain in Egypt more than 215 years. If Galatians is true, I am right.

Strange that Mr. Talmage should belittle the miracles. The trouble with this defender of the faith is that he cares nothing for facts. He makes the strangest statements, and cares the least for proof, of any man I know. I can account for what he says of me only upon the supposition that he has not read my lectures. He may have been misled by the pirated editions. Persons have stolen my lectures, printed the same ones under various names, and filled them with mistakes and things I never said. Mr. C. P. Farrell, of Washington, is my only authorized publisher. Yet Mr. Talmage prefers to answer the mistakes of literary thieves, and charge their ignorance to me.

Question. Did you ever attack the character of Queen Victoria, or did you draw any parallel between her and George Eliot, calculated to depreciate the reputation of the Queen?

Answer. I never said a word against Victoria. The fact is, I am not acquainted with her—never met her in my life, and know but little of her. I never happened to see her "in plain clothes, reading the "Bible to the poor in the lane,"—neither did I ever hear her sing. I most cheerfully admit that her reputation is good in the neighborhood where she resides. In one of my lectures I drew a parallel between George Eliot and Victoria. I was showing the difference between a woman who had won her position in the world of thought, and one who was queen by chance. This is what I said:

"It no longer satisfies the ambition of a great man
" to be a king or emperor. The last Napoleon was
" not satisfied with being the Emperor of the French.
" He was not satisfied with having a circlet of gold
" about his head—he wanted some evidence that he
" had something of value in his head. So he wrote
" the life of Julius Cæsar that he might become a
" member of the French Academy. The emperors,
" the kings, the popes, no longer tower above their
" fellows. Compare King William with the philoso-
" pher Hæckel. The king is one of the 'anointed

" ' of the Most High '—as they claim—one upon
" whose head has been poured the divine petroleum
" of authority. Compare this king with Hæckel, who
" towers an intellectual Colossus above the crowned
" mediocrity. Compare George Eliot with Queen
" Victoria. The queen is clothed in garments given
" her by blind fortune and unreasoning chance, while
" George Eliot wears robes of glory, woven in the
" loom of her own genius. The world is beginning
" to pay homage to intellect, to genius, to heart."

I said not one word against Queen Victoria, and did not intend to even intimate that she was not an excellent woman, wife and mother. I was simply trying to show that the world was getting great enough to place a genius above an accidental queen. Mr. Talmage, true to the fawning, cringing spirit of orthodoxy, lauds the living queen and cruelly maligns the genius dead. He digs open the grave of George Eliot, and tries to stain the sacred dust of one who was the greatest woman England has produced. He calls her " an adultress." He attacks her because she was an atheist—because she abhorred Jehovah, denied the inspiration of the Bible, denied the dogma of eternal pain, and with all her heart despised the Presbyterian creed. He hates her because she was great and brave and free—because she lived without "faith" and died without fear—because she dared to give her honest thought, and grandly bore the taunts and slanders of the Christian world.

George Eliot tenderly carried in her heart the burdens of our race. She looked through pity's tears upon the faults and frailties of mankind. She knew the springs and seeds of thought and deed, and saw, with cloudless eyes, through all the winding ways of greed, ambition and deceit, where folly vainly plucks with thorn-pierced hands the fading flowers of selfish joy—the highway of eternal right. Whatever her relations may have been—no matter what I think, or others say, or how much all regret the one mistake in all her self-denying, loving life—I feel and know that in the court where her own conscience sat as judge, she stood acquitted—pure as light and stainless as a star.

How appropriate here, with some slight change, the wondrously poetic and pathetic words of Laertes at Ophelia's grave:

> Leave her i' the earth;
> And from her fair and unpolluted flesh
> May violets spring! I tell thee, churlish priest,
> A ministering angel shall this woman be,
> When thou liest howling!

I have no words with which to tell my loathing for a man who violates a noble woman's grave.

Question. Do you think that the spirit in which Mr. Talmage reviews your lectures is in accordance with the teachings of Christianity?

Answer. I think that he talks like a true Presbyterian. If you will read the arguments of Calvin against the doctrines of Castalio and Servetus, you will see that Mr. Talmage follows closely in the footsteps of the founder of his church. Castalio was such a wicked and abandoned wretch, that he taught the innocence of honest error. He insisted that God would not eternally damn a man for being honestly mistaken. For the utterance of such blasphemous sentiments, abhorrent to every Christian mind, Calvin called him " a dog of Satan, and a child of hell." In short, he used the usual arguments. Castalio was banished, and died in exile. In the case of Servetus, after all the epithets had been exhausted, an appeal was made to the stake, and the blasphemous wretch was burned to ashes.

If you will read the life of John Knox, you will find that Mr. Talmage is as orthodox in his methods of dealing with infidels, as he is in his creed. In my opinion, he would gladly treat unbelievers now, as the Puritans did the Quakers, as the Episcopalians did the Presbyterians, as the Presbyterians did the Baptists, and as the Catholics have treated all heretics. Of course, all these sects will settle their differences in heaven. In the next world, they will laugh at the crimes they committed in this.

The course pursued by Mr. Talmage is consistent. The pulpit cannot afford to abandon the weapons of falsehood and defamation. Candor sows the seeds of doubt. Fairness is weakness. The only way to successfully uphold the religion of universal love, is to denounce all Freethinkers as blasphemers, adulterers, and criminals. No matter how generous they may appear to be, no matter how fairly they may deal with their fellow-men, rest assured that they are actuated by the lowest and basest motives. Infidels who outwardly live honest and virtuous lives, are inwardly vicious, virulent and vile. After all, morality is only a veneering. God is not deceived with the varnish of good works. We know that the natural man is totally depraved, and that until he has been regenerated by the spirit of God, he is utterly incapable of a good action. The generosity of the unbeliever is, in fact, avarice. His honesty is only a form of larceny. His love is only hatred. No matter how sincerely he may love his wife,—how devoted he may be to his children,—no matter how ready he may be to sacrifice even his life for the good of mankind, God, looking into his very heart, finds it only a den of hissing snakes, a lair of wild, ferocious beasts, a cage of unclean birds.

The idea that God will save a man simply because he is honest and generous, is almost too preposterous for serious refutation. No man should rely upon his own goodness. He should plead the virtue of another. God, in his infinite justice, damns a good man on his own merits, and saves a bad man on the merits of another. The repentant murderer will be an angel of light, while his honest and unoffending victim will be a fiend in hell.

A little while ago, a ship, disabled, was blown about the Atlantic for eighty days. Everything had been eaten. Nothing remained but bare decks and hunger. The crew consisted of Captain Kruger and nine others. For nine days, nothing had been eaten. The captain, taking a revolver in his hand, said: "Mates, some " one must die for the rest. I am willing to sacrifice " myself for you." One of his comrades grasped his hand, and implored him to wait one more day. The next morning, a sail was seen upon the horizon, and the dying men were rescued.

To an ordinary man,—to one guided by the light of

reason,—it is perfectly clear that Captain Kruger was about to do an infinitely generous action. Yet Mr. Talmage will tell us that if that captain was not a Christian, and if he had sent the bullet crashing through his brain in order that his comrades might eat his body, and live to reach their wives and homes,—his soul, from that ship, would have gone, by dark and tortuous ways, down to the prison of eternal pain.

Is it possible that Christ would eternally damn a man for doing exactly what Christ would have done, had he been infinitely generous, under the same circumstances? Is not self-denial in a man as praiseworthy as in a God? Should a God be worshiped, and a man be damned, for the same action?

According to Mr. Talmage, every soldier who fought for our country in the Revolutionary war, who was not a Christian, is now in hell. Every soldier, not a Christian, who carried the flag of his country to victory—either upon the land or sea, in the war of 1812, is now in hell. Every soldier, not a Christian, who fought for the preservation of this Union,—to break the chains of slavery—to free four millions of people —to keep the whip from the naked back—every man who did this—every one who died at Andersonville and Libby, dreaming that his death would help make the lives of others worth living, is now a lost and wretched soul. These men are now in the prison of God,—a prison in which the cruelties of Libby and Andersonville would be regarded as mercies,—in which famine would be a joy.

THIRD INTERVIEW.

THIRD INTERVIEW.

SINNER. *Is God infinite in wisdom and power?*
PARSON. *He is.*
SINNER. *Does he at all times know just what ought to be done?*
PARSON. *He does.*
SINNER. *Does he always do just what ought to be done?*
PARSON. *He does.*
SINNER. *Why do you pray to him?*
PARSON. *Because he is unchangeable.*

Question. I want to ask you a few questions about Mr. Talmage's third sermon. What do you think of it?

Answer. I often ask myself the questions: Is there anything in the occupation of a minister,—anything in his surroundings, that makes him incapable of treating an opponent fairly, or decently? Is there anything in the doctrine of universal forgiveness that compels a man to speak of one who differs with him only in terms of disrespect and hatred? Is it necessary for those who profess to love the whole world, to hate the few they come in actual contact with?

Mr. Talmage, no doubt, professes to love all mankind,—Jew and Gentile, Christian and Pagan. No doubt, he believes in the missionary effort, and thinks we should do all in our power to save the soul of the most benighted savage; and yet he shows anything but affection for the "heathen" at home. He loves the ones he never saw,—is real anxious for their welfare,—but for the ones he knows, he exhibits only scorn and hatred. In one breath, he tells us that Christ loves us, and in the next, that we are "wolves "and dogs." We are informed that Christ forgave even his murderers, but that now he hates an honest unbeliever with all his heart. He can forgive the ones who drove the nails into his hands and feet,—the one who thrust the spear through his quivering flesh,—but he cannot forgive the man who entertains an honest doubt about the "scheme of salvation." He regards the man who thinks, as a "mouth-maker "at heaven." Is it possible that Christ is less forgiving in heaven than he was in Jerusalem? Did he excuse murderers then, and does he damn thinkers now? Once he pitied even thieves; does he now abhor an intellectually honest man?

Question. Mr. Talmage seems to think that you have no right to give your opinion about the Bible.

Do you think that laymen have the same right as ministers to examine the Scriptures?

Answer. If God only made a revelation for preachers, of course we will have to depend on the preachers for information. But the preachers have made the mistake of showing the revelation. They ask us, the laymen, to read it, and certainly there is no use of reading it, unless we are permitted to think for ourselves while we read. If after reading the Bible we believe it to be true, we will say so, if we are honest. If we do not believe it, we will say so, if we are honest.

But why should God be so particular about our believing the stories in his book? Why should God object to having his book examined? We do not have to call upon legislators, or courts, to protect Shakespeare from the derision of mankind. Was not God able to write a book that would command the love and admiration of the world? If the God of Mr. Talmage is infinite, he knew exactly how the stories of the Old Testament would strike a gentleman of the nineteenth century. He knew that many would have their doubts,—that thousands of them— and I may say most of them,—would refuse to believe that a miracle had ever been performed.

Now, it seems to me that he should either have left the stories out, or furnished evidence enough to convince the world. According to Mr. Talmage, thousands of people are pouring over the Niagara of unbelief into the gulf of eternal pain. Why does not God furnish more evidence? Just in proportion as man has developed intellectually, he has demanded additional testimony. That which satisfies a barbarian, excites only the laughter of a civilized man. Certainly God should furnish evidence in harmony with the spirit of the age. If God wrote his Bible for the average man, he should have written it in such a way that it would have carried conviction to the brain and heart of the average man; and he should have made no man in such a way that he could not, by any possibility, believe it. There certainly should be a harmony between the Bible and the human brain. If I do not believe the Bible, whose fault is it? Mr. Talmage insists that his God wrote the Bible for me and made me. If this is true, the book and the man should agree. There is no sense in God writing a book for me and then making me in such a way that I cannot believe his book.

Question. But Mr. Talmage says the reason why you hate the Bible is, that your soul is poisoned; that the Bible " throws you into a rage precisely as pure " water brings on a paroxysm of hydrophobia."

Answer. Is it because the mind of the infidel is poisoned, that he refuses to believe that an infinite God commanded the murder of mothers, maidens and babes? Is it because their minds are impure, that they refuse to believe that a good God established the institution of human slavery, or that he protected it when established? Is it because their minds are vile, that they refuse to believe that an infinite God established or protected polygamy? Is it a sure sign of an impure mind, when a man insists that God never waged wars of extermination against his helpless children? Does it show that a man has been entirely given over to the devil, because he refuses to believe that God ordered a father to sacrifice his son? Does it show that a heart is entirely without mercy, simply because a man denies the justice of eternal pain?

I denounce many parts of the Old Testament because they are infinitely repugnant to my sense of justice,—because they are bloody, brutal and infamous,—because they uphold crime and destroy human liberty. It is impossible for me to imagine a greater monster than the God of the Old Testament. He is unworthy of my worship. He commands only my detestation, my execration, and my passionate hatred. The God who commanded the murder of children is an infamous fiend. The God who believed in polygamy, is worthy only of contempt. The God who established slavery should be hated by every free man. The Jehovah of the Jews was simply a barbarian, and the Old Testament is mostly the barbarous record of a barbarous people.

If the Jehovah of the Jews is the real God, I do not wish to be his friend. From him I neither ask, nor expect, nor would I be willing to receive, even an eternity of joy. According to the Old Testament, he established a government,—a political state,—and yet, no civilized country to-day would re-enact these laws of God.

Question. What do you think of the explanation given by Mr. Talmage of the stopping of the sun and moon in the time of Joshua, in order that a battle might be completed?

Answer. Of course, if there is an infinite God, he could have stopped the sun and moon. No one pretends to prescribe limits to the power of the infinite. Even admitting that such a being existed, the question whether he did stop the sun and moon, or not, still remains.   According to the account, these planets were stopped, in order that Joshua might continue the pursuit of a routed enemy. I take it for granted that a being of infinite wisdom would not waste any force,—that he would not throw away any "omnipotence," and that, under ordinary circumstances, he would husband his resources. I find that this spirit exists, at least in embryo, in Mr. Talmage. He proceeds to explain this miracle. He does not assert that the earth was stopped on its axis, but suggests "refraction" as a way out of the difficulty. Now, while the stopping of the earth on its axis accounts for the sun remaining in the same relative position, it does not account for the stoppage of the moon. The moon has a motion of its own, and even if the earth had been stopped in its rotary motion, the moon would have gone on. The Bible tells us that the moon was stopped. One would suppose that the sun would have given sufficient light for all practical purposes. Will Mr. Talmage be kind enough to explain the stoppage of the moon? Every one knows that the moon is somewhat obscure when the sun is in the midst of the heavens. The moon when compared with the sun at such a time, is much like one of the discourses of Mr. Talmage side by side with a chapter from Humboldt;—it is useless.

In the same chapter in which the account of the stoppage of the sun and moon is given, we find that God cast down from heaven great hailstones on Joshua's enemies. Did he get out of hailstones? Had he no "omnipotence" left? Was it necessary for him to stop the sun and moon and depend entirely upon the efforts of Joshua? Would not the force employed in stopping the rotary motion of the earth have been sufficient to destroy the enemy? Would not a millionth part of the force necessary to stop the moon, have pierced the enemy's centre, and rolled up both his flanks? A resort to lightning would have been, in my judgment, much more economical and rather more effective. If he had simply opened the earth, and swallowed them, as he did Korah and his company, it would have been a vast saving of "omnipotent" muscle. Yet, the foremost orthodox minister of the Presbyterian Church,—the one who calls all unbelievers " wolves and dogs," and " brazen " fools," in his effort to account for this miracle, is driven to the subterfuge of an " optical illusion."

We are seriously informed that "God probably " changed the nature of the air," and performed this feat of ledgerdemain through the instrumentality of " refraction." It seems to me it would have been fully

as easy to have changed the nature of the air breathed by the enemy, so that it would not have supported life. He could have accomplished this by changing only a little air, in that vicinity; whereas, according to the Talmagian view, he changed the atmosphere of the world. Or, a small " local flood " might have done the work. The optical illusion and refraction view, ingenious as it may appear, was not original with Mr. Talmage. The Rev. Henry M. Morey, of South Bend, Indiana, used, upon this subject, the following language; " The phenomenon was simply
" optical. The rotary motion of the earth was not
" disturbed, but the light of the sun was prolonged by
" the same laws of refraction and reflection by which
" the sun now appears to be above the horizon when
" it is really below. The medium through which the
" sun's rays passed, might have been miraculously
" influenced so as to have caused the sun to linger
" above the horizon long after its usual time for dis-
" appearance."

I pronounce the opinion of Mr. Morey to be the ripest product of Christian scholarship. According to the Morey-Talmage view, the sun lingered somewhat above the horizon. But this is inconsistent with the Bible account. We are not told in the Scriptures that the sun "lingered above the horizon," but that it "stood " still in the midst of heaven for about a whole day." The trouble about the optical-illusion view is, that it makes the day too long. If the air was miraculously changed, so that it refracted the rays of the sun, while the earth turned over as usual for about a whole day, then, at the end of that time, the sun must have been again visible in the east. It would then naturally shine twelve hours more, so that this miraculous day must have been at least thirty-six hours in length. There were first twelve hours of natural light, then twelve hours of refracted and reflected light, and then twelve hours more of natural light. This makes the day too long. So, I say to Mr. Talmage, as I said to Mr. Morey: If you will depend a little less on refraction, and a little more on reflection, you will see that the whole story is a barbaric myth and foolish fable.

For my part, I do not see why God should be pleased to have me believe a story of this character. I can hardly think that there is great joy in heaven over another falsehood swallowed. I can imagine that a man may deny this story, and still be an excellent citizen, a good father, an obliging neighbor, and in all respects a just and truthful man. I can also imagine that a man may believe this story, and yet assassinate a President of the United States.

I am afraid that Mr. Talmage is beginning to be touched, in spite of himself, with some new ideas. He tells us that worlds are born and that worlds die. This is not exactly the Bible view. You would think that he imagined that a world was naturally produced,—that the aggregation of atoms was natural, and that disintegration came to worlds, as to men, through old age. Yet this is not the Bible view. According to the Bible, these worlds were not born,—they were created out of "nothing," or out of "omnipotence," which is much the same. According to the Bible, it took this infinite God six days to make this atom called earth; and according to the account, he did not work nights,—he worked from the mornings to the evenings,—and I suppose rested nights, as he has since that time on Sundays.

Admitting that the battle which Joshua fought was exceedingly important—which I do not think—is it not a little strange that this God, in all subsequent battles of the world's history, of which we know anything, has maintained the strictest neutrality? The earth turned as usual at Yorktown, and at Gettysburg the moon pursued her usual course; and so far as I know, neither at Waterloo nor at Sedan were there any peculiar freaks of "re-fraction" or "reflection."

Question. Mr. Talmage tells us that there was in the early part of this century a dark day, when workmen went home from their fields, and legislatures and courts adjourned, and that the darkness of that day has not yet been explained. What is your opinion about that?

Answer. My opinion is, that if at that time we had been at war with England, and a battle had been commenced in the morning, and in the afternoon the American forces had been driven from their position and were hard pressed by the enemy, and if the day had become suddenly dark, and so dark that the Americans were thereby enabled to escape, thousands of theologians of the calibre of Mr. Talmage would have honestly believed that there had been an interposition of divine Providence. No battle was fought that day, and consequently, even the ministers are looking for natural causes. In olden times, when the heavens were visited by comets, war, pestilence and famine were predicted. If wars came, the prediction was remembered; if nothing happened, it was forgotten. When eclipses visited the sun and moon, the barbarian fell upon his knees, and accounted for the phenomena by the wickedness of his neighbor. Mr. Talmage tells us that his father was terrified by the meteoric shower that visited our earth in 1833. The terror of the father may account for the credulity of the son. Astronomers will be surprised to read the declaration of Mr. Talmage that the meteoric shower has never been explained. Meteors visit the earth every year of its life, and in a certain portion of the orbit they are always expected, and they always come. Mr. Newcomb has written a work on astronomy that all ministers ought to read.

Question. Mr. Talmage also charges you with "making light of holy things," and seems to be astonished that you should ridicule the anointing oil of Aaron?

Answer. I find that the God who had no time to say anything on the subject of slavery, and who found no room upon the tables of stone to say a word against polygamy, and in favor of the rights of woman, wife and mother, took time to give a recipe for making hair oil. And in order that the priests might have the exclusive right to manufacture this oil, decreed the penalty of death on all who should infringe. I admit that I am incapable of seeing the beauty of this symbol. Neither could I ever see the necessity of Masons putting oil on the corner-stone of a building. Of course, I do not know the exact chemical effect that oil has on stone, and I see no harm in laughing at such a ceremony. If the oil does good, the laughter will do no harm; and if the oil will do no harm, the laughter will do no good. Personally, I am willing that Masons should put oil on all stones; but, if Masons should insist that I must believe in the efficacy of the ceremony, or be eternally damned, I would have about the same feeling toward the Masons that I now have toward Mr. Talmage. I presume that at one time the putting of oil on a corner-stone had some meaning; but that it ever did any good, no sensible man will insist. It is a custom to break a bottle of champagne over the bow of a newly-launched ship, but I have never considered this ceremony important to the commercial interests of the world.

I have the same opinion about putting oil on stones, as about putting water on heads. For my part, I see no good in the rite of baptism. Still, it may do no harm, unless people are immersed during cold weather. Neither have I the slightest objection to the baptism of anybody; but if people tell me that I must be baptized or suffer eternal agony, then I deny it. If they say that baptism does any earthly good, I deny it. No one objects to any harmless ceremony; but the moment it is insisted that a ceremony is necessary, the reason of which no man can see, then the practice of the ceremony becomes hurtful, for the reason that it is maintained only at the expense of intelligence and manhood.

It is hurtful for people to imagine that they can please God by any ceremony whatever. If there is any God, there is only one way to please him, and that is, by a conscientious discharge of your obligations to your fellow-men. Millions of people imagine that they can please God by wearing certain kinds of cloth. Think of a God who can be pleased with a coat of a certain cut! Others, to earn a smile of heaven, shave their heads, or trim their beards, or perforate their ears or lips or noses. Others maim and mutilate their bodies. Others think to please God by simply shutting their eyes, by swinging censers, by lighting candles, by repeating poor Latin, by making a sign of the cross with holy water, by ringing bells, by going without meat, by eating fish, by getting hungry, by counting beads, by making themselves miserable Sundays, by looking solemn, by refusing to marry, by hearing sermons; and others imagine that they can please God by calumniating unbelievers.

There is an old story of an Irishman who, when dying, sent for a priest. The reputation of the dying man was so perfectly miserable, that the priest refused to administer the rite of extreme unction. The priest therefore asked him if he could recollect any decent action that he had ever done. The dying man said that he could not. "Very well," said the priest, "then you will have to be damned." In a moment, the pinched and pale face brightened, and he said to the priest: "I have thought of one good " action." "What is it?" asked the priest. And the dying man said, "Once I killed a gauger."

I suppose that in the next world some ministers, driven to extremes, may reply: "Once I told a lie " about an infidel."

Question. You see that Mr. Talmage still sticks to the whale and Jonah story. What do you think of his argument, or of his explanation, rather, of that miracle?

Answer. The edge of his orthodoxy seems to be crumbling. He tells us that "there is in the mouth " of the common whale a cavity large enough for a " man to live in without descent into his stomach,"— and yet Christ says, that Jonah was in the whale's belly, not in his mouth. But why should Mr. Talmage say that? We are told in the sacred account that "God prepared a great fish" for the sole purpose of having Jonah swallowed. The size of the present whale has nothing to do with the story. No matter whether the throat of the whale of to-day is large or small,—that has nothing to do with it. The simple story is, that God prepared a fish and had Jonah swallowed. And yet Mr. Talmage throws out the suggestion that probably this whale held Jonah in his mouth for three days and nights. I admit that Jonah's chance for air would have been a little better in his mouth, and his chance for water a little worse. Probably the whale that swallowed Jonah was the same fish spoken of by Procopius,—both accounts being entitled, in my judgment, to equal credence. I am a little surprised that Mr. Talmage forgot to mention the fish spoken of by Munchausen—an equally reliable author,—and who has given, not simply the bald fact that a fish swallowed a ship, but was good enough to furnish the details. Mr. Talmage should remember that out of Jonah's biography grew the habit of calling any remarkable lie, "a fish "story." There is one thing that Mr. Talmage should not forget; and that is, that miracles should not be explained. Miracles are told simply to be believed, not to be understood.

Somebody suggested to Mr. Talmage that, in all probability, a person in the stomach of a whale would be digested in less than three days. Mr. Talmage, again showing his lack of confidence in God, refusing to believe that God could change the nature of gastric juice,—having no opportunity to rely upon "refraction or reflection," frankly admits that Jonah had to save himself by keeping on the constant go and jump. This gastric-juice theory of Mr. Talmage is an abandonment of his mouth hypothesis. I do not wonder that Mr. Talmage thought of the mouth theory. Possibly, the two theories had better be united—so that we may say that Jonah, when he got tired of the activity necessary to avoid the gastric juice, could have strolled into the mouth for a rest. What a picture! Jonah sitting on the edge of the lower jaw, wiping the perspiration and the gastric juice from his anxious face, and vainly looking through the open mouth for signs of land!

In this story of Jonah, we are told that "the Lord "spake unto the fish." In what language? It must be remembered that this fish was only a few hours old. He had been prepared during the storm, for the sole purpose of swallowing Jonah. He was a fish of exceedingly limited experience. He had no hereditary knowledge, because he did not spring from ancestors; consequently, he had no instincts. Would such a fish understand any language? It may be contended that the fish, having been made for the occasion, was given a sufficient knowledge of language to understand an ordinary commandment; but, if Mr. Talmage is right, I think an order to the fish would have been entirely unnecessary. When we take into consideration that a thing the size of a man had been promenading up and down the stomach of this fish for three days and three nights, successfully baffling the efforts of gastric juice, we can readily believe that the fish was as anxious to have Jonah go, as Jonah was to leave.

But the whale part is, after all, not the most wonderful portion of the book of Jonah. According to this wonderful account, "the word of the Lord came "to Jonah," telling him to "go and cry against the "city of Nineveh;" but Jonah, instead of going, endeavored to evade the Lord by taking ship for Tarshish. As soon as the Lord heard of this, he "sent out a great wind into the sea," and frightened the sailors to that extent that after assuring themselves, by casting lots, that Jonah was the man, they threw him into the sea. After escaping from the whale, he went to Nineveh, and delivered his pretended message from God. In consequence of his message, Jonah having no credentials from God,—nothing certifying to his official character, the King of Nineveh covered himself with sack-cloth and sat down in some ashes. He then caused a decree to be issued that every man and beast should abstain from food and water; and further, that every man and beast should be covered with sack-cloth. This was done in the hope that Jonah's God would repent, and turn away his fierce anger. When we take into consideration the fact that the people of Nineveh were not Hebrews, and had not the slightest confidence in the God of the Jews — knew no more of, and cared no more for, Jehovah than we now care for Jupiter, or Neptune; the effect produced by the proclamation of Jonah is, to say the least of it, almost incredible.

We are also informed, in this book, that the moment God saw all the people sitting in the ashes, and all the animals covered with sack-cloth, he repented. This failure on the part of God to destroy the unbelievers displeased Jonah exceedingly, and he was very angry. Jonah was much like the modern minister, who seems always to be personally aggrieved if the pestilence and famine prophesied by him do not come. Jonah was displeased to that degree, that he asked God to kill him. Jonah then went out of the city, even after God had repented, made him a booth and sat under it, in the shade, waiting to see what would become of the city. God then "prepared a gourd, and made it to come up " over Jonah that it might be a shadow over his " head to deliver him from his grief." And then we have this pathetic line : " So Jonah was exceedingly " glad of the gourd."

God having prepared a fish, and also prepared a gourd, proposed next morning to prepare a worm. And when the sun rose next day, the worm that God had prepared, "smote the gourd, so that " it withered." I can hardly believe that an infinite being prepared a worm to smite a gourd so that it withered, in order to keep the sun from the bald head of a prophet. According to the account, after sunrise, and after the worm had smitten the gourd, " God prepared a vehement east " wind." This was not an ordinary wind, but one prepared expressly for that occasion. After the wind had been prepared, " the sun beat upon the head of " Jonah, and he fainted, and wished in himself to " die." All this was done in order to convince Jonah that a man who would deplore the loss of a gourd, ought not to wish for the destruction of a city.

Is it possible for any intelligent man now to believe that the history of Jonah is literally true? For my part, I cannot see the necessity either of believing it, or of preaching it. It has nothing to do with honesty, with mercy, or with morality. The bad may believe it, and the good may hold it in contempt. I do not see that civilization has the slightest interest in the fish, the gourd, the worm, or the vehement east wind.

Does Mr. Talmage think that it is absolutely necessary to believe *all* the story? Does he not think it probable that a God of infinite mercy, rather than damn the soul of an honest man to hell forever, would waive, for instance, the worm,—provided he believed in the vehement east wind, the gourd and the fish?

Mr. Talmage, by insisting on the literal truth of the Bible stories, is doing Christianity great harm. Thousands of young men will say: "I can't become "a Christian if it is necessary to believe the adven- "tures of Jonah." Mr. Talmage will put into the paths of multitudes of people willing to do right, anxious to make the world a little better than it is,— this stumbling block. He could have explained it, called it an allegory, poetical license, a child of the oriental imagination, a symbol, a parable, a poem, a dream, a legend, a myth, a divine figure, or a great truth wrapped in the rags and shreds and patches of seeming falsehood. His efforts to belittle the miracle, to suggest the mouth instead of the stomach,—to suggest that Jonah took deck passage, or lodged in the forecastle instead of in the cabin or steerage,— to suggest motion as a means of avoiding digestion, is a serious theological blunder, and may cause the loss of many souls.

If Mr. Talmage will consult with other ministers, they will tell him to let this story alone—that he will simply " provoke investigation and discussion"—two things to be avoided. They will tell him that they are not willing their salary should hang on so slender a thread, and will advise him not to bother his gourd about Jonah's. They will also tell him that in this age of the world, arguments cannot be answered by " a vehement east wind."

Some people will think that it would have been just as easy for God to have pulled the gourd up, as to have prepared a worm to bite it.

Question. Mr. Talmage charges that you have said there are indecencies in the Bible. Are you still of that opinion?

Answer. Mr. Talmage endeavors to evade the charge, by saying that " there are things in the Bible " not intended to be read, either in the family circle, " or in the pulpit, but nevertheless they are to be " read." My own judgment is, that an infinite being should not inspire the writing of indecent things. It will not do to say, that the Bible description of sin " warns and saves." There is nothing in the history of Tamar calculated to " warn and save ;" and the same may be said of many other passages in the Old Testament. Most Christians would be glad to know that all such passages are interpolations. I regret that Shakespeare ever wrote a line that could not be read any where, and by any person. But Shakespeare, great as he was, did not rise entirely above his time. So of most poets. Nearly all have stained their pages with some vulgarity; and I am sorry for it, and hope the time will come when we shall have an edition of all the great writers and poets from which every such passage is eliminated.

It is with the Bible as with most other books. It is a mingling of good and bad. There are many exquisite passages in the Bible,—many good laws,—many wise sayings,—and there are many passages that should never have been written. I do not propose to throw away the good on account of the bad, neither do I propose to accept the bad on account of the good. The Bible need not be taken as an entirety. It is the business of every man who reads it, to discriminate between that which is good and that which is bad. There are also many passages neither good nor bad,—wholly and totally indifferent —conveying no information—utterly destitute of ideas,—and as to these passages, my only objection to them is that they waste time and paper.

I am in favor of every passage in the Bible that conveys information. I am in favor of every wise proverb, of every verse coming from human experience and that appeals to the heart of man. I am in favor of every passage that inculcates justice, generosity, purity, and mercy. I am satisfied that much of the historical part is false. Some of it is probably true. Let us have the courage to take the true, and throw the false away. I am satisfied that many of the passages are barbaric, and many of them are good. Let us have the wisdom to accept the good and to reject the barbaric.

No system of religion should go in partnership with barbarism. Neither should any Christian feel it his duty to defend the savagery of the past. The philosophy of Christ must stand independently of the mistakes of the Old Testament. We should do justice whether a woman was made from a rib or from "omnipotence." We should be merciful whether the flood was general, or local. We should be kind and obliging whether Jonah was swallowed by a fish or not. The miraculous has nothing to do with the moral. Intelligence is of more value than inspiration. Brain is better than Bible. Reason is above all religion. I do not believe that any civilized human being clings to the Bible on account of its barbaric passages. I am candid enough to believe that every Christian in the world would think more of the Bible, if it had not upheld slavery, if it had denounced polygamy, if it had cried out against wars of extermination, if it had spared women and babes, if it had upheld everywhere, and at all times, the standard of justice and mercy. But when it is claimed that the book is perfect, that it is inspired, that it is, in fact, the work of an infinitely wise and good God,—then it should be without a defect. There should not be within its lids an impure word; it should not express an impure thought. There should not be one word in favor of injustice, not one word in favor of slavery, not one word in favor of wars of extermination. There must be another revision of the Scriptures. The chaff must be thrown away. The dross must be rejected; and only that be retained which is in exact harmony with the brain and heart of the greatest and the best.

Question. Mr. Talmage charges you with unfairness, because you account for the death of art in Palestine, by the commandment which forbids the making of graven images.

Answer. I have said that that commandment was the death of art, and I say so still. I insist that by reason of that commandment, Palestine produced no painter and no sculptor until after the destruction of

Jerusalem. Mr. Talmage, in order to answer that statement, goes on to show that hundreds and thousands of pictures were produced in the Middle Ages. That is a departure in pleading. Will he give us the names of the painters that existed in Palestine from Mount Sinai to the destruction of the temple? Will he give us the names of the sculptors between those times? Mohammed prohibited his followers from making any representation of human or animal life, and as a result, Mohammedans have never produced a painter nor a sculptor, except in the portrayal and chiseling of vegetable forms. They were confined to trees and vines, and flowers. No Mohammedan has portrayed the human face or form. But the commandment of Jehovah went farther than that of Momammed, and prevented portraying the image of anything. The assassination of art was complete.

There is another thing that should not be forgotten. We are indebted for the encouragement of art, not to the Protestant Church; if indebted to any, it is to the Catholic. The Catholic adorned the cathedral with painting and statue—not the Protestant. The Protestants opposed music and painting, and refused to decorate their temples. But if Mr. Talmage wishes to know to whom we are indebted for art, let him read the mythology of Greece and Rome. The early Christians destroyed paintings and statues. They were the enemies of all beauty. They hated and detested every expression of art. They looked upon the love of statues as a form of idolatry. They looked upon every painting as a remnant of Paganism. They destroyed all upon which they could lay their ignorant hands. Hundred of years afterwards, the world was compelled to search for the fragments that Christian fury had left. The Greeks filled the world with beauty. For every stream and mountain and cataract they had a god or goddess. Their sculptors impersonated every dream and hope, and their mythology feeds, to-day, the imagination of mankind. The Venus de Milo is the impersonation of beauty, in ruin—the sublimest fragment of the ancient world. Our mythology is infinitely unpoetic and barren—our deity an old bachelor from eternity, who once believed in indiscriminate massacre. Upon the throne of our heaven, woman finds no place. Our mythology is destitute of the maternal.

Question. Mr. Talmage denies your statement that the Old Testament humiliates woman. He also denies that the New Testament says anything against woman. How is it?

Answer. Of course, I never considered a book upholding polygamy to be the friend of woman. Eve, according to that book, is the mother of us all, and yet the inspired writer does not tell us how long she lived,—does not even mention her death,—makes not the slightest reference as to what finally became of her. Methuselah lived nine hundred and sixty-nine years, and yet, there is not the slightest mention made of Mrs. Methuselah. Enoch was translated, and his widow is not mentioned. There is not a word about Mrs. Seth, or Mrs. Enos, or Mrs. Cainan, or Mrs. Mahalaleel, or Mrs. Jared. We do not know the name of Mrs. Noah, and I believe not the name of a solitary woman is given from the creation of Eve—with the exception of two of Lamech's wives—until Sarai is mentioned as being the wife of Abram.

If you wish really to know the Bible estimation of woman, turn to the fourth and fifth verses of the twelfth chapter of Leviticus, in which a woman, for the crime of having borne a son, is unfit to touch a hallowed thing, or to come in the holy sanctuary for thirty-three days; but if a woman was the mother of a girl, then she became totally unfit to enter the sanctuary, or pollute with her touch a hallowed thing, for sixty-six days. The pollution was twice as great when she had borne a daughter.

It is a little difficult to see why it is a greater crime to give birth to a daughter than to a son. Surely, a law like that did not tend to the elevation of woman. You will also find in the same chapter that a woman had to offer a pigeon, or a turtle-dove, as a sin offering, in order to expiate the crime of having become a mother. By the Levitical law, a mother was unclean. The priest had to make an atonement for her.

If there is, beneath the stars, a figure of complete and perfect purity, it is a mother holding in her arms her child. The laws respecting women, given by commandment of Jehovah to the Jews, were born of barbarism, and in this day and age should be regarded only with detestation and contempt. The twentieth and twenty-first verses of the nineteenth chapter of Leviticus show that the same punishment was not meted to men and women guilty of the same crime.

The real explanation of what we find in the Old Testament degrading to woman, lies in the fact, that the overflow of Love's mysterious Nile—the sacred source of life—was, by its savage authors, deemed unclean.

Question. But what have you to say about the women of the Bible, mentioned by Mr. Talmage, and held up as examples for all time of all that is sweet and womanly?

Answer. I believe that Esther is his principal heroine. Let us see who she was.

According to the book of Esther, Ahasuerus who was king of Persia, or some such place, ordered Vashti his queen to show herself to the people and the princes, because she was "exceedingly fair " to look upon." For some reason—modesty perhaps—she refused to appear. And thereupon the king " sent letters into all his provinces and to every " people after their language, that every man should " bear rule in his own house ;" it being feared that if it should become public that Vashti had disobeyed, all other wives might follow her example. The king also, for the purpose of impressing upon all women the necessity of obeying their husbands, issued a decree that " Vashti should come no more before " him," and that he would " give her royal estate " unto another." This was done that " all the " wives should give to their husbands honor, both to " great and small."

After this, " the king appointed officers in all the

"provinces of his kingdom that they might gather "together all the fair young virgins," and bring them to his palace, put them in the custody of his chamberlain, and have them thoroughly washed. Then the king was to look over the lot and take each day the one that pleased him best until he found the one to put in the place of Vashti. A fellow by the name of Mordecai, living in that part of the country, hearing of the opportunity to sell a girl, brought Esther, his uncle's daughter,—she being an orphan, and very beautiful—to see whether she might not be the lucky one.

The remainder of the second chapter of this book, I do not care to repeat. It is sufficient to say that Esther at last was chosen.

The king at this time did not know that Esther was a Jewess. Mordecai her kinsman, however, discovered a plot to assassinate the king, and Esther told the king, and the two plotting gentlemen were hanged on a tree.

After a while, a man by the name of Haman was made Secretary of State, and everybody coming in his presence bowed except Mordecai. Mordecai was probably depending on the influence of Esther. Haman finally became so vexed, that he made up his mind to have all the Jews in the kingdom destroyed. (The number of Jews at that time in Persia must have been immense.) Haman thereupon requested the king to have an order issued to destroy all the Jews, and in consideration of the order, proposed to pay ten thousand talents of silver. And thereupon, letters were written to the governors of the various provinces, sealed with the king's ring, sent by post in all directions, with instructions to kill all the Jews, both young and old—little children and women,—in one day. (One would think that the king copied this order from another part of the Old Testament, or had found an original by Jehovah.) The people immediately made preparations for the killing. Mordecai clothed himself with sack-cloth, and Esther called upon one of the king's chamberlains, and she finally got the history of the affair, as well as a copy of the writing, and thereupon made up her mind to go in and ask the king to save her people.

At that time, Bismarck's idea of government being in full force, any one entering the king's presence without an invitation, was liable to be put to death. And in case any one did go in to see the king, if the king failed to hold out his golden sceptre, his life was not spared. Notwithstanding this order, Esther put on her best clothes, and stood in the inner court of the king's house, while the king sat on his royal throne. When the king saw her standing in the court, he held out his sceptre, and Esther drew near, and he asked her what she wished; and thereupon she asked that the king and Haman might take dinner with her that day, and it was done. While they were feasting, the king again asked Esther what she wanted; and her second request was, that they would come and dine with her once more. When Haman left the palace that day, he saw Mordecai again at the gate, standing as stiffly as usual, and it filled Haman with indignation. So Haman, taking the advice of his wife, made a gallows fifty cubits high, for the special benefit of Mordecai. The next day, when Haman went to see the king, the king, having the night before refreshed his memory in respect to the service done him by Mordecai, asked Haman what ought to be done for the man whom the king wished to honor. Haman, supposing of course that the king referred to him, said that royal purple ought to be brought forth, such as the king wore, and the horse that the king rode on, and the crown-royal should be set on the man's head;—that one of the most noble princes should lead the horse, and as he went through the streets, proclaim: "Thus "shall it be done to the man whom the king de-"lighteth to honor."

Thereupon the king told Haman that Mordecai was the man that the king wished to honor. And Haman was forced to lead this horse, backed by Mordecai, through the streets, shouting: "This shall "be done to the man whom the king delighteth to "honor." Immediately afterward, he went to the banquet that Esther had prepared, and the king again asked Esther her petition. She then asked for the salvation of her people; stating at the same time, that if her people had been sold into slavery, she would have held her tongue; but since they were about to be killed, she could not keep silent. The king asked her who had done this thing; and Esther replied that it was the wicked Haman.

Thereupon one of the chamberlains, remembering the gallows that had been made for Mordecai, mentioned it, and the king immediately ordered that Haman be hanged thereon; which was done. And Mordecai immediately became Secretary of State. The order against the Jews was then rescinded; and Ahasuerus, willing to do anything that Esther desired, hanged all of Haman's folks. He not only did this, but he immediately issued an order to all the Jews allowing them to kill the other folks. And the Jews got together throughout one hundred and twenty-seven provinces, "and such was their power, "that no man could stand against them; and there- "upon the Jews smote all their enemies with the "stroke of the sword, and with slaughter and de- "struction, and did whatever they pleased to those "who hated them." And in the palace of the king, the Jews slew and destroyed five hundred men, besides ten sons of Haman; and in the rest of the provinces, they slew seventy-five thousand people. And after this work of slaughter, the Jews had a day of gladness and feasting.

One can see from this, what a beautiful Bible character Esther was—how filled with all that is womanly, gentle, kind and tender!

This story is one of the most unreasonable, as well as one of the most heartless and revengeful, in the whole Bible. Ahasuerus was a monster, and Esther equally infamous; and yet, this woman is held up for the admiration of mankind by a Brooklyn pastor. There is this peculiarity about the book of Esther: the name of God is not mentioned in it, and the deity is not referred to, directly or indirectly;—yet it is claimed to be an inspired book. If Jehovah wrote it, he certainly cannot be charged with egotism.

I most cheerfully admit that the book of Ruth is quite a pleasant story, and the affection of Ruth for her mother-in-law exceedingly touching, but I am of opinion that Ruth did many things that would be regarded as somewhat indiscreet, even in the city of Brooklyn.

All I can find about Hannah is, that she made a little coat for her boy Samuel, and brought it to him from year to year. Where he got his vest and pantaloons we are not told. But this fact seems hardly enough to make her name immortal.

So also Mr. Talmage refers us to the wonderful woman Abigail. The story about Abigail, told in plain English, is this: David sent some of his followers to Nabal, Abigail's husband, and demanded food. Nabal, who knew nothing about David, and cared less, refused. Abigail heard about it, and took food to David and his servants. She was very much struck, apparently, with David and David with her. A few days afterward Nabal died—supposed to have been killed by the Lord—but probably poisoned; and thereupon David took Abigail to wife. The whole matter should have been investigated by the grand jury.

We are also referred to Dorcas, who no doubt was a good woman—made clothes for the poor and gave alms, as millions have done since then. It seems that this woman died. Peter was sent for, and thereupon raised her from the dead, and she is never mentioned any more. Is it not a little strange that a woman who had been actually raised from the dead, should have so completely passed out of the memory of her time, that when she died the second time, she was entirely unnoticed?

Is it not astonishing that so little is in the New Testament concerning the mother of Christ? My own opinion is, that she was an excellent woman, and the wife of Joseph; and that Joseph was the actual father of Christ. I think there can be no reasonable doubt that such was the opinion of the authors of the original gospels. Upon any other hypothesis, it is impossible to account for their having given the genealogy of Joseph to prove that Christ was of the blood of David. The idea that he was the Son of God, or in any way miraculously produced, was an afterthought, and is hardly entitled now to serious consideration. The gospels were written so long after the death of Christ, that very little was known of him, and substantially nothing of his parents. How is it that not one word is said about the death of Mary—not one word about the death of Joseph? How did it happen that Christ did not visit his mother after his resurrection? The first time he speaks to his mother is when he was twelve years old. His mother having told him that she and his father had been seeking him, he replied: "How is it that ye sought me: wist ye not that I must be about my Father's business?"

The second time was at the marriage feast in Cana, when he said to her: "Woman, what have I to do with thee?" And the third time was at the cross, when "Jesus, seeing his mother standing by the disciple whom he loved, said to her: Woman, behold thy son;" and to the disciple: "Behold thy mother." And this is all.

The best thing about the Catholic Church is the deification of Mary,—and yet this is denounced by Protestantism as idolatry. There is something in the human heart that prompts man to tell his faults more freely to the mother than to the father. The cruelty of Jehovah is softened by the mercy of Mary.

Is it not strange that none of the disciples of Christ

said anything about their parents,—that we know absolutely nothing of them? Is there any evidence that they showed any particular respect even for the mother of Christ?

Mary Magdalen is, in many respects, the tenderest and most loving character in the New Testament. According to the account, her love for Christ knew no abatement,—no change—true even in the hopeless shadow of the cross. Neither did it die with his death. She waited at the sepulchre; she hasted in the early morning to his tomb, and yet the only comfort Christ gave to this true and loving soul lies in these strangely cold and heartless words: "Touch "me not."

There is nothing tending to show that the women spoken of in the Bible were superior to the ones we know. There are to-day millions of women making coats for their sons,—hundreds of thousands of women, true not simply to innocent people, falsely accused, but to criminals. Many a loving heart is as true to the gallows as Mary was to the cross. There are hundreds of thousands of women accepting poverty and want and dishonor, for the love they bear unworthy men; hundreds and thousands, hundreds and thousands, working day and night, with strained eyes and tired hands, for husbands and children,—clothed in rags, housed in huts and hovels, hoping day after day for the angel of death. There are thousands of women in Christian England, working in iron, laboring in the fields and toiling in mines. There are hundreds and thousands in Europe, everywhere, doing the work of men—deformed by toil, and who would become simply wild and ferocious beasts, except for the love they bear for home and child.

You need not go back four thousand years for heroines. The world is filled with them to-day. They do not belong to any nation, nor to any religion, nor exclusively to any race. Wherever woman is found, they are found.

There is no description of any women in the Bible that equal thousands and thousands of women known to-day. The women mentioned by Mr. Talmage fall almost infinitely below, not simply those in real life, but the creations of the imagination found in the world of fiction. They will not compare with the women born of Shakespeare's brain. You will find none like Isabella, in whose spotless life, love and reason blended into perfect truth; nor Juliet, within whose heart passion and purity met, like white and red within the bosom of a rose; nor Cordelia, who chose to suffer loss rather than show her wealth of love with those who gilded dross with golden words in hope of gain; nor Miranda, who told her love as freely as a flower gives its bosom to the kisses of the sun; nor Imogene, who asked: "What is it to be false?" nor Hermione, who bore with perfect faith and hope the cross of shame, and who at last forgave with all her heart; nor Desdemona, her innocence so perfect and her love so pure, that she was incapable of suspecting that another could suspect, and sought with dying words to hide her lover's crime.

If we wish to find what the Bible thinks of woman, all that is necessary to do is to read it. We will find that everywhere she is spoken of simply as property, — as belonging absolutely to the man. We will find that whenever a man got tired of his wife, all he had to do was to give her a writing of divorcement, and that then the mother of his children became a houseless and a homeless wanderer. We will find that men were allowed to have as many wives as they could get, either by courtship, purchase, or conquest. The Jewish people in the olden time were in many respects like their barbarian neighbors.

If we read the New Testament, we will find in the

epistle of Paul to Timothy, the following gallant passages:

"Let the woman learn in silence, with all "subjection."

"But I suffer not a woman to teach, nor to usurp "authority over the man, but to be in silence."

And for these kind, gentle and civilized remarks, the apostle Paul gives the following reasons:

"For Adam was first formed, then Eve."

"And Adam was not deceived, but the woman "being deceived was in the transgression."

Certainly women ought to feel under great obligation to the apostle Paul.

In the fifth chapter of the same epistle, Paul, advising Timothy as to what kind of people he should admit into his society or church, uses the following language:

"Let not a widow be taken into the number under "threescore years old, having been the wife of one "man."

"But the younger widows refuse, for when they "have begun to wax wanton against Christ, they will "marry."

This same Paul did not seem to think polygamy wrong, except in a bishop. He tells Timothy that:

"A bishop must be blameless, the husband of *one* "wife."

He also lays down the rule that a deacon should be the husband of *one* wife, leaving us to infer that the other members might have as many as they could get.

In the second epistle to Timothy, Paul speaks of "grandmother Lois," who was referred to in such extravagant language by Mr. Talmage, and nothing is said touching her character in the least. All her virtues live in the imagination, and in the imagination alone.

Paul, also, in his epistle to the Ephesians, says:

"Wives, submit yourselves unto your own hus-"bands, as unto the Lord. For the husband is the "head of the wife, even as Christ is the head of the "church."

"Therefore, as the church is subject unto Christ, "so let the wives be to their own husbands, in "everything."

You will find, too, that in the seventh chapter of First Corinthians, Paul laments that all men are not bachelors like himself, and in the second verse of that chapter he gives the only reason for which he was willing that men and women should marry. He advised all the unmarried, and all widows, to remain as he was. In the ninth verse of this same chapter is a slander too vulgar for repetition,—an estimate of woman and of woman's love so low and vile, that every woman should hold the inspired author in infinite abhorrence.

Paul sums up the whole matter, however, by telling those who have wives or husbands, to stay with them—as necessary evils only to be tolerated—but sincerely regrets that anybody was ever married; and finally says that:

"They that have wives should be as though they "had none;" because, in his opinion:

"He that is unmarried careth for the things that "belong to the Lord, how he may please the Lord; "but he that is married careth for the things that are "of the world, how he may please his wife."

"There is this difference also," he tells us, "be-"tween a wife and a virgin. The unmarried woman "careth for the things of the Lord, that she may be "holy both in body and in spirit; but she that is "married careth for the things of the world, how she "may please her husband."

Of course, it is contended that these things have tended to the elevation of woman.

The idea that it is better to love the Lord than to

love your wife, or your husband, is infinitely absurd. Nobody ever did love the Lord,—nobody can—until he becomes acquainted with him.

Saint Paul also tells us that " Man is the image " and glory of God ; but woman is the glory of " man ;" and for the purpose of sustaining this position, says :

"For the man is not of the woman, but the woman " of the man ; neither was the man created for the " woman, but the woman for the man."

Of course, we can all see that man could have gotten along well enough without woman, but woman, by no possibility, could have gotten along without man. And yet, this is called " inspired ;" and this apostle Paul is supposed to have known more than all the people now upon the earth. No wonder Paul at last was constrained to say : "We are fools for " Christ's sake."

Question. How do you account for the present condition of woman in what is known as "the civilized "world," unless the Bible has bettered her condition?

Answer. We must remember that thousands of things enter into the problem of civilization. Soil, climate, and geographical position, united with countless other influences, have resulted in the civilization of our time. If we want to find what the influence of the Bible has been, we must ascertain the condition of Europe when the Bible was considered as absolutely true, and when it wielded its greatest influence.

Christianity as a form of religion had actual possession of Europe during the Middle Ages. At that time, it exerted its greatest power. Then it had the opportunity of breaking the shackles from the limbs of woman. Christianity found the Roman matron a free woman. Polygamy was never known in Rome; and although divorces were allowed by law, the Roman state had been founded for more than five hundred years before either a husband or a wife asked for a divorce. From the foundation of Christianity,—I mean from the time it became the force in the Roman state,—woman, as such, went down in the scale of civilization. The sceptre was taken from her hands, and she became once more the slave and serf of man. The men also were made slaves, and woman has regained her liberty by the same means that man has regained his,—by wresting authority from the hands of the church. While the church had power, the wife and mother was not considered as good as the begging nun; the husband and father was far below the vermin-covered monk; homes were of no value compared with the cathedral; for God had to have a house, no matter how many of his children were wanderers. During all the years in which woman has struggled for equal liberty with man, she has been met with the Bible doctrine that she is the inferior of the man; that Adam was made first, and Eve afterwards; that man was not made for woman, but that woman was made for man.

I find that in this day and generation, the meanest men have the lowest estimate of woman; that the greater the man is, the grander he is, the more he thinks of mother, wife and daughter. I also find that just in the proportion that he has lost confidence in the polygamy of Jehovah and in the advice and philosophy of Saint Paul, he believes in the rights and liberties of woman. As a matter of fact, men have risen from a perusal of the Bible, and murdered their wives. They have risen from reading its pages, and inflicted cruel and even mortal blows upon their children. Men have risen from reading the Bible and torn the flesh of others with red-hot pincers. They have laid down the sacred volume long enough to pour molten lead into the ears of others. They have stopped reading the sacred Scriptures for a sufficient time to incarcerate their fellow-men, to load them with chains, and then they have gone back to their reading, allowing their victims to die in darkness and despair. Men have stopped reading the Old Testament long enough to drive a stake into the ground and collect a few fagots and burn an honest man. Even ministers have denied themselves the privilege of reading the sacred book long enough to tell falsehoods about their fellow-men. There is no crime that Bible readers and Bible believers and Bible worshipers and Bible defenders have not committed. There is no meanness of which some Bible reader, believer, and defender, has not been guilty. Bible believers and Bible defenders have filled the world with calumnies and slanders. Bible believers and Bible defenders have not only whipped their wives, but they have murdered them; they have murdered their children. I do not say that reading the Bible will necessarily make men dishonest, but I do say, that reading the Bible will not prevent their committing crimes. I do not say that believing the Bible will necessarily make men commit burglary, but I do say that a belief in the Bible has caused men to persecute each other, to imprison each other, and to burn each other.

Only a little while ago, a British clergyman murdered his wife. Only a little while ago, an American Protestant clergyman whipped his boy to death because the boy refused to say a prayer.

The Rev. Mr. Crowley not only believed the Bible, but was licensed to expound it. He had been "called" to the ministry, and upon his head had been laid the holy hands; and yet, he deliberately starved orphans, and while looking upon their sunken eyes and hollow cheeks, sung pious hymns and quoted with great unction: " Suffer little chil-
" dren to come unto me."

As a matter of fact, in the last twenty years, more money has been stolen by Christian cashiers, Christian presidents, Christian directors, Christian trustees and Christian statesmen, than by all other convicts in all the penitentiaries in all the Christian world.

The assassin of Henry the Fourth was a Bible reader and a Bible believer. The instigators of the massacre of St. Bartholomew were believers in your sacred Scriptures. The men who invested their money in the slave-trade believed themselves filled with the Holy Ghost, and read with rapture the Psalms of David and the Sermon on the Mount. The murderers of Scotch Presbyterians were believers in Revelation, and the

Presbyterians, when they murdered others, were also believers. Nearly every man who expiates a crime upon the gallows is a believer in the Bible. For a thousand years, the daggers of assassination and the swords of war were blest by priests—by the believers in the sacred Scriptures. The assassin of President Garfield is a believer in the Bible, a hater of infidelity, a believer in personal inspiration, and he expects in a few weeks to join the winged and redeemed in heaven.

If a man would follow, to-day, the teachings of the Old Testament, he would be a criminal. If he would follow strictly the teachings of the New, he would be insane.

FOURTH INTERVIEW.

FOURTH INTERVIEW.

SON. *There is no devil.*
MOTHER. *I know there is.*
SON. *How do you know?*
MOTHER. *Because they make pictures that look just like him.*
SON. *But, mother—*
MOTHER. *Don't "mother" me! You are trying to disgrace your parents.*

Question. I want to ask you a few questions about Mr. Talmage's fourth sermon against you, entitled: "The Meanness of Infidelity," in which he compares you to Jehoiakim, who had the temerity to throw some of the writings of the weeping Jeremiah into the fire?

Answer. So far as I am concerned, I really regret that a second edition of Jeremiah's roll was gotten out. It would have been far better for us all, if it had been left in ashes. There was nothing but curses and prophecies of evil, in the sacred roll that

Jehoiakim burned. The Bible tells us that Jehovah became exceedingly wroth because of the destruction of this roll, and pronounced a curse upon Jehoiakim and upon Palestine. I presume it was on account of the burning of that roll that the king of Babylon destroyed the chosen people of God. It was on account of that sacrilege that the Lord said of Jehoiakim: "He shall have none to sit upon the "throne of David; and his dead body shall be cast "out in the day to the heat, and in the night to the "frost." Any one can see how much a dead body would suffer under such circumstances. Imagine an infinitely wise, good and powerful God taking vengeance on the corpse of a barbarian king! What joy there must have been in heaven as the angels watched the alternate melting and freezing of the dead body of Jehoiakim!

Jeremiah was probably the most accomplished croaker of all time. Nothing satisfied him. He was a prophetic pessimist,—an ancient Bourbon. He was only happy when predicting war, pestilence and famine. No wonder Jehoiakim despised him, and hated all he wrote.

One can easily see the character of Jeremiah from the following occurrence: When the Babylonians had succeeded in taking Jerusalem, and in sacking the city, Jeremiah was unfortunately taken prisoner; but Captain Nebuzaradan came to Jeremiah, and told him that he would let him go, because he had prophesied against his own country. He was regarded as a friend by the enemy.

There was, at that time, as now, the old fight between the church and the civil power. Whenever a king failed to do what the priests wanted, they immediately prophesied overthrow, disaster, and defeat. Whenever the kings would hearken to their voice, and would see to it that the priests had plenty to eat and drink and wear, then they all declared that Jehovah would love that king, would let him live out all his days, and allow his son to reign in his stead. It was simply the old conflict that is still being waged, and it will be carried on until universal civilization does away with priestcraft and superstition.

The priests in the days of Jeremiah were the same as now. They sought to rule the State. They pretended that, at their request, Jehovah would withhold or send the rain; that the seasons were within their power; that they with bitter words could blight the fields and curse the land with want and death. They gloried then, as now, in the exhibition of God's wrath.

In prosperity, the priests were forgotten. Success scorned them; Famine flattered them; Health laughed at them; Pestilence prayed to them; Disaster was their only friend.

These old prophets prophesied nothing but evil, and consequently, when anything bad happened, they claimed it as a fulfillment, and pointed with pride to the fact that they had, weeks or months, or years before, foretold something of that kind. They were really the originators of the phrase, "I told you so!"

There was a good old Methodist class-leader that lived down near a place called Liverpool, on the Illinois river. In the spring of 1861 the old man, telling his experience, among other things said, that he had lived there by the river for more than thirty years, and he did not believe that a year had passed that there were not hundreds of people during the hunting season shooting ducks on Sunday; that he had told his wife thousands of times that no good would come of it; that evil would come of it; "And " now," said the old man, raising his voice with the importance of the announcement, " war is upon us!"

Question. Do you wish, as Mr. Talmage says, to destroy the Bible—to have all the copies burned to ashes? What do you wish to have done with the Bible?

Answer. I want the Bible treated exactly as we treat other books—preserve the good and throw away the foolish and the hurtful. I am fighting the doctrine of inspiration. As long as it is believed that the Bible is inspired, that book is the master—no mind is free. With that belief, intellectual liberty is impossible. With that belief, you can investigate only at the risk of losing your soul. The Catholics have a pope. Protestants laugh at them, and yet the pope is capable of intellectual advancement. In addition to this, the pope is mortal, and the church cannot be afflicted with the same idiot forever. The Protestants have a book for their pope. The book cannot advance. Year after year, and century after century, the book remains as ignorant as ever. It is only made better by those who believe in its inspiration giving better meanings to the words than their ancestors did. In this way it may be said that the Bible grows a little better.

Why should we have a book for a master? That which otherwise might be a blessing, remains a curse. If every copy of the Bible were destroyed, all that is good in that book would be reproduced in a single day. Leave every copy of the Bible as it is, and have every human being believe in its inspiration, and intellectual liberty would cease to exist. The whole race, from that moment, would go back toward the night of intellectual death.

The Bible would do more harm if more people really believed it, and acted in accordance with its teachings. Now and then a Freeman puts the knife to the heart of his child. Now and then an assassin relies upon some sacred passage; but, as a rule, few men believe the Bible to be absolutely true.

There are about fifteen hundred million people in the world. There are not two million who have read the Bible through. There are not two hundred million who ever saw the Bible. There are not five hundred million who ever heard that such a book exists.

Christianity is claimed to be a religion for all mankind. It was founded more than eighteen centuries ago; and yet, not one human being in three has ever heard of it. As a matter of fact, for more than fourteen centuries and-a-half after the crucifixion of Christ, this hemisphere was absolutely unknown. There was not a Christian in the world who knew there was such a continent as ours, and all the inhabitants of this, the New World, were deprived of the gospel for fourteen centuries and-a-half, and knew nothing of its blessings until they were informed by Spanish murderers and marauders. Even in the United States, Christianity is not keeping pace with the increase of population. When we take into consideration that it is aided by the momentum of eighteen centuries, is it not wonderful that it is not to-day holding its own? The reason of this is, that we are beginning to understand the Scriptures. We are beginning to see, and to see clearly, that they are simply of human origin, and that the Bible bears the marks of the barbarians who wrote it. The best educated among the clergy admit that we know but little as to the origin of the gospels; that we do not positively know the author of one of them; that it is really a matter of doubt as to who wrote the five books attributed to Moses. They admit now, that Isaiah was written by more than one person; that Solomon's Song was not written by that king; that Job is, in all probability, not a Jewish book; that Ecclesiastes must have been written by a Freethinker, and by one who had his doubts about the immortality of the soul. The best biblical students of the so-called orthodox world now admit that several stories were united to make the gospel of Saint Luke; that Hebrews is a selection from many fragments, and that no human being, not afflicted with delirium tremens, can understand the book of Revelation.

I am not the only one engaged in the work of destruction. Every Protestant who expresses a doubt as to the genuineness of a passage, is destroying the Bible. The gentlemen who have endeavored to treat hell as a question of syntax, and to prove that eternal punishment depends upon grammar, are helping to bring the Scriptures into contempt. Hundreds of years ago, the Catholics told the Protestant world that it was dangerous to give the Bible to the people. The Catholics were right; the Protestants were wrong. To read is to think. To think is to investigate. To investigate is, finally, to deny. That book should have been read only by priests. Every copy should have been under the lock and key of bishop, cardinal and pope. The common people should have received the Bible from the lips of the ministers. The world should have been kept in ignorance. In that way, and in that way only, could the pulpit have maintained its power. He who teaches a child the alphabet sows the seeds of heresy. I have lived to see the schoolhouse in many a village larger than the church. Every man who finds a fact, is the enemy of theology. Every man who expresses an honest thought is a soldier in the army of intellectual liberty.

Question. Mr. Talmage thinks that you laugh too much,—that you exhibit too much mirth, and that no one should smile at sacred things?

Answer. The church has always feared ridicule. The minister despises laughter. He who builds upon ignorance and awe, fears intelligence and mirth. The theologians always begin by saying: "Let us be "solemn." They know that credulity and awe are twins. They also know that while Reason is the pilot of the soul, Humor carries the lamp. Whoever has the sense of humor fully developed, cannot, by any possibility, be an orthodox theologian. He would be his own laughing stock. The most absurd stories, the most laughable miracles, read in a solemn, stately way, sound to the ears of ignorance and awe like truth. It has been the object of the church for eighteen hundred years to prevent laughter.

A smile is the dawn of a doubt.

Ministers are always talking about death, and coffins, and dust, and worms,—the cross in this life, and the fires of another. They have been the enemies of human happiness. They hate to hear even the laughter of children. There seems to have been a bond of sympathy between divinity and dyspepsia, between theology and indigestion. There is a certain pious hatred of pleasure, and those who have been "born again" are expected to despise "the transitory joys of this fleeting life." In this, they follow the example of their prophets, of whom they proudly say: "They never smiled."

Whoever laughs at a holy falsehood, is called a "scoffer." Whoever gives vent to his natural feelings is regarded as a "blasphemer," and whoever examines the Bible as he examines other books, and relies upon his reason to interpret it, is denounced as a "reprobate."

Let us respect the truth, let us laugh at miracles, and above all, let us be candid with each other.

Question. Mr. Talmage charges that you have, in your lectures, satirized your early home; that you have described with bitterness the Sundays that were forced upon you in your youth; and that in various ways you have denounced your father as a "tyrant," or a "bigot," or a "fool"?

Answer. I have described the manner in which Sunday was kept when I was a boy. My father for many years regarded the Sabbath as a sacred day. We kept Sunday as most other Christians did. I think that my father made a mistake about that day. I have no doubt he was honest about it, and really believed that it was pleasing to God for him to keep the Sabbath as he did.

I think that Sunday should not be a day of gloom, of silence and despair, or a day in which to hear that the chances are largely in favor of your being eternally damned. That day, in my opinion, should be one of joy; a day to get acquainted with your wife and children; a day to visit the woods, or the sea, or the murmuring stream; a day to gather flowers, to visit the graves of your dead, to read old poems, old letters, old books; a day to rekindle the fires of friendship and love.

Mr. Talmage says that my father was a Christian, and he then proceeds to malign his memory. It seems to me that a living Christian should at least tell the truth about one who sleeps the silent sleep of death.

I have said nothing, in any of my lectures, about my father, or about my mother, or about any of my relatives. I have not the egotism to bring them forward. They have nothing to do with the subject in hand. That my father was mistaken upon the subject of religion, I have no doubt. He was a good, a brave and honest man. I loved him living, and I love him dead. I never said to him an unkind word, and in my heart there never was of him an unkind thought. He was grand enough to say to me, that I had the same right to my opinion that he had to his. He was great enough to tell me to read the Bible for myself, to be honest with myself, and if after reading it I concluded it was not the word of God, that it was my duty to say so.

My mother died when I was but a child; and from that day—the darkest of my life—her memory has been within my heart a sacred thing, and I have felt, through all these years, her kisses on my lips.

I know that my parents—if they are conscious now—do not wish me to honor them at the expense of my manhood. I know that neither my father nor my mother would have me sacrifice upon their graves my honest thought. I know that I can only please them by being true to myself, by defending what I believe is good, by attacking what I believe is bad. Yet this minister of Christ is cruel enough, and malicious enough, to attack the reputation of the dead. What he says about my father is utterly and unqualifiedly false.

Right here, it may be well enough for me to say, that long before my father died, he threw aside, as unworthy of a place in the mind of an intelligent man, the infamous dogma of eternal fire; that he regarded with abhorrence many passages in the Old Testament; that he believed man, in another world, would have the eternal opportunity of doing right, and that the pity of God would last as long as the suffering of man. My father and my mother were good, in spite of the Old Testament. They were merciful, in spite of the one frightful doctrine in the New. They did not need the religion of Presbyterianism. Presbyterianism never made a human being better. If there is anything that will freeze the generous current of the soul, it is Calvinism. If there is any creed that will destroy charity, that will keep the tears of pity from the cheeks of men and women, it is Presbyterianism. If there is any doctrine calculated to make man bigoted, unsympathetic, and cruel, it is the doctrine of predestination. Neither my father, nor my mother, believed in the damnation of babes, nor in the inspiration of John Calvin.

Mr. Talmage professes to be a Christian. What effect has the religion of Jesus Christ had upon him? Is he the product—the natural product—of Christianity? Does the real Christian violate the sanctity of death? Does the real Christian malign the memory of the dead? Does the good Christian defame unanswering and unresisting dust?

But why should I expect kindness from a Christian? Can a minister be expected to treat with fairness a man whom his God intends to damn? If a good God is going to burn an infidel forever, in the world to come, surely a Christian should have the right to persecute him a little here.

What right has a Christian to ask anybody to love his father, or mother, or wife, or child? According to the gospels, Christ offered a reward to any one who would desert his father or his mother. He offered a premium to gentlemen for leaving their wives, and tried to bribe people to abandon their little children. He offered them happiness in this world, and a hundred fold in the next, if they would turn a deaf ear to the supplications of a father, the beseeching cry of a wife, and would leave the outstretched arms of babes. They were not even allowed to bury their fathers and their mothers. At that time they were expected to prefer Jesus to their wives and children. And now an orthodox minister says that a man ought not to express his honest thoughts, because they do not happen to be in accord with the belief of his father or mother.

Suppose Mr. Talmage should read the Bible carefully and without fear, and should come to the honest conclusion that it is not inspired, what course would he pursue for the purpose of honoring his parents? Would he say, "I cannot tell the truth, I must lie, "for the purpose of shedding a halo of glory around "the memory of my mother"? Would he say: "Of "course, my father and mother would a thousand "times rather have their son a hypocritical Christian "than an honest, manly unbeliever"? This might please Mr. Talmage, and accord perfectly with his view, but I prefer to say, that my father wished me to be an honest man. If he is in "heaven" now, I am sure that he would rather hear me attack the "inspired" word of God, honestly and bravely, than to hear me, in the solemn accents of hypocrisy, defend what I believe to be untrue.

I may be mistaken in the estimate angels put upon human beings. It may be that God likes a pretended follower better than an honest, outspoken man—one who is an infidel simply because he does not understand this God. But it seems to me, in my unregenerate condition, touched and tainted as I am by original sin, that a God of infinite power and wisdom ought to be able to make a man brave enough to have an opinion of his own. I cannot conceive of God taking any particular pride in any hypocrite he has ever made. Whatever he may say through his ministers, or whatever the angels may repeat, a manly devil stands higher in my estimation than an unmanly angel. I do not mean by this, that there are any unmanly angels, neither do I pretend that there are any manly devils. My meaning is this: If I have a Creator, I can only honor him by being true to myself, and kind and just to my fellow-men. If I wish to shed lustre upon my father and mother, I can only do so by being absolutely true to myself. Never will I lay the wreath of hypocrisy upon the tombs of those I love.

Mr. Talmage takes the ground that we must defend the religious belief of our parents. He seems to forget that all parents do not believe exactly alike, and that everybody has at least two parents. Now, suppose that the father is an infidel, and the mother a Christian, what must the son do? Must he "drive " the ploughshare of contempt through the grave of " the father," for the purpose of honoring the mother; or must he drive the ploughshare through the grave of the mother to honor the father; or must he compromise, and talk one way and believe another? If Mr. Talmage's doctrine is correct, only persons who have no knowledge of their parents can have liberty of opinion. Foundlings would be the only free people. I do not suppose that Mr. Talmage would go so far as to say that a child would be bound by the religion of the person upon whose door-steps he was found. If he does not, then over every foundling hospital should be these words: "Home of Intel-"lectual Liberty."

Question. Do you suppose that we will care nothing in the next world for those we loved in this? Is it worse in a man than in an angel, to care nothing for his mother?

Answer. According to Mr. Talmage, a man can be perfectly happy in heaven, with his mother in hell. He will be so entranced with the society of Christ, that he will not even inquire what has become of his wife. The Holy Ghost will keep him in such a state of happy wonder, of ecstatic joy, that the names, even, of his children will never invade his memory. It may be that I am lacking in filial affection, but I would much rather be in hell, with my parents in heaven, than be in heaven with my parents in hell. I think a thousand times more of my parents than I do of Christ. They knew me, they worked for me, they loved me, and I can imagine no heaven, no state of perfect bliss for me, in which they have no share. If God hates me, because I love them, I cannot love him.

I cannot truthfully say that I look forward with any great degree of joy, to meeting with Haggai and Habakkuk; with Jeremiah, Nehemiah, Obadiah, Zechariah or Zephaniah; with Ezekiel, Micah, or Malachi; or even with Jonah. From what little I have read of their writings, I have not formed a very high opinion of the social qualities of these gentlemen.

I want to meet the persons I have known: and if there is another life, I want to meet the really and the truly great—men who have been broad enough to be tender, and great enough to be kind.

Because I differ with my parents, because I am convinced that my father was wrong in some of his religious opinions, Mr. Talmage insists that I disgrace my parents. How did the Christian religion commence? Did not the first disciples advocate theories that their parents denied? Were they not false,—in his sense of the word,—to their fathers and mothers? How could there have been any progress in this world, if children had not gone beyond their parents? Do you consider that the inventor of a steel plow cast a slur upon his father who scratched the ground with a wooden one? I do not consider that an invention by the son is a slander upon the father; I regard each invention simply as an improvement; and every father should be exceedingly proud of an ingenious son. If Mr. Talmage has a son, it will be impossible for him to honor his father except by differing with him.

It is very strange that Mr. Talmage, a believer in Christ, should object to any man for not loving his mother and his father, when his Master, according to the gospel of Saint Luke, says: "If any man " come to me, and hate not his father, and mother, " and wife, and children, and brethren, and sis- " ters, yea, and his own life also, he cannot be my " disciple."

According to this, I have to make my choice between my wife, my children, and Jesus Christ. I have concluded to stand by my folks—both in this world, and in "the world to come."

Question. Mr. Talmage asks you whether, in your judgment, the Bible was a good, or an evil, to your parents?

Answer. I think it was an evil. The worst thing about my father was his religion. He would have been far happier, in my judgment, without it. I think I get more real joy out of life than he did. He was a man of a very great and tender heart. He was continually thinking—for many years of his life—of the thousands and thousands going down to eternal fire. That doctrine filled his days with gloom, and his eyes with tears. I think that my father and mother would have been far happier had they believed as I do. How any one can get any joy out of the Christian religion is past my comprehension. If that religion is true, hundreds of millions are now in hell, and thousands of millions yet unborn will be. How such a fact can form any part of the "glad tidings of great joy," is amazing to me. It is impossible for me to love a being who would create countless millions for eternal pain. It is impossible for me to worship the God of the Bible, or the God of Calvin, or the God of the Westminster Catechism.

Question. I see that Mr. Talmage challenges you to read the fourteenth chapter of Saint John. Are you willing to accept the challenge; or have you ever read that chapter?

Answer. I do not claim to be very courageous, but I have read that chapter, and am very glad that Mr. Talmage has called attention to it. According to the gospels, Christ did many miracles. He healed the sick, gave sight to the blind, made the lame walk, and raised the dead. In the fourteenth chapter of Saint John, twelfth verse, I find the following:

"Verily, verily, I say unto you: He that believeth
"on me, the works that I do shall he do also; and
"greater works than these shall he do, because I go
"unto my Father."

I am willing to accept that as a true test of a believer. If Mr. Talmage really believes in Jesus Christ, he ought to be able to do at least as great miracles as Christ is said to have done. Will Mr. Talmage have the kindness to read the fourteenth chapter of John, and then give me some proof, in accordance with that chapter, that he is a believer in Jesus Christ? Will he have the kindness to perform a miracle?—for instance, produce a "local flood," make a worm to smite a gourd, or "prepare a fish"?

Can he do anything of that nature? Can he even cause a "vehement east wind"? What evidence, according to the Bible, can Mr. Talmage give of his belief? How does he prove that he is a Christian? By hating infidels and maligning Christians? Let Mr. Talmage furnish the evidence, according to the fourteenth chapter of Saint John, or forever after hold his peace.

He has my thanks for calling my attention to the fourteenth chapter of Saint John.

Question. Mr. Talmage charges that you are attempting to destroy the "chief solace of the world," without offering any substitute. How do you answer this?

Answer. If he calls Christianity the "chief solace" "of the world," and if by Christianity he means that all who do not believe in the inspiration of the Scriptures, and have no faith in Jesus Christ, are to be eternally damned, then I admit that I am doing the best I can to take that "solace" from the human heart. I do not believe that the Bible, when properly understood, is, or ever has been, a comfort to any human being. Surely, no good man can be comforted by reading a book in which he finds that a large majority of mankind have been sentenced to eternal fire. In the doctrine of total depravity there is no "solace." In the doctrine of "election" there can be no joy until the returns are in, and a majority found for you.

Question. Mr. Talmage says that you are taking away the world's medicines, and in place of anæsthetics, in place of laudanum drops, you read an essay to the man in pain, on the absurdities of morphine and nervines in general.

Answer. It is exactly the other way. I say, let us depend upon morphine, not upon prayer. Do not send for the minister—take a little laudanum. Do not read your Bible,—chloroform is better. Do not waste your time listening to meaningless sermons, but take real, genuine soporifics.

I regard the discoverer of ether as a benefactor. I look upon every great surgeon as a blessing to mankind. I regard one doctor, skilled in his profession, of more importance to the world than all the orthodox ministers.

Mr. Talmage should remember that for hundreds of years, the church fought, with all its power, the science of medicine. Priests used to cure diseases by selling little pieces of paper covered with cabalistic marks. They filled their treasuries by the sale of holy water. They healed the sick by relics—the teeth and ribs of saints, the finger-nails of departed worthies, and the hair of glorified virgins. Infidelity said: " end for the doctor." Theology said: " Stick "to the priest." Infidelity,—that is to say, science,—said: "Vaccinate him." The priest said: "Pray;— " I will sell you a charm." The doctor was regarded as a man who was endeavoring to take from God his means of punishment. He was supposed to spike the artillery of Jehovah, to wet the powder of the Almighty, and to steal the flint from the musket of heavenly retribution.

Infidelity has never relied upon essays, it has never relied upon words, it has never relied upon prayers, it has never relied upon angels or gods; it has relied upon the honest efforts of men and women. It has relied upon investigation, observation, experience, and above all, upon human reason.

We, in America, know how much prayers are worth. We have lately seen millions of people upon their knees. What was the result?

In the olden times, when a plague made its appearance, the people fell upon their knees and died.

When pestilence came, they rushed to their cathedrals, they implored their priests—and died. God had no pity upon his ignorant children. At last, Science came to the rescue. Science,—not in the attitude of prayer, with closed eyes, but in the attitude of investigation, with open eyes,—looked for and discovered some of the laws of health. Science found that cleanliness was far better than godliness. It said: Do not spend your time in praying;—clean your houses, clean your streets, clean yourselves. This pestilence is not a punishment. Health is not simply a favor of the gods. Health depends upon conditions, and when the conditions are violated, disease is inevitable, and no God can save you. Health depends upon your surroundings, and when these are favorable, the roses are in your cheeks.

We find in the Old Testament that God gave to Moses a thousand directions for ascertaining the presence of leprosy. Yet it never occurred to this God to tell Moses how to cure the disease. Within the lids of the Old Testament, we have no information upon a subject of such vital importance to mankind.

It may, however, be claimed by Mr. Talmage, that this statement is a little too broad, and I will therefore give one recipe that I find in the fourteenth chapter of Leviticus:

"Then shall the priest command to take for him that is to be cleansed two birds alive and clean, and cedar wood, and scarlet, and hyssop; and the priest shall command that one of the birds be killed in an earthen vessel over running water. As for the living bird, he shall take it, and the cedar wood, and the scarlet, and the hyssop, and shall dip them and the living bird in the blood of the bird that was killed over the running water. And he shall sprinkle upon him that is to be cleansed from the leprosy seven times, and shall pronounce him clean, and shall let the living bird loose into the open field."

Prophets were predicting evil—filling the country with their wails and cries, and yet it never occurred to them to tell one solitary thing of the slightest importance to mankind. Why did not these inspired men tell us how to cure some of the diseases that have decimated the world? Instead of spending forty days and forty nights with Moses, telling him how to build a large tent, and how to cut the garments of priests, why did God not give him a little useful information in respect to the laws of health?

Mr. Talmage must remember that the church has invented no anodynes, no anæsthetics, no medicines, and has affected no cures. The doctors have not been inspired. All these useful things men have discovered for themselves, aided by no prophet and by no divine Savior. Just to the extent that man has depended upon the other world, he has failed to make the best of this. Just in the proportion that he has depended on his own efforts, he has advanced. The church has always said:

"Consider the lilies of the field; they toil not, " neither do they spin." " Take no thought for the " morrow." Whereas, the real common sense of this world has said: "No matter whether lilies toil and spin, or not, if you would succeed, you must work, you must take thought for the morrow, you must look beyond the present day, you must provide for your wife and your children."

What can I be expected to give as a substitute for perdition? It is enough to show that it does not exist. What does a man want in place of a disease? Health. And what is better calculated to increase the happiness of mankind than to know that the doctrine of eternal pain is infinitely and absurdly false?

Take theology from the world, and natural Love remains, Science is still here, Music will not be lost, the page of History will still be open, the walls of the world will still be adorned with Art, and the niches rich with Sculpture.

Take theology from the world, and we all shall have a common hope,—and the fear of hell will be removed from every human heart.

Take theology from the world, and millions of men will be compelled to earn an honest living. Impudence will not tax credulity. The vampire of hypocrisy will not suck the blood of honest toil.

Take theology from the world, and the churches can be schools, and the cathedrals universities.

Take theology from the world, and the money wasted on superstition will do away with want.

Take theology from the world, and every brain will find itself without a chain.

There is a vast difference between what is called infidelity and theology.

Infidelity is honest. When it reaches the confines of reason, it says : " I know no further."

Infidelity does not palm its guess upon an ignorant world as a demonstration.

Infidelity proves nothing by slander—establishes nothing by abuse.

Infidelity has nothing to hide. It has no " holy " of holies," except the abode of truth. It has no curtain that the hand of investigation has not the right to draw aside. It lives in the cloudless light, in the very noon, of human eyes.

Infidelity has no bible to be blasphemed. It does not cringe before an angry God.

Infidelity says to every man: Investigate for yourself. There is no punishment for unbelief.

Infidelity asks no protection from legislatures. It wants no man fined because he contradicts its doctrines.

Infidelity relies simply upon evidence—not evidence of the dead, but of the living.

Infidelity has no infallible pope. It relies only upon infallible fact. It has no priest except the interpreter of Nature. The universe is its church. Its bible is everything that is true. It implores every man to verify every word for himself, and it implores him to say, if he does not believe it, that he does not.

Infidelity does not fear contradiction. It is not afraid of being laughed at. It invites the scrutiny of all doubters, of all unbelievers. It does not rely upon awe, but upon reason. It says to the whole world: It is dangerous *not* to think. It is dangerous *not* to be honest. It is dangerous *not* to investigate. It is dangerous *not* to follow where your reason leads.

Infidelity requires every man to judge for himself. Infidelity preserves the manhood of man.

Question. Mr. Talmage also says that you are trying to put out the light-houses on the coast of the next world; that you are "about to leave everybody "in darkness at the narrows of death"?

Answer. There can be no necessity for these light-houses, unless the God of Mr. Talmage has planted rocks and reefs within that unknown sea. If there is no hell, there is no need of any light-house on the shores of the next world; and only those are interested in keeping up these pretended light-houses who are paid for trimming invisible wicks and supplying the lamps with allegorical oil. Mr. Talmage is one of these light-house keepers, and he knows that if it is ascertained that the coast is not dangerous, the light-house will be abandoned, and the keeper will have to find employment elsewhere. As a matter of fact, every church is a useless light house. It warns us only against breakers that do not exist. Whenever a mariner tells one of the keepers that there is no danger, then all the keepers combine to destroy the reputation of that mariner.

No one has returned from the other world to tell us whether they have light-houses on that shore or not; or whether the light-houses on this shore—one of which Mr. Talmage is tending—have ever sent a cheering ray across the sea.

Nature has furnished every human being with a light more or less brilliant, more or less powerful. That light is Reason; and he who blows that light out, is in utter darkness. It has been the business of the church for centuries to extinguish the lamp of the mind, and to convince the people that their own reason is utterly unreliable. The church has asked all men to rely only upon the light of the church.

Every priest has been not only a light-house but a guide-board. He has threatened eternal damnation to all who travel on some other road. These guide-boards have been toll-gates, and the principal reason why the churches have wanted people to go their road is, that tolls might be collected. They have regarded unbelievers as the owners of turnpikes do people who go 'cross lots. The toll-gate man always tells you that other roads are dangerous—filled with quagmires and quicksands.

Every church is a kind of insurance society, and proposes, for a small premium, to keep you from eternal fire. Of course, the man who tells you that there is to be no fire, interferes with the business, and is denounced as a malicious meddler and blasphemer. The fires of this world sustain the same relation to insurance companies that the fires of the next do to the churches.

Mr. Talmage also insists that I am breaking up the "life-boats." Why should a ship built by infinite wisdom, by an infinite shipbuilder, carry life-boats? The reason we have life-boats now is, that we are not entirely sure of the ship. We know that man has not yet found out how to make a ship that can certainly brave all the dangers of the deep. For this reason we carry life-boats. But infinite wisdom must surely build ships that do not need life-boats. Is there to be a wreck at last? Is God's ship to go down in storm and darkness? Will it be necessary at last to forsake his ship and depend upon life-boats?

For my part, I do not wish to be rescued by a lifeboat. When the ship, bearing the whole world, goes down, I am willing to go down with it—with my wife, with my children, and with those I have loved. I will not slip ashore in an orthodox canoe with somebody else's folks,—I will stay with my own.

What a picture is presented by the church! A few in life's last storm are to be saved; and the saved, when they reach shore, are to look back with joy upon the great ship going down to the eternal depths! This is what I call the unutterable meanness of orthodox Christianity.

Mr. Talmage speaks of the "meanness of in-"fidelity."

The meanness of orthodox Christianity permits the husband to be saved, and to be ineffably happy, while the wife of his bosom is suffering the tortures of hell.

The meanness of orthodox Christianity tells the boy that he can go to heaven and have an eternity of bliss, and that this bliss will not even be clouded by the fact that the mother who bore him writhes in eternal pain.

The meanness of orthodox Christianity allows a soul to be so captivated with the companionship of angels as to forget all the old loves and friendships of this world.

The meanness of orthodox Christianity, its unspeakable selfishness, allows a soul in heaven to exult in the fact of its own salvation, and at the same time to care nothing for the damnation of all the rest.

The orthodox Christian says that if he can only save his little soul, if he can barely squeeze into heaven, if he can only get past Saint Peter's gate, if he can by hook or crook climb up the opposite bank of Jordan, if he can get a harp in his hand, it matters not to him what becomes of brother or sister, father or mother, wife or child. He is willing that they should burn if he can sing.

Oh, the unutterable meanness of orthodox Christianity, the infinite heartlessness of the orthodox angels, who with tearless eyes will forever gaze upon the agonies of those who were once blood of their blood and flesh of their flesh!

Mr. Talmage describes a picture of the scourging of Christ, painted by Rubens, and he tells us that he was so appalled by this picture—by the sight of the naked back, swollen and bleeding—that he could not have lived had he continued to look; yet this same man, who could not bear to gaze upon a painted pain, expects to be perfectly happy in heaven, while countless billions of actual—not painted—men, women, and children writhe—not in a pictured flame, but in the real and quenchless fires of hell.

Question. Mr. Talmage also claims that we are indebted to Christianity for schools, colleges, universities, hospitals and asylums?

Answer. This shows that Mr. Talmage has not read the history of the world. Long before Christianity had a place, there were vast libraries. There were thousands of schools before a Christian existed on the earth. There were hundreds of hospitals before a line of the New Testament was written. Hundreds of years before Christ, there were hospitals in India,—not only for men, women and children, but even for beasts. There were hospitals in Egypt long before Moses was born. They knew enough then to cure insanity with music. They surrounded the insane with flowers, and treated them with kindness.

The great libraries at Alexandria were not Christian. The most intellectual nation of the Middle Ages was not Christian. While Christians were imprisoning people for saying that the earth is round, the Moors in Spain were teaching geography with globes. They had even calculated the circumference of the earth by the tides of the Red Sea.

Where did education come from? For a thousand

years Christianity destroyed books and paintings and statues. For a thousand years Christianity was filled with hatred toward every effort of the human mind. We got paper from the Moors. Printing had been known thousands of years before, in China. A few manuscripts, containing a portion of the literature of Greece, a few enriched with the best thoughts of the Roman world, had been preserved from the general wreck and ruin wrought by Christian hate. These became the seeds of intellectual progress. For a thousand years Christianity controlled Europe. The Mohammedans were far in advance of the Christians with hospitals and asylums and institutions of learning.

Just in proportion that we have done away with what is known as orthodox Christianity, humanity has taken its place. Humanity has built all the asylums, all the hospitals. Humanity, not Christianity, has done these things. The people of this country are all willing to be taxed that the insane may be cared for, that the sick, the helpless, and the destitute may be provided for, not because they are Christians, but because they are humane; and they are not humane because they are Christians.

The colleges of this country have been poisoned by

theology, and their usefulness almost destroyed. Just in proportion that they have gotten from ecclesiastical control, they have become a good. That college, today, which has the most religion has the least true learning; and that college which is the nearest free, does the most good. Colleges that pit Moses against modern geology, that undertake to overthrow the Copernican system by appealing to Joshua, have done, and are doing, very little good in this world.

Suppose that in the first century Pagans had said to Christians: Where are your hospitals, where are your asylums, where are your works of charity, where are your colleges and universities?

The Christians undoubtedly would have replied: We have not been in power. There are but few of us. We have been persecuted to that degree that it has been about as much as we could do to maintain ourselves.

Reasonable Pagans would have regarded such an answer as perfectly satisfactory. Yet that question could have been asked of Christianity after it had held the reins of power for a thousand years, and Christians would have been compelled to say: We have no universities, we have no colleges, we have no real asylums.

The Christian now asks of the atheist: Where is your asylum, where is your hospital, where is your university? And the atheist answers: There have been but few atheists. The world is not yet sufficiently advanced to produce them. For hundreds and hundreds of years, the minds of men have been darkened by the superstitions of Christianity. Priests have thundered against human knowledge, have denounced human reason, and have done all within their power to prevent the real progress of mankind.

You must also remember that Christianity has made more lunatics than it ever provided asylums for. Christianity has driven more men and women crazy than all other religions combined. Hundreds and thousands and millions have lost their reason in contemplating the monstrous falsehoods of Christianity. Thousands of mothers, thinking of their sons in hell—thousands of fathers, believing their boys and girls in perdition, have lost their reason.

So, let it be distinctly understood, that Christianity has made ten lunatics—twenty—one hundred—where it has provided an asylum for one.

Mr. Talmage also speaks of the hospitals. When we take into consideration the wars that have been waged on account of religion, the countless thousands who have been maimed and wounded, through all the years, by wars produced by theology—then I say that Christianity has not built hospitals enough to take care of her own wounded—not enough to take care of one in a hundred. Where Christianity has bound up the wounds of one, it has pierced the bodies of a hundred others with sword and spear, with bayonet and ball. Where she has provided one bed in a hospital, she has laid away a hundred bodies in bloody graves.

Of course I do not expect the church to do anything but beg. Churches produce nothing. They are like the lilies of the field. " They toil not, neither " do they spin, yet Solomon in all his glory was not " arrayed like most of them."

The churches raise no corn nor wheat. They simply collect tithes. They carry the alms' dish. They pass the plate. They take toll. Of course a mendicant is not expected to produce anything. He does not support,—he is supported. The church does not help. She receives, she devours, she consumes, and she produces only discord. She exchanges mistakes for provisions, faith for food, prayers for pence. The church is a beggar. But we have this consolation: In this age of the world, this beggar is not on horseback, and even the walking is not good.

Question. Mr. Talmage says that infidels have done no good?

Answer. Well, let us see. In the first place, what is an "infidel"? He is simply a man in advance of his time. He is an intellectual pioneer. He is the dawn of a new day. He is a gentleman with an idea of his own, for which he gave no receipt to the church. He is a man who has not been branded as the property of some one else. An "infidel" is one who has made a declaration of independence. In other words, he is a man who has had a doubt. To have a doubt means that you have thought upon the subject—that you have investigated the question; and he who investigates any religion will doubt.

All the advance that has been made in the religious world has been made by "infidels," by "heretics," by "skeptics," by doubters,—that is to say, by thoughtful men. The doubt does not come from the ignorant members of your congregations. Heresy is not born of stupidity,—it is not the child of the brainless. He who is so afraid of hurting the reputation of his father and mother that he refuses to advance, is not a "heretic." The "heretic" is not true to falsehood. Orthodoxy is. He who stands faithfully by a mistake is "orthodox." He who, discovering that it is a mistake, has the courage to say so, is an "infidel."

An infidel is an intellectual discoverer—one who finds new isles, new continents, in the vast realm of thought. The dwellers on the orthodox shore denounce this brave sailor of the seas as a buccaneer.

And yet we are told that the thinkers of new thoughts have never been of value to the world. Voltaire did more for human liberty than all the orthodox ministers living and dead. He broke a thousand times more chains than Luther. Luther simply substituted his chain for that of the Catholics. Voltaire had none. The Encyclopædists of France did more for liberty than all the writers upon theology. Bruno did more for mankind than millions of "be- "lievers." Spinoza contributed more to the growth of the human intellect than all the orthodox theologians.

Men have not done good simply because they have believed this or that doctrine. They have done good in the intellectual world as they have thought and secured for others the liberty to think and to express their thoughts. They have done good in the physical world by teaching their fellows how to triumph over the obstructions of nature. Every man who has taught his fellow-man to think, has been a benefactor. Every one who has supplied his fellow-men with facts, and insisted upon their right to think, has been a blessing to his kind.

Mr. Talmage, in order to show what Christians have done, points us to Whitefield, Luther, Oberlin, Judson, Martyn, Bishop McIlvaine and Hannah More. I would not for one moment compare George Whitefield with the inventor of movable type, and there is no parallel between Frederick Oberlin and the inventor of paper; not the slightest between Martin Luther and the discoverer of the New World; not the least between Adoniram Judson and the inventor of the reaper, nor between Henry Martyn and the discoverer of photography. Of what use to the world was Bishop McIlvaine, compared with the inventor of needles? Of what use were a hundred such priests compared with the inventor of matches, or even of clothes-pins? Suppose that Hannah More had never lived? about the same number would read her writings now. It is hardly fair to compare her with the inventor of the steamship?

The progress of the world—its present improved condition—can be accounted for only by the discoveries of genius, only by men who have had the courage to express their honest thoughts.

After all, the man who invented the telescope found out more about heaven than the closed eyes of prayer had ever discovered. I feel absolutely certain that the inventor of the steam engine was a greater benefactor to mankind than the writer of the Presbyterian creed. I may be mistaken, but I think that railways have done more to civilize mankind, than any system of theology. I believe that the printing press has done more for the world than the pulpit. It is my opinion that the discoveries of Kepler did a thousand times more to enlarge the minds of men than the prophecies of Daniel. I feel under far greater obligation to Humboldt than to Haggai. The inventor of the plow did more good than the maker of the first rosary—because, say what you will, plowing is better than praying; we can live by plowing without praying, but we can not live by praying without plowing. So I put my faith in the plow.

As Jehovah has ceased to make garments for his children,—as he has stopped making coats of skins,

I have great respect for the inventors of the spinning-jenny and the sewing machine. As no more laws are given from Sinai, I have admiration for the real statesmen. As miracles have ceased, I rely on medicine, and on a reasonable compliance with the conditions of health.

I have infinite respect for the inventors, the thinkers, the discoverers, and above all, for the unknown millions who have, without the hope of fame, lived and labored for the ones they loved.

FIFTH INTERVIEW.

FIFTH INTERVIEW.

PARSON. *You had better join the church; it is the safer way.*
SINNER. *I can't live up to your doctrines, and you know it.*
PARSON. *Well, you can come as near it in the church as out; and forgiveness will be easier if you join us.*
SINNER. *What do you mean by that?*
PARSON. *I will tell you. If you join the church, and happen to backslide now and then, Christ will say to his Father: "That man is a "friend of mine, and you may charge his account to me."*

QUESTION. What have you to say about the fifth sermon of the Rev. Mr. Talmage in reply to you?

Answer. The text from which he preached is: "Do men gather grapes of thorns, or figs of thistles?" I am compelled to answer these questions in the negative. That is one reason why I am an infidel. I do not believe that anybody can gather grapes of thorns, or figs of thistles. That is exactly my doctrine. But the doctrine of the church is, that you can. The church says, that just at the last, no matter if you have spent your whole life in raising thorns and thistles, in planting and watering and hoeing and plowing thorns and thistles—that just at the last, if you will repent, between hoeing the last thistle and taking the last breath, you can reach out the white and palsied hand of death and gather from every thorn a cluster of grapes and from every thistle an abundance of figs. The church insists that in this way you can gather enough grapes and figs to last you through all eternity.

My doctrine is, that he who raises thorns must harvest thorns. If you sow thorns, you must reap thorns; and there is no way by which an innocent being can have the thorns you raise thrust into his brow, while you gather his grapes.

But Christianity goes even further than this. It insists that a man can plant grapes and gather thorns. Mr. Talmage insists that, no matter how good you are, no matter how kind, no matter how much you love your wife and children, no matter how many self-denying acts you do, you will not be allowed to eat of the grapes you raise; that God will step between you and the natural consequences of your goodness, and not allow you to reap what you sow.

Mr. Talmage insists, that if you have no faith in the Lord Jesus Christ, although you have been good here, you will reap eternal pain as your harvest; that the effect of honesty and kindness will not be peace and joy, but agony and pain. So that the church does insist not only that you can gather grapes from thorns, but thorns from grapes.

I believe exactly the other way. If a man is a good man here, dying will not change him, and he will land on the shore of another world—if there is one—the same good man that he was when he left this; and I do not believe there is any God in this universe who can afford to damn a good man. This God will say to this man: You loved your wife, your children, and your friends, and I love you. You treated others with kindness; I will treat you in the same way. But Mr. Talmage steps up to his God, nudges his elbow, and says: Although he was a very good man, he belonged to no church; he was a blasphemer; he denied the whale story, and after I explained that Jonah was only in the whale's mouth, he still denied it; and thereupon Mr. Talmage expects that his infinite God will fly in a passion, and in a perfect rage will say: What! did he deny that story? Let him be eternally damned!

Not only this, but Mr. Talmage insists that a man may have treated his wife like a wild beast; may have trampled his child beneath the feet of his rage; may have lived a life of dishonesty, of infamy, and yet, having repented on his dying bed, having made his peace with God through the intercession of his Son, he will be welcomed in heaven with shouts of joy. I deny it. I do not believe that angels can be so quickly made from rascals. I have but little confidence in repentance without restitution, and a husband who has driven a wife to insanity and death by his cruelty—afterward repenting and finding himself in heaven, and missing his wife,—were he worthy to be an angel, would wander through all the gulfs of hell until he clasped her once again.

Now, the next question is, What must be done with those who are sometimes good and sometimes bad? That is my condition. If there is another world, I expect to have the same opportunity of behaving myself that I have here. If, when I get there, I fail to act as I should, I expect to reap what I sow. If, when I arrive at the New Jerusalem, I go into the thorn business, I expect to harvest what I plant. If I am wise enough to start a vineyard, I expect to have grapes in the early fall. But if I do there as I have done here — plant some grapes and some thorns, and harvest them together — I expect to fare very much as I have fared here. But I expect year by year to grow wiser, to plant fewer thorns every spring, and more grapes.

Question. Mr. Talmage charges that you have taken the ground that the Bible is a cruel book, and has produced cruel people?

Answer. Yes, I have taken that ground, and I maintain it. The Bible was produced by cruel people, and in its turn it has produced people like its authors. The extermination of the Canaanites was cruel. Most of the laws of Moses were bloodthirsty and cruel. Hundreds of offences were punishable by death, while now, in civilized countries, there are only two crimes for which the punishment is capital. I charge that Moses and Joshua and David and Samuel and Solomon were cruel. I believe that to read and believe the Old Testament naturally makes a man careless of human life. That book has produced hundreds of religious wars, and it has furnished the battle-cries of bigotry for fifteen hundred years.

The Old Testament is filled with cruelty, but its cruelty stops with this world, its malice ends with death; whenever its victim has reached the grave, revenge is satisfied. Not so with the New Testament. It pursues its victim forever. After death, comes hell; after the grave, the worm that never dies. So that, as a matter of fact, the New Testament is infinitely more cruel than the Old.

Nothing has so tended to harden the human heart as the doctrine of eternal punishment, and that passage: "He that believeth and is baptized shall be " saved, and he that believeth not shall be damned," has shed more blood than all the other so-called " sacred books " of all this world.

I insist that the Bible is cruel. The Bible invented instruments of torture. The Bible laid the foundations of the Inquisition. The Bible furnished the fagots and the martyrs. The Bible forged chains not only for the hands, but for the brains of men. The Bible was at the bottom of the massacre of St. Bartholomew. Every man who has been persecuted for religion's sake has been persecuted by the Bible. That sacred book has been a beast of prey.

The truth is, Christians have been good in spite of the Bible. The Bible has lived upon the reputations of good men and good women,—men and women who were good notwithstanding the brutality they found upon the inspired page. Men have said: "My mother "believed in the Bible; my mother was good; there- "fore, the Bible is good," when probably the mother never read a chapter in it.

The Bible produced the Church of Rome, and Torquemada was a product of the Bible. Philip of Spain and the Duke of Alva were produced by the Bible. For thirty years Europe was one vast battle-field, and the war was produced by the Bible. The revocation of the Edict of Nantes was produced by the sacred Scriptures. The instruments of torture—the pincers, the thumb-screws, the racks, were produced by the word of God. The Quakers of New England were whipped and burned by the Bible—their children were stolen by the Bible. The slave-ship had for its sails the leaves of the Bible. Slavery was upheld in the United States by the Bible. The Bible was the auction-block. More than this, worse than this, infinitely beyond the computation of imagination, the despotisms of the old world all rested and still rest upon the Bible. "The powers that be" were supposed to have been "ordained of God;" and he who rose against his king periled his soul.

In this connection, and in order to show the state of society when the church had entire control of civil and ecclesiastical affairs, it may be well enough to read the following, taken from the New York *Sun* of March 21, 1882. From this little extract, it will be easy in the imagination to re-organize the government that then existed, and to see clearly the state of society at that time. This can be done upon the same principle that one scale tells of the entire fish, or one bone of the complete animal:

"From records in the State archives of Hesse-
" Darmstadt, dating back to the thirteenth century,
" it appears that the public executioner's fee for boiling
" a criminal in oil was twenty-four florins; for decapi-
" tating with the sword, fifteen florins and-a-half; for
" quartering, the same; for breaking on the wheel,
" five florins, thirty kreuzers; for tearing a man to
" pieces, eighteen florins. Ten florins per head was
" his charge for hanging, and he burned delinquents
" alive at the rate of fourteen florins apiece. For ap-
" plying the 'Spanish boot' his fee was only two
" florins. Five florins were paid to him every time he
" subjected a refractory witness to the torture of the
" rack. The same amount was his due for 'branding
" 'the sign of the gallows with a red-hot iron upon
" 'the back, forehead, or cheek of a thief,' as well as
" for 'cutting off the nose and ears of a slanderer or

"'blasphemer.' Flogging with rods was a cheap punishment, its remuneration being fixed at three florins, thirty kreuzers."

The Bible has made men cruel. It is a cruel book. And yet, amidst its thorns, amidst its thistles, amidst its nettles and its swords and pikes, there are some flowers, and these I wish, in common with all good men, to save.

I do not believe that men have ever been made merciful in war by reading the Old Testament. I do not believe that men have ever been prompted to break the chain of a slave by reading the Pentateuch. The question is not whether Florence Nightingale and Miss Dix were cruel. I have said nothing about John Howard, nothing about Abbott Lawrence. I say nothing about people in this connection. The question is: Is the Bible a cruel book? not: Was Miss Nightingale a cruel woman? There have been thousands and thousands of loving, tender and charitable Mohammedans. Mohammedan mothers love their children as well as Christian mothers can. Mohammedans have died in defence of the Koran— died for the honor of an impostor. There were millions of charitable people in India—millions in Egypt—and I am not sure that the world has ever produced people who loved one another better than the Egyptians.

I think there are many things in the Old Testament calculated to make man cruel. Mr. Talmage asks: "What has been the effect upon your children? As they have become more and more fond of the Scriptures have they become more and more fond of tearing off the wings of flies and pinning grasshoppers and robbing birds' nests?"

I do not believe that reading the bible would make them tender toward flies or grasshoppers. According to that book, God used to punish animals for the crimes of their owners. He drowned the animals in a flood. He visited cattle with disease. He bruised them to death with hailstones—killed them by the thousand. Will the reading of these things make children kind to animals? So, the whole system of sacrifices in the Old Testament is calculated to harden the heart. The butchery of oxen and lambs, the killing of doves, the perpetual destruction of life, the continual shedding of blood—these things, if they have any tendency, tend only to harden the heart of childhood.

The Bible does not stop simply with the killing of animals. The Jews were commanded to kill their neighbors—not only the men, but the women; not only the women, but the babes. In accordance with the command of God, the Jews killed not only their neighbors, but their own brothers; and according to this book, which is the foundation, as Mr. Talmage believes, of all mercy, men were commanded to kill their wives because they differed with them on the subject of religion.

Nowhere in the world can be found laws more unjust and cruel than in the Old Testament.

Question. Mr. Talmage wants you to tell where the cruelty of the Bible crops out in the lives of Christians?

Answer. In the first place, millions of Christians have been persecutors. Did they get the idea of persecution from the Bible? Will not every honest man admit that the early Christians, by reading the Old Testament, became convinced that it was not only their privilege, but their duty, to destroy heathen nations? Did they not, by reading the same book, come to the conclusion that it was their solemn duty to extirpate heresy and heretics? According to the New Testament, nobody could be saved unless he believed in the Lord Jesus Christ. The early Christians believed this dogma. They also believed that they had a right to defend themselves and their children from "heretics."

We all admit that a man has a right to defend his children against the assaults of a would-be murderer, and he has the right to carry this defence to the extent of killing the assailant. If we have the right to kill people who are simply trying to kill the bodies of our children, of course we have the right to kill them when they are endeavoring to assassinate, not simply their bodies, but their souls. It was in this way Christians reasoned. If the Testament is right, their reasoning was correct. Whoever believes the New Testament literally—whoever is satisfied that it is absolutely the word of God, will become a persecutor. All religious persecution has been, and is, in exact harmony with the teachings of the Old and New Testaments. Of course I mean with some of the teachings. I admit that there are passages in both the Old and New Testaments against persecution. These are passages quoted only in time of peace. Others are repeated to feed the flames of war.

I find, too, that reading the Bible and believing the Bible do not prevent even ministers from telling falsehoods about their opponents. I find that the Rev. Mr. Talmage is willing even to slander the dead,— that he is willing to stain the memory of a Christian, and that he does not hesitate to give circulation to what he knows to be untrue. Mr. Talmage has himself, I believe, been the subject of a church trial. How many of the Christian witnesses against him, in his judgment, told the truth? Yet they were all Bible readers and Bible believers. What effect, in his judgment, did the reading of the Bible have upon his enemies? Is he willing to admit that the testimony of a Bible reader and believer is true? Is he willing to accept the testimony even of ministers? —of his brother ministers? Did reading the Bible make them bad people? Was it a belief in the Bible that colored their testimony? Or, was it a belief in the Bible that made Mr. Talmage deny the truth of their statements?

Question. Mr. Talmage charges you with having said that the Scriptures are a collection of polluted writings?

Answer. I have never said such a thing. I have said, and I still say, that there are passages in the Bible unfit to be read—passages that never should have been written—passages, whether inspired or uninspired, that can by no possibility do any human being any good. I have always admitted that there are good passages in the Bible—many good, wise and just laws—many things calculated to make men better—many things calculated to make men worse. I admit that the Bible is a mixture of good and bad, of truth and falsehood, of history and fiction, of sense and nonsense, of virtue and vice, of aspiration and revenge, of liberty and tyranny.

I have never said anything against Solomon's Song. I like it better than I do any book that precedes it, because it touches upon the human. In the desert of murder, wars of extermination, polygamy, concubinage and slavery, it is an oasis where the trees grow, where the birds sing, and where human love blossoms and fills the air with perfume. I do not regard that book as obscene. There are many things in it that are beautiful and tender, and it is calculated to do good rather than harm.

Neither have I any objection to the book of Ecclesiastes—except a few interpolations in it. That book was written by a Freethinker, by a philosopher. There is not the slightest mention of God in it, nor of another state of existence. All portions in which

God is mentioned are interpolations. With some of this book I agree heartily. I believe in the doctrine of enjoying yourself, if you can, to-day. I think it foolish to spend all your years in heaping up treasures, not knowing but he who will spend them is to be an idiot. I believe it is far better to be happy with your wife and child now, than to be miserable here, with angelic expectations in some other world.

Mr. Talmage is mistaken when he supposes that all Bible believers have good homes, that all Bible readers are kind in their families. As a matter of fact, nearly all the wife-whippers of the United States are orthodox. Nine-tenths of the people in the penitentiaries are believers. Scotland is one of the most orthodox countries in the world, and one of the most intemperate. Hundreds and hundreds of women are arrested every year in Glasgow for drunkenness. Visit the Christian homes in the manufacturing districts of England. Talk with the beaters of children and whippers of wives, and you will find them believers. Go into what is known as the "Black "Country," and you will have an idea of the Christian civilization of England.

Let me tell you something about the "Black "Country." There women work in iron; there women do the work of men. Let me give you an instance: A commission was appointed by Parliament to examine into the condition of the women in the " Black " Country," and a report was made. In that report I read the following:

" A superintendent of a brickyard where women " were engaged in carrying bricks from the yard to " the kiln, said to one of the women:

"' Eliza, you don't appear to be very uppish this " morning.'"

"' Neither would you be very uppish, sir,' she re-" plied, 'if you had had a child last night.'"

This gives you an idea of the Christian civilization of England.

England and Ireland produce most of the prize-fighters. The scientific burglar is a product of Great Britain. There is not the great difference that Mr. Talmage supposes, between the morality of Pekin and of New York. I doubt if there is a city in the world with more crime according to the population than New York, unless it be London, or it may be Dublin, or Brooklyn, or possibly Glasgow, where a man too pious to read a newspaper published on Sunday, stole millions from the poor.

I do not believe there is a country in the world

where there is more robbery than in Christian lands—no country where more cashiers are defaulters, where more presidents of banks take the money of depositors, where there is more adulteration of food, where fewer ounces make a pound, where fewer inches make a yard, where there is more breach of trust, more respectable larceny under the name of embezzlement, or more slander circulated as gospel.

Question. Mr. Talmage insists that there are no contradictions in the Bible—that it is a perfect harmony from Genesis to Revelation—a harmony as perfect as any piece of music ever written by Beethoven or Handel?

Answer. Of course, if God wrote it, the Bible ought to be perfect. I do not see why a minister should be so perfectly astonished to find that an inspired book is consistent with itself throughout. Yet the truth is, the Bible is infinitely inconsistent.

Compare the two systems—the system of Jehovah and that of Jesus. In the Old Testament the doctrine of "an eye for an eye and a tooth for a tooth" was taught. In the New Testament, "forgive your " enemies," and "pray for those who despitefully " use you and persecute you." In the Old Testament it is kill, burn, massacre, destroy; in the New forgive. The two systems are inconsistent, and one is just about as far wrong as the other. To live for and thirst for revenge, to gloat over the agony of an enemy, is one extreme; to "resist not evil" is the other extreme; and both these extremes are equally distant from the golden mean of justice.

The four gospels do not even agree as to the terms of salvation. And yet, Mr. Talmage tells us that there are four cardinal doctrines taught in the Bible— the goodness of God, the fall of man, the sympathetic and forgiving nature of the Savior, and two destinies—one for believers and the other for unbelievers. That is to say:

1. That God is good, holy and forgiving.
2. That man is a lost sinner.
3. That Christ is "all sympathetic," and ready to take the whole world to his heart.
4. Heaven for believers and hell for unbelievers.

First. I admit that the Bible says that God is good and holy. But this Bible also tells what God did, and if God did what the Bible says he did, then I insist that God is not good, and that he is not holy, or forgiving. According to the Bible, this good God believed in religious persecution; this good

God believed in extermination, in polygamy, in concubinage, in human slavery; this good God commanded murder and massacre, and this good God could only be mollified by the shedding of blood. This good God wanted a butcher for a priest. This good God wanted husbands to kill their wives—wanted fathers and mothers to kill their children. This good God persecuted animals on account of the crimes of their owners. This good God killed the common people because the king had displeased him. This good God killed the babe even of the maid behind the mill, in order that he might get even with a king. This good God committed every possible crime.

Second. The statement that man is a lost sinner is not true. There are thousands and thousands of magnificent Pagans—men ready to die for wife, or child, or even for friend, and the history of Pagan countries is filled with self-denying and heroic acts. If man is a failure, the infinite God, if there be one, is to blame. Is it possible that the God of Mr. Talmage could not have made man a success? According to the Bible, his God made man knowing that in about fifteen hundred years he would have to drown all his descendants.

Why would a good God create a man that he knew would be a sinner all his life, make hundreds of thousands of his fellow-men unhappy, and who at last would be doomed to an eternity of suffering? Can such a God be good? How could a devil have done worse?

Third. If God is infinitely good, is he not fully as sympathetic as Christ? Do you have to employ Christ to mollify a being of infinite mercy? Is Christ any more willing to take to his heart the whole world than his Father is? Personally, I have not the slightest objection in the world to anybody believing in an infinitely good and kind God—not the slightest objection to any human being worshiping an infinitely tender and merciful Christ—not the slightest objection to people preaching about heaven, or about the glories of the future state—not the slightest.

Fourth. I object to the doctrine of two destinies for the human race. I object to the infamous falsehood of eternal fire. And yet, Mr. Talmage is endeavoring to poison the imagination of men, women and children with the doctrine of an eternal hell. Here is what he preaches, taken from the " Constitu-
" tion of the Presbyterian Church of the United
" States : "

"By the decrees of God, for the manifestation of
"his glory, some men and angels are predestinated
"to everlasting life, and others foreordained to ever-
"lasting death."

That is the doctrine of Mr. Talmage. He worships a God who damns people "for the manifesta-"tion of his glory,"—a God who made men, knowing that they would be damned—a God who damns babes simply to increase his reputation with the angels. This is the God of Mr. Talmage. Such a God I abhor, despise and execrate.

Question. What does Mr. Talmage think of mankind? What is his opinion of the "unconverted"? How does he regard the great and glorious of the earth, who have not been the victims of his particular superstition? What does he think of some of the best the earth has produced?

Answer. I will tell you how he looks upon all such. Read this from his "Confession of Faith:"

"Our first parents, being seduced by the subtlety
"of the tempter, sinned in eating the forbidden fruit.
"By this sin, they fell from their original righteous-
"ness and communion with God, and so became
"dead in sin, and wholly defiled in all the faculties

"and parts of soul and body; and they being the
"root of all mankind, the guilt of this sin was
"imputed, and the same death in sin and corrupted
"nature conveyed to all their posterity. From this
"original corruption—whereby we are utterly indis-
"posed, disabled, and made opposite to all good,
"and wholly inclined to all evil, do proceed all actual
"transgressions."

This is Mr. Talmage's view of humanity.

Why did his God make a devil? Why did he allow the devil to tempt Adam and Eve? Why did he leave innocence and ignorance at the mercy of subtlety and wickedness? Why did he put "the "tree of the knowledge of good and evil" in the garden? For what reason did he place temptation in the way of his children? Was it kind, was it just, was it noble, was it worthy of a good God? No wonder Christ put into his prayer: "Lead us not "into temptation."

At the time God told Adam and Eve not to eat, why did he not tell them of the existence of Satan? Why were they not put upon their guard against the serpent? Why did not God make his appearance just before the sin, instead of just after. Why did he not play the role of a Savior instead of that of a detective? After he found that Adam and Eve had sinned—knowing as he did that they were then totally corrupt—knowing that all their children would be corrupt, knowing that in fifteen hundred years he would have to drown millions of them, why did he not allow Adam and Eve to perish in accordance with natural law, then kill the devil, and make a new pair?

When the flood came, why did he not drown all? Why did he save for seed that which was "perfectly "and thoroughly corrupt in all its parts and facul-"ties"? If God had drowned Noah and his sons and their families, he could have then made a new pair, and peopled the world with men not "wholly " defiled in all their faculties and parts of soul and " body."

Jehovah learned nothing by experience. He persisted in his original mistake. What would we think of a man who finding that a field of wheat was worthless, and that such wheat never could be raised with profit, should burn all of the field with the exception of a few sheaves, which he saved for seed? Why save such seed? Why should God have preserved Noah, knowing that he was totally corrupt, and that he would again fill the world with infamous people—people incapable of a good action? He must have known at that time, that by preserving Noah, the Canaanites would be produced, that these same Canaanites would have to be murdered, that the babes in the cradles would have to be strangled. Why did he produce them? He knew at that time, that Egypt would result from the salvation of Noah, that the Egyptians would have to be nearly destroyed, that he would have to kill their first-born, that he would have to visit even their cattle with disease and hailstones. He knew also that the Egyptians would oppress his chosen people for two hundred and fifteen years, that they would upon the back of toil inflict the lash. Why did he preserve Noah? He should have drowned all, and started with a new pair. He should have warned them against the devil, and he might have succeeded, in that way, in covering the world with gentlemen and ladies, with real men and real women.

We know that most of the people now in the world are not Christians. Most who have heard the gospel of Christ have rejected it, and the Presbyterian Church tells us what is to become of all these people. This is the "glad tidings of great joy." Let us see:

"All mankind, by their fall, lost communion with God, are under his wrath and curse, and so made liable to all the miseries of this life, to death itself, and to the pains of hell forever."

According to this good Presbyterian doctrine, all that we suffer in this world, is the result of Adam's fall. The babes of to-day suffer for the crime of the first parents. Not only so; but God is angry at us for what Adam did. We are under the wrath of an infinite God, whose brows are corrugated with eternal hatred.

Why should God hate us for being what we are and necessarily must have been? A being that God made—the devil—for whose work God is responsible, according to the Bible wrought this woe. God of his own free will must have made the devil. What did he make him for? Was it necessary to have a devil in heaven? God, having infinite power, can of course destroy this devil to-day. Why does he permit him to live? Why did he allow him to thwart his plans? Why did he permit him to pollute the innocence of Eden? Why does he allow him now to wrest souls by the million from the redeeming hand of Christ?

According to the Scriptures, the devil has always

been successful. He enjoys himself. He is called "the prince of the power of the air." He has no conscientious scruples. He has miraculous power. All miraculous power must come of God, otherwise it is simply in accordance with nature. If the devil can work a miracle, it is only with the consent and by the assistance of the Almighty. Is the God of Mr. Talmage in partnership with the devil? Do they divide profits?

We are also told by the Presbyterian Church—I quote from their Confession of Faith—that "there is no sin so small but it deserves damnation." Yet Mr. Talmage tells us that God is good, that he is filled with mercy and loving-kindness. A child nine or ten years of age commits a sin, and thereupon it deserves eternal damnation. That is what Mr. Talmage calls, not simply justice, but mercy; and the sympathetic heart of Christ is not touched. The same being who said: "Suffer little children to come unto me," tells us that a child, for the smallest sin, deserves to be eternally damned. The Presbyterian Church tells us that infants, as well as adults, in order to be saved, need redemption by the blood of Christ, and regeneration by the Holy Ghost.

I am charged with trying to take the consolation

of this doctrine from the world. I am a criminal because I am endeavoring to convince the mother that her child does not deserve eternal punishment. I stand by the graves of those who "died in their "sins," by the tombs of the "unregenerate," over the ashes of men who have spent their lives working for their wives and children, and over the sacred dust of soldiers who died in defence of flag and country, and I say to their friends—I say to the living who loved them, I say to the men and women for whom they worked, I say to the children whom they educated, I say to the country for which they died: These fathers, these mothers, these wives, these husbands, these soldiers are not in hell.

Question. Mr. Talmage insists that the Bible is scientific, and that the real scientific man sees no contradiction between revelation and science; that, on the contrary, they are in harmony. What is your understanding of this matter?

Answer. I do not believe the Bible to be a scientific book. In fact, most of the ministers now admit that it was not written to teach any science. They admit that the first chapter of Genesis is not geologically true. They admit that Joshua knew nothing of science. They admit that four-footed birds did not exist in the days of Moses. In fact, the only way they can avoid the unscientific statements of the Bible, is to assert that the writers simply used the common language of their day, and used it, not with the intention of teaching any scientific truth, but for the purpose of teaching some moral truth. As a matter of fact, we find that moral truths have been taught in all parts of this world. They were taught in India long before Moses lived; in Egypt long before Abraham was born; in China thousands of years before the flood. They were taught by hundreds and thousands and millions before the Garden of Eden was planted.

It would be impossible to prove the truth of a revelation simply because it contained moral truths. If it taught immorality, it would be absolutely certain that it was not a revelation from an infinitely good being. If it taught morality, it would be no reason for even suspecting that it had a divine origin. But if the Bible had given us scientific truths; if the ignorant Jews had given us the true theory of our solar system; if from Moses we had learned the nature of light and heat; if from Joshua we had learned something of electricity; if the minor prophets had given us the distances to other planets; if the orbits of the stars had been marked by the barbarians of that day, we might have admitted that they must have been inspired. If they had said anything in advance of their day: if they had plucked from the night of ignorance one star of truth, we might have admitted the claim of inspiration; but the Scriptures did not rise above their source, did not rise above their ignorant authors—above the people who believed in wars of extermination, in polygamy, in concubinage, in slavery, and who taught these things in their " sacred Scriptures."

The greatest men in the scientific world have not been, and are not, believers in the inspiration of the Scriptures. There has been no greater astronomer than Laplace. There is no greater name than Humboldt. There is no living scientist who stands higher than Charles Darwin. All the professors in all the religious colleges in this country rolled into one, would not equal Charles Darwin. All the cowardly apologists for the cosmogony of Moses do not amount to as much in the world of thought as Ernst Hæckel. There is no orthodox scientist the equal of Tyndall or Huxley. There is not one in this country the equal of John Fiske. I insist, that the foremost men to-day in the scientific world reject the dogma of inspiration. They reject the science of the Bible, and hold in utter contempt the astronomy of Joshua, and the geology of Moses.

Mr. Talmage tells us " that Science is a boy and " Revelation is a man." Of course, like the most he says, it is substantially the other way. Revelation, so-called, was the boy. Religion was the lullaby of the cradle, the ghost-story told by the old woman, Superstition. Science is the man. Science asks for demonstration. Science impels us to investigation, and to verify everything for ourselves. Most professors of American colleges, if they were not afraid of losing their places, if they did not know that Christians were bad enough now to take the bread from their mouths, would tell their students that the Bible is not a scientific book.

I admit that I have said :

1. That the Bible is *cruel*.
2. That in many passages it is *impure*.
3. That it is *contradictory*.
4. That it is *unscientific*.

Let me now prove these propositions one by one.
First. The Bible is *cruel*.

I have opened it at random, and the very first

chapter that has struck my eye is the sixth of First Samuel. In the nineteenth verse of that chapter, I find the following:

"And he smote the men of Bethshemesh, because "they had looked into the ark of the Lord; even he "smote of the people fifty thousand and three-score "and ten men."

All this slaughter was because some people had looked into a box that was carried upon a cart. Was that cruel?

I find, also, in the twenty-fourth chapter of Second Samuel, that David was moved by God to number Israel and Judah. God put it into his heart to take a census of his people, and thereupon David said to Joab, the captain of his host:

"Go now through all the tribes of Israel, from "Dan even to Beersheba, and number ye the people, "that I may know the number of the people."

At the end of nine months and twenty days, Joab gave the number of the people to the king, and there were at that time, according to that census, "eight hundred thousand valiant men that drew the "sword," in Israel, and in Judah, "five hundred "thousand men," making a total of thirteen hundred thousand men of war. The moment this census was taken, the wrath of the Lord waxed hot against David, and thereupon he sent a seer, by the name of Gad, to David, and asked him to choose whether he would have seven years of famine, or fly three months before his enemies, or have three days of pestilence. David concluded that as God was so merciful as to give him a choice, he would be more merciful than man, and he chose the pestilence.

Now, it must be remembered that the sin of taking the census had not been committed by the people, but by David himself, inspired by God, yet the people were to be punished for David's sin. So, when David chose the pestilence, God immediately killed "seventy thousand men, from Dan even to " Beersheba."

"And when the angel stretched out his hand upon " Jerusalem to destroy it, the Lord repented him of " the evil, and said to the angel that destroyed the " people, It is enough; stay now thine hand."

Was this cruel?

Why did a God of infinite mercy destroy seventy thousand men? Why did he fill his land with widows and orphans, because King David had taken the census? If he wanted to kill anybody, why did he not kill David? I will tell you why. Because at that time, the people were considered as the property of the king. He killed the people precisely as he killed the cattle. And yet, I am told that the Bible is not a cruel book.

In the twenty-first chapter of Second Samuel, I find that there were three years of famine in the days of David, and that David inquired of the Lord the reason of the famine; and the Lord told him that it was because Saul had slain the Gibeonites. Why did not God punish Saul instead of the people? And David asked the Gibeonites how he should make atonement, and the Gibeonites replied that they wanted no silver nor gold, but they asked that seven of the sons of Saul might be delivered unto them, so that they could hang them before the Lord, in Gibeah. And David agreed to the proposition, and thereupon he delivered to the Gibeonites the two sons of Rizpah, Saul's concubine, and the five sons of Michal, the daughter of Saul, and the Gibeonites hanged all seven of them together. And Rizpah, more tender than them all, with a woman's heart of love kept lonely vigil by the dead, "from the beginning of har-
" vest until water dropped upon them out of heaven,
" and suffered neither the birds of the air to rest upon
" them by day, nor the beast of the field by night."

I want to know if the following, from the fifteenth chapter of First Samuel, is inspired:

"Thus saith the Lord of hosts; I remember that which Amalek did to Israel, how he laid wait for him in the way when he came up from Egypt. Now go and smite Amalek, and utterly destroy all that they have, and spare them not, but slay both man and woman, infant and suckling, ox and sheep, camel and ass."

We must remember that those he was commanded to slay had done nothing to Israel. It was something done by their forefathers, hundreds of years before; and yet they are commanded to slay the women and children and even the animals, and to spare none.

It seems that Saul only partially carried into execution this merciful command of Jehovah. He spared the life of the king. He "utterly destroyed all the people with the edge of the sword," but he kept alive the best of the sheep and oxen and of the fatlings and lambs. Then God spake unto Samuel and told him that he was very sorry he had made Saul king, because he had not killed all the animals, and because he had spared Agag; and Samuel asked Saul: "What meaneth this bleating of sheep in mine ears, and the lowing of the oxen which I hear?"

Are stories like this calculated to make soldiers merciful?

So I read in the sixth chapter of Joshua, the fate of the city of Jericho: "And they utterly destroyed "all that was in the city, both man and woman, "young and old, and ox, and sheep, and ass, with the "edge of the sword. And they burnt the city with "fire, and all that was therein." But we are told that one family was saved by Joshua, out of the general destruction: "And Joshua saved Rahab, the harlot, "alive, and her father's household, and all that she "had." Was this fearful destruction an act of mercy?

It seems that they saved the money of their victims: "the silver and gold and the vessels of brass "and of iron they put into the treasury of the house "of the Lord."

After all this pillage and carnage, it appears that there was a suspicion in Joshua's mind that somebody was keeping back a part of the treasure. Search was made, and a man by the name of Achan admitted that he had sinned against the Lord, that he had seen a Babylonish garment among the spoils, and two hundred shekels of silver and a wedge of gold of fifty shekels' weight, and that he took them and hid them in his tent. For this atrocious crime it seems that the Lord denied any victories to the Jews until they found out the wicked criminal. When they discovered poor Achan, "they took him and his sons "and his daughters, and his oxen and his asses and "his sheep, and all that he had, and brought them unto "the valley of Achor; and all Israel stoned him with "stones and burned them with fire after they had "stoned them with stones."

After Achan and his sons and his daughters and his herds had been stoned and burned to death, we are told that "the Lord turned from the fierceness of "his anger."

And yet it is insisted that this God "is merciful, "and that his loving-kindness is over all his works."

In the eighth chapter of this same book, the infinite God, "creator of heaven and earth and all that is "therein," told his general, Joshua, to lay an ambush for a city—to "lie in wait against the city, even be-"hind the city; go not very far from the city, but be "ye all ready." He told him to make an attack and then to run, as though he had been beaten, in order that the inhabitants of the city might follow, and thereupon his reserves that he had ambushed might rush into the city and set it on fire. God Almighty planned the battle. God himself laid the snare. The whole programme was carried out. Joshua made believe that he was beaten, and fled, and then the soldiers in ambush rose out of their places, entered the city, and set it on fire. Then came the slaughter. They "utterly destroyed all the inhabit-"ants of Ai," men and maidens, women and babes, sparing only their king till evening, when they hanged him on a tree, then "took his carcase down "from the tree and cast it at the entering of the "gate, and raised thereon a great heap of stones "which remaineth unto this day." After having done all this, "Joshua built an altar unto the Lord "God of Israel, and offered burnt offerings unto the "Lord." I ask again, was this cruel?

Again I ask, was the treatment of the Gibeonites cruel when they sought to make peace but were denied, and cursed instead; and although permitted to live, were yet made slaves? Read the mandate consigning them to bondage: "Now therefore ye "are cursed, and there shall none of you be freed "from being bondmen and hewers of wood and "drawers of water for the house of my God."

Is it possible, as recorded in the tenth chapter of Joshua, that the Lord took part in these battles, and cast down great hail-stones from the battlements of heaven upon the enemies of the Israelites, so that " they were more who died with hail-stones, than " they whom the children of Israel slew with the " sword"?

Is it possible that a being of infinite power would exercise it in that way instead of in the interest of kindness and peace?

I find, also, in this same chapter, that Joshua took Makkedah and smote it with the edge of the sword, that he utterly destroyed all the souls that were therein, that he allowed none to remain.

I find that he fought against Libnah, and smote it with the edge of the sword, and utterly destroyed all the souls that were therein, and allowed none to remain, and did unto the king as he did unto the king of Jericho.

I find that he also encamped against Lachish, and that God gave him that city, and that he " smote it " with the edge of the sword, and all the souls that " were therein," sparing neither old nor young, helpless women nor prattling babes.

He also vanquished Horam, King of Gezer, " and " smote him and his people until he left him none " remaining."

He encamped against the city of Eglon, and killed every soul that was in it, at the edge of the sword, just as he had done to Lachish and all the others.

He fought against Hebron, "and took it and " smote it with the edge of the sword, and the king " thereof,"—and it appears that several cities, their number not named, were included in this slaughter, for Hebron " and all the cities thereof and all the " souls that were therein," were utterly destroyed.

He then waged war against Debir and took it, and more unnumbered cities with it, and all the souls that were therein shared the same horrible fate—he did not leave a soul alive.

And this chapter of horrors concludes with this song of victory:

" So Joshua smote all the country of the hills, and " of the south, and of the vale, and of the springs, " and all their kings: he left none remaining, but " utterly destroyed all that breathed, as the Lord " God of Israel commanded. And Joshua smote " them from Kadeshbarnea even unto Gaza, and all the " country of Goshen, even unto Gibeon. And all these " kings and their land did Joshua take at one time, ' because the Lord God of Israel fought for Israel."

Was God, at that time, merciful?

I find, also, in the twenty-first chapter that many kings met, with their armies, for the purpose of overwhelming Israel, and the Lord said unto Joshua: "Be not afraid because of them, for to-morrow about "this time I will deliver them all slain before Israel. "I will hough their horses and burn their chariots "with fire." Were animals so treated by the command of a merciful God?

Joshua captured Hazor, and smote all the souls that were therein with the edge of the sword, there was not one left to breathe; and he took all the cities of all the kings that took up arms against him, and utterly destroyed all the inhabitants thereof. He took the cattle and spoils as prey unto himself, and smote every man with the edge of the sword; and not only so, but left not a human being to breathe.

I find the following directions given to the Israelites who were waging a war of conquest. They are in the twentieth chapter of Deuteronomy, from the tenth to the eighteenth verses:

"When thou comest nigh unto a city to fight "against it, then proclaim peace unto it. And it "shall be, if it make thee an answer of peace, and "open unto thee, then it shall be that all the people "that is found therein shall be tributaries unto thee, and they shall serve thee. And if it will make no peace with thee, but will war against thee, then thou shalt besiege it. And when the Lord thy God hath delivered it into thine hands, thou shalt smite every male thereof with the edge of the sword; but the women, and the little ones, and the cattle, and all that is in the city, even the spoil thereof, shalt thou take unto thyself; and thou shalt eat the spoil of thine enemies, which the Lord thy God hath given thee. Thus shalt thou do unto all the cities which are very far off from thee, which are not of the cities of these nations."

It will be seen from this that people could take their choice between death and slavery, provided these people lived a good ways from the Israelites. Now, let us see how they were to treat the inhabitants of the cities near to them:

"But of the cities of these people which the Lord thy God doth give thee for an inheritance, thou shalt save alive nothing that breatheth. But thou shalt utterly destroy them; namely, the Hittites, and the Amorites, the Canaanites, and the Perizzites, the Hivites and the Jebusites, as the Lord thy God hath commanded thee."

It never occurred to this merciful God to send missionaries to these people. He built them no schoolhouses, taught them no alphabet, gave them no book; they were not supplied even with a copy of the Ten Commandments. He did not say "Reform," but "Kill;" not "Educate," but "Destroy." He gave them no Bible, built them no church, sent them no preachers. He knew when he made them that he would have to have them murdered. When he created them he knew that they were not fit to live; and yet, this is the infinite God who is infinitely merciful and loves his children better than an earthly mother loves her babe.

In order to find just how merciful God is, read the twenty-eighth chapter of Deuteronomy, and see what he promises to do with people who do not keep all of his commandments and all of his statutes. He curses them in their basket and store, in the fruit of their body, in the fruit of their land, in the increase of their cattle and sheep. He curses them in the city and in the field, in their coming in and their going out. He curses them with pestilence, with consumption, with fever, with inflammation, with extreme burning, with sword, with blasting, with mildew. He tells them that the heavens shall be as brass over their heads and the earth as iron under their feet; that the rain shall be powder and dust and shall come down on them and destroy them; that they shall flee seven ways before their enemies; that their carcasses shall be meat for the fowls of the air, and the beasts of the earth; that he will smite them with the botch of Egypt, and with the scab, and with the itch, and with madness and blindness and astonishment; that he will make them grope at noonday; that they shall be oppressed and spoiled evermore; that one shall betroth a wife and another shall have her; that they shall build a house and not dwell in it; plant a vineyard and others shall eat the grapes; that their sons and daughters shall be given to their enemies; that he will make them mad for the sight of their eyes; that he will smite them in the knees and in the legs with a sore botch that cannot be healed, and from the sole of the foot to the top of the head; that they shall be a by-word among all nations; that they shall sow much seed and gather but little; that the locusts shall consume their crops; that they shall plant vineyards and drink no wine,—that they shall gather grapes, but worms shall eat them; that they shall raise olives but have no oil; beget sons and daughters, but they shall go into captivity; that all the trees and fruit of the land shall be devoured by locusts, and that all these curses shall pursue them and overtake them, until they be destroyed; that they shall be slaves to their enemies, and be constantly in hunger and thirst and nakedness, and in want of all things. And as though this were not enough, the Lord tells them that he will bring a nation against them swift as eagles, a nation fierce and savage, that will show no mercy and no favor to old or young, and leave them neither corn, nor wine, nor oil, nor flocks, nor herds; and this nation shall besiege them in their cities until they are reduced to the necessity of eating the flesh of their own sons and daughters; so that the men would eat their wives and their children, and women eat their husbands and their own sons and daughters, and their own babes.

All these curses God pronounced upon them if they did not observe to do all the words of the law that were written in his book.

This same merciful God threatened that he would bring upon them all the diseases of Egypt—every sickness and every plague; that he would scatter them from one end of the earth to the other; that they should find no rest; that their lives should hang in perpetual doubt; that in the morning they would say: Would God it were evening! and in the evening, Would God it were morning! and that he would finally take them back to Egypt where they should be again sold for bondmen and bondwomen.

This curse, the foundation of the *Anathema maranatha;* this curse, used by the pope of Rome to prevent the spread of thought; this curse used even by the Protestant Church; this curse born of barbarism and of infinite cruelty, is now said to have issued from the lips of an infinitely merciful God. One would suppose that Jehovah had gone insane; that he had divided his kingdom like Lear, and from the darkness of insanity had launched his curses upon a world.

In order that there may be no doubt as to the mercy of Jehovah, read the thirteenth chapter of Deuteronomy:

"If thy brother, the son of thy mother, or thy
" son, or thy daughter, or the wife of thy bosom, or
" thy friend, which is as thine own soul, entice thee
" secretly, saying, Let us go and serve other gods,
" which thou hast not known, thou nor thy fathers;
" * * * thou shalt not consent unto him, nor
" hearken unto him; neither shall thine eyes pity him,
" neither shalt thou spare, neither shalt thou conceal

"him; but thou shalt surely kill him: thine hand
"shall be first upon him to put him to death, and
"afterwards the hand of all the people; and thou
"shalt stone him with stones that he die, because he
"hath sought to entice thee away from the Lord thy
"God."

This, according to Mr. Talmage, is a commandment of the infinite God. According to him, God ordered a man to murder his own son, his own wife, his own brother, his own daughter, if they dared even to suggest the worship of some other God than Jehovah. For my part, it is impossible not to despise such a God—a God not willing that one should worship what he must. No one can control his admiration, and if a savage at sunrise falls upon his knees and offers homage to the great light of the East, he cannot help it. If he worships the moon, he cannot help it. If he worships fire, it is because he cannot control his own spirit. A picture is beautiful to me in spite of myself. A statue compels the applause of my brain. The worship of the sun was an exceedingly natural religion, and why should a man or woman be destroyed for kneeling at the fireside of the world?

No wonder that this same God, in the very next chapter of Deuteronomy to that quoted, says to his

chosen people: "Ye shall not eat of anything that
" dieth of itself: thou shalt give it unto the stranger
" that is within thy gates, that he may eat it; or thou
" mayest sell it unto an alien: for thou art a holy
" people unto the Lord thy God."

What a mingling of heartlessness and thrift—the religion of sword and trade!

In the seventh chapter of Deuteronomy, Jehovah gives his own character. He tells the Israelites that there are seven nations greater and mightier than themselves, but that he will deliver them to his chosen people, and that they shall smite them and utterly destroy them; and having some fear that a drop of pity might remain in the Jewish heart, he says:

" Thou shalt make no covenant with them, nor
" show mercy unto them. * * * Know therefore
" that the Lord thy God, he is God, the faithful God,
" which keepeth covenant and mercy with them that
" love him and keep his commandments to a thousand
" generations, and repayeth them that hate him to
" their face, to destroy them: he will not be slack to
" him that hateth him, he will repay him to his face."
This is the description which the merciful, long-suffering Jehovah gives of himself.

So, he promises great prosperity to the Jews if

they will only obey his commandments, and says: "And the Lord will take away from thee all sickness, and will put none of the evil diseases of Egypt upon thee, but will lay them upon all them that hate thee. And thou shalt consume all the people which the Lord thy God shall deliver thee; thine eye shall have no pity upon them."

Under the immediate government of Jehovah, mercy was a crime. According to the law of God, pity was weakness, tenderness was treason, kindness was blasphemy, while hatred and massacre were virtues.

In the second chapter of Deuteronomy we find another account tending to prove that Jehovah is a merciful God. We find that Sihon, king of Heshbon, would not let the Hebrews pass by him, and the reason given is, that "the Lord God hardened his spirit and made his heart obstinate, that he might deliver him into the hand" of the Hebrews. Sihon, his heart having been hardened by God, came out against the chosen people, and God delivered him to them, and "they smote him, and his sons, and all his people, and took all his cities, and utterly destroyed the men and, the women, and the little ones of every city: they left none to remain." And in this same chapter this same God promises that the dread and fear of his chosen people should be "upon all the "nations that are under the whole heaven," and that they should "tremble and be in anguish because of" the Hebrews.

Read the thirty-first chapter of Numbers, and see how the Midianites were slain. You will find that "the children of Israel took all the women of Midian "captives, and their little ones," that they took "all "their cattle, and all their flocks, and all their goods," that they slew all the males, and burnt all their cities and castles with fire, that they brought the captives and the prey and the spoil unto Moses and Eleazar the priest; that Moses was wroth with the officers of his host because they had saved all the women alive, and thereupon this order was given: "Kill "every male among the little ones, and kill every "woman, * * * but all the women children "keep alive for yourselves."

After this, God himself spake unto Moses, and said: "Take the sum of the prey that was taken, "both of man and of beast, thou and Eleazar the "priest * * * and divide the prey into two "parts, between those who went to war, and between "all the congregation, and levy a tribute unto the

"Lord, one soul of five hundred of the persons, and the cattle; take it of their half and give it to the priest for an offering * * * and of the children of Israel's half, take one portion of fifty of the persons and the animals and give them unto the Levites. * * * And Moses and the priest did as the Lord had commanded." It seems that they had taken six hundred and seventy-five thousand sheep, seventy-two thousand beeves, sixty-one thousand asses, and thirty-two thousand women children and maidens. And it seems, by the fortieth verse, *that the Lord's tribute of the maidens was thirty-two,*—the rest were given to the soldiers and to the congregation of the Lord.

Was anything more infamous ever recorded in the annals of barbarism? And yet we are told that the Bible is an inspired book, that it is not a cruel book, and that Jehovah is a being of infinite mercy.

In the twenty-fifth chapter of Numbers we find that the Israelites had joined themselves unto Baal-Peor, and thereupon the anger of the Lord was kindled against them, as usual. No being ever lost his temper more frequently than this Jehovah. Upon this particular occasion, "the Lord said unto Moses, "Take all the heads of the people, and hang them

"up before the Lord against the sun, that the fierce
"anger of the Lord may be turned away from Israel."
And thereupon "Moses said unto the judges of Israel,
"Slay ye every one his men that were joined unto
"Baal-peor."

Just as soon as these people were killed, and their heads hung up before the Lord against the sun, and a horrible double murder of a too merciful Israelite and a Midianitish woman, had been committed by Phinehas, the son of Eleazar, "the plague was stayed "from the children of Israel." Twenty-four thousand had died. Thereupon, "the Lord spake unto Moses "and said"—and it is a very merciful commandment —"Vex the Midianites and smite them."

In the twenty-first chapter of Numbers is more evidence that God is merciful and compassionate.

The children of Israel had become discouraged. They had wandered so long in the desert that they finally cried out: "Wherefore have ye brought us "up out of Egypt to die in the wilderness? There "is no bread, there is no water, and our soul loatheth "this light bread." Of course they were hungry and thirsty. Who would not complain under similar circumstances? And yet, on account of this complaint, the God of infinite tenderness and compassion sent serpents among them, and these serpents bit them—bit the cheeks of children, the breasts of maidens, and the withered faces of age. Why would a God do such an infamous thing? Why did he not, as the leader of this people, his chosen children, feed them better? Certainly an infinite God had the power to satisfy their hunger and to quench their thirst. He who overwhelmed a world with water, certainly could have made a few brooks, cool and babbling, to follow his chosen people through all their journeying. He could have supplied them with miraculous food.

How fortunate for the Jews that Jehovah was not revengeful, that he was so slow to anger, so patient, so easily pleased. What would they have done had he been exacting, easily incensed, revengeful, cruel, or blood-thirsty?

In the sixteenth chapter of Numbers, an account is given of a rebellion. It seems that Korah, Dathan and Abiram got tired of Moses and Aaron. They thought the priests were taking a little too much upon themselves. So Moses told them to have two hundred and fifty of their men bring their censers and put incense in them before the Lord, and stand in the door of the tabernacle of the congregation with Moses and Aaron. That being done, the Lord appeared, and told Moses and Aaron to separate themselves from the people, that he might consume them all in a moment. Moses and Aaron, having a little compassion, begged God not to kill everybody. The people were then divided, and Dathan and Abiram came out and stood in the door of their tents with their wives and their sons and their little children. And Moses said :

"Hereby ye shall know that the Lord hath sent
"me to do all these works; for I have not done them
"of my mine own mind. If these men die the
"common death of all men, or if they be visited
"after the common visitation of all men, then the
"Lord hath not sent me. But if the Lord make a
"new thing, and the earth open her mouth and
"swallow them up, with all that appertain unto them,
"and they go down quick into the pit, then ye shall
"understand that these men have provoked the
"Lord." The moment he ceased speaking, "the
"ground clave asunder that was under them; and
"the earth opened her mouth and swallowed them up,
"and their houses, and all the men that appertained
"unto Korah, and all their goods. They, and all that
"appertained to them went down alive into the pit,

"and the earth closed upon them, and they perished "from among the congregation."

This, according to Mr. Talmage, was the act of an exceedingly merciful God, prompted by infinite kindness, and moved by eternal pity. What would he have done had he acted from motives of revenge? What would he have done had he been remorselessly cruel and wicked?

In addition to those swallowed by the earth, the two hundred and fifty men that offered the incense were consumed by "a fire that came out from the "Lord." And not only this, but the same merciful Jehovah wished to consume all the people, and he would have consumed them all, only that Moses prevailed upon Aaron to take a censer and put fire therein from off the altar of incense and go quickly to the congregation and make an atonement for them. He was not quick enough. The plague had already begun; and before he could possibly get the censers and incense among the people, fourteen thousand and seven hundred had died of the plague. How many more might have died, if Jehovah had not been so slow to anger and so merciful and tender to his children, we have no means of knowing.

In the thirteenth chapter of the same book of

Numbers, we find that some spies were sent over into the promised land, and that they brought back grapes and figs and pomegranates, and reported that the whole land was flowing with milk and honey, but that the people were strong, that the cities were walled, and that the nations in the promised land were mightier than the Hebrews. They reported that all the people they met were men of a great stature, that they had seen "the giants, the sons of Anak " which come of giants," compared with whom the Israelites were "in their own sight as grasshoppers, " and so were we in their sight." Entirely discouraged by these reports, "all the congregation lifted up " their voice and cried, and the people wept that " night * * * and murmured against Moses and " against Aaron, and said unto them: Would God " that we had died in the land of Egypt! or would " God we had died in this wilderness!" Some of them thought that it would be better to go back,— that they might as well be slaves in Egypt as to be food for giants in the promised land. They did not want their bones crunched between the teeth of the sons of Anak.

Jehovah got angry again, and said to Moses: " How long will these people provoke me? * * *

"I will smite them with pestilence, and disinherit "them." But Moses said: Lord, if you do this, the Egyptians will hear of it, and they will say that you were not able to bring your people into the promised land. Then he proceeded to flatter him by telling him how merciful and long-suffering he had been. Finally, Jehovah concluded to pardon the people this time, but his pardon depended upon the violation of his promise, for he said: "They shall "not see the land which I sware unto their fathers, "neither shall any of them that provoked me see it; "but my servant Caleb, * * * him will I bring "into the land." And Jehovah said to the people: "Your carcasses shall fall in this wilderness, and all "that were numbered of you according to your "whole number, from twenty years old and upward, "which have murmured against me, ye shall not "come into the land concerning which I sware to "make you dwell therein, save Caleb the son of "Jephunneh, and Joshua the son of Nun. But your "little ones, which ye said should be a prey, them "will I bring in, and they shall know the land "which ye have despised. But as for you, your "carcasses shall fall in this wilderness. And your "children shall wander in the wilderness forty

" years * * * until your carcasses be wasted in
" the wilderness."

And all this because the people were afraid of giants, compared with whom they were but as grasshoppers.

So we find that at one time the people became exceedingly hungry. They had no flesh to eat. There were six hundred thousand men of war, and they had nothing to feed on but manna. They naturally murmured and complained, and thereupon a wind from the Lord went forth and brought quails from the sea, (quails are generally found in the sea,) " and let them fall by the camp, as it were a day's
" journey on this side, and as it were a day's journey
" on the other side, round about the camp, and as it
" were two cubits high upon the face of the earth.
" And the people stood up all that day, and all that
" night, and all the next day, and they gathered the
" quails. * * * And while the flesh was yet be-
" tween their teeth, ere it was chewed, the wrath of
" the Lord was kindled against the people, and the
" Lord smote the people with a very great plague."

Yet he is slow to anger, long-suffering, merciful and just.

In the thirty-second chapter of Exodus, is the account of the golden calf. It must be borne in mind that the worship of this calf by the people was before the Ten Commandments had been given to them. Christians now insist that these commandments must have been inspired, because no human being could have constructed them,—could have conceived of them.

It seems, according to this account, that Moses had been up in the mount with God, getting the Ten Commandments, and that while he was there the people had made the golden calf. When he came down and saw them, and found what they had done, having in his hands the two tables, the work of God, he cast the tables out of his hands, and broke them beneath the mount. He then took the calf which they had made, ground it to powder, strewed it in the water, and made the children of Israel drink of it. And in the twenty-seventh verse we are told what the Lord did:
" Thus saith the Lord God of Israel: Put every man
" his sword by his side, and go in and out from gate
" to gate throughout the camp, and slay every man
" his brother, and every man his companion, and
" every man his neighbor. And the children of Levi
" did according to the word of Moses; and there fell
" of the people that day about three thousand men."

The reason for this slaughter is thus given : "For " Moses had said : Consecrate yourselves to-day to " the Lord, even every man upon his son, and upon " his brother, that he may bestow upon you a blessing " this day."

Now, it must be remembered that there had not been as yet a promulgation of the commandment " Thou shalt have no other gods before me." This was a punishment for the infraction of a law before the law was known—before the commandment had been given. Was it cruel, or unjust?

Does the following sound as though spoken by a God of mercy : "I will make mine arrows drunk " with blood, and my sword shall devour flesh"? And yet this is but a small part of the vengeance and destruction which God threatens to his enemies, as recorded in the thirty-second chapter of the book of Deuteronomy.

In the sixty-eighth Psalm is found this merciful passage : "That thy foot may be dipped in the blood " of thine enemies, and the tongue of thy dogs in the " same."

So we find in the eleventh chapter of Joshua the reason why the Canaanites and other nations made war upon the Jews. It is as follows : "For it was of

"the Lord to harden their hearts that they should
"come against Israel in battle, that he might destroy
"them utterly, and that they might have no favor, but
"that he might destroy them."

Read the thirtieth chapter of Exodus and you will find that God gave to Moses a recipe for making the oil of holy anointment, and in the thirty-second verse we find that no one was to make any oil like it; and in the next verse it is declared that whoever compounded any like it, or whoever put any of it on a stranger, should be cut off from the Lord's people.

In the same chapter, a recipe is given for perfumery, and it is declared that whoever shall make any like it, or that smells like it, shall suffer death.

In the next chapter, it is decreed that if any one fails to keep the Sabbath "he shall be surely put to death."

There are in the Pentateuch hundreds and hundreds of passages showing the cruelty of Jehovah. What could have been more cruel than the flood? What more heartless than to overwhelm a world? What more merciless than to cover a shoreless sea with the corpses of men, women and children?

The Pentateuch is filled with anathemas, with curses, with words of vengeance, of jealousy, of hatred, and brutality. By reason of these passages, millions of people have plucked from their hearts the flowers of pity and justified the murder of women and the assassination of babes.

In the second chapter of Second Kings we find that the prophet Elisha was on his way to a place called Bethel, and as he was going, there came forth little children out of the city and mocked him and said: "Go up thou bald head; Go up thou bald " head! And he turned back and looked on them " and cursed them in the name of the Lord. And " there came forth two she bears out of the wood and " tare forty and two children of them."

Of course he obtained his miraculous power from Jehovah; and there must have been some communication between Jehovah and the bears. Why did the bears come? How did they happen to be there? Here is a prophet of God cursing children in the name of the Lord, and thereupon these children are torn in fragments by wild beasts.

This is the mercy of Jehovah; and yet I am told that the Bible has nothing cruel in it; that it preaches only mercy, justice, charity, peace; that all hearts are softened by reading it; that the savage nature of man is melted into tenderness and pity by it, and that only the totally depraved can find evil in it.

And so I might go on, page after page, book after book, in the Old Testament, and describe the cruelties committed in accordance with the commands of Jehovah.

But all the cruelties in the Old Testament are absolute mercies compared with the hell of the New Testament. In the Old Testament God stops with the grave. He seems to have been satisfied when he saw his enemies dead, when he saw their flesh rotting in the open air, or in the beaks of birds, or in the teeth of wild beasts. But in the New Testament, vengeance does not stop with the grave. It begins there, and stops never. The enemies of Jehovah are to be pursued through all the ages of eternity. There is to be no forgiveness—no cessation, no mercy, nothing but everlasting pain.

And yet we are told that the author of hell is a being of infinite mercy.

Second. All intelligent Christians will admit that there are many passages in the Bible that, if found in the Koran, they would regard as impure and immoral.

It is not necessary for me to specify the passages, nor to call the attention of the public to such things. I am willing to trust the judgment of every honest reader, and the memory of every biblical student.

The Old Testament upholds polygamy. That is infinitely impure. It sanctions concubinage. That is impure; nothing could or can be worse. Hundreds of things are publicly told that should have remained unsaid. No one is made better by reading the history of Tamar, or the biography of Lot, or the memoirs of Noah, of Dinah, of Sarah and Abraham, or of Jacob and Leah and Rachel and others that I do not care to mention. No one is improved in his morals by reading these things.

All I mean to say is, that the Bible is like other books produced by other nations in the same stage of civilization. What one age considers pure, the next considers impure. What one age may consider just, the next may look upon as infamous. Civilization is a growth. It is continually dying, and continually being born. Old branches rot and fall, new buds appear. It is a perpetual twilight, and a perpetual dawn—the death of the old, and the birth of the new.

I do not say, throw away the Bible because there are some foolish passages in it, but I say, throw away the foolish passages. Don't throw away wisdom because it is found in company with folly; but do not say that folly is wisdom, because it is found in its company. All that is true in the Bible is true whether it is inspired or not. All that is true did not need to be inspired. Only that which is not true needs the assistance of miracles and wonders. I read the Bible as I read other books. What I believe to be good, I admit is good; what I think is bad, I say is bad; what I believe to be true, I say is true, and what I believe to be false, I denounce as false.

Third. Let us see whether there are any contradictions in the Bible.

A little book has been published, called "Self "Contradictions of the Bible," by J. P. MENDUM, of *The Boston Investigator.* I find many of the apparent contradictions of the Bible noted in this book.

We all know that the Pentateuch is filled with the commandments of God upon the subject of sacrificing animals. We know that God declared, again and again, that the smell of burning flesh was a sweet savor to him. Chapter after chapter is filled with directions how to kill the beasts that were set apart for sacrifices; what to do with their blood, their flesh and their fat. And yet, in the seventh chapter of Jeremiah, all this is expressly denied, in the following language: " For I spake not unto your fathers, nor commanded " them in the day that I brought them out of the land " of Egypt, concerning burnt offerings or sacrifices."

And in the sixth chapter of Jeremiah, the same Jehovah says: "Your burnt offerings are not ac-
" ceptable, nor your sacrifices sweet unto me."

In the Psalms, Jehovah derides the idea of sacrifices, and says: " Will I eat of the flesh of
" bulls, or drink the blood of goats? Offer unto God
" thanksgiving, and pay thy vows unto the Most
" High."

So I find in Isaiah the following: " Bring no more
" vain oblations; incense is an abomination unto me;
" the new moons and sabbaths, the calling of as-
" semblies, I cannot away with; it is iniquity, even
" the solemn meeting. Your new moons and your
" appointed feasts my soul hateth; they are a trouble
" to me; I am weary to bear them." "To what
" purpose is the multitude of your sacrifices unto me?
" saith the Lord. I am full of the burnt offerings of
" rams, and the fat of fed beasts; and I delight not
" in the blood of bullocks, or of lambs, or of he goats.
" When ye come to appear before me, who hath re-
" quired this at your hand?"

So I find in James: " Let no man say when he is
" tempted: I am tempted of God; for God cannot be
" tempted with evil, neither tempteth he any man;"
and yet in the twenty-second chapter of Genesis I

find this: "And it came to pass after these things, "that God did tempt Abraham."

In Second Samuel we see that he tempted David. He also tempted Job, and Jeremiah says: "O Lord, "thou hast deceived me, and I was deceived." To such an extent was Jeremiah deceived, that in the fourteenth chapter and eighteenth verse we find him crying out to the Lord: "Wilt thou be altogether "unto me as a liar?"

So in Second Thessalonians: "For these things "God shall send them strong delusions, that they "should believe a lie."

So in First Kings, twenty-second chapter: "Behold, "the Lord hath put a lying spirit in the mouth of all "these thy prophets, and the Lord hath spoken evil "concerning thee."

So in Ezekiel: "And if the prophet be deceived "when he hath spoken a thing, I, the Lord, have de-"ceived that prophet."

So I find: "Thou shalt not bear false witness;" and in the book of Revelation: "All liars shall have "their part in the lake which burneth with fire and "brimstone;" yet in First Kings, twenty-second chapter, I find the following: "And the Lord said: "Who shall persuade Ahab, that he may go up and "fall at Ramoth-Gilead? And one said on this "manner, and another said on that manner. And "there came forth a spirit and stood before the Lord, "and said: I will persuade him. And the Lord said "unto him: Wherewith? And he said: I will go "forth, and I will be a lying spirit in the mouth of all "his prophets. And he said: Thou shalt persuade "him, and prevail also. Go forth, and do so."

In the Old Testament we find contradictory laws about the same thing, and contradictory accounts of the same occurrences.

In the twentieth chapter of Exodus we find the first account of the giving of the Ten Commandments. In the thirty-fourth chapter another account of the same transaction is given. These two accounts could not have been written by the same person. Read them, and you will be forced to admit that both of them cannot by any possibility be true. They differ in so many particulars, and the commandments themselves are so different, that it is impossible that both can be true.

So there are two histories of the creation. If you will read the first and second chapters of Genesis, you will find two accounts inconsistent with each other, both of which cannot be true. The first account ends with the third verse of the second chapter of Genesis. By the first account, man and woman were made at the same time, and made last of all. In the second account, not to be too critical, all the beasts of the field were made before Eve was, and Adam was made before the beasts of the field; whereas in the first account, God made all the animals before he made Adam. In the first account there is nothing about the rib or the bone or the side,—that is only found in the second account. In the first account, there is nothing about the Garden of Eden, nothing about the four rivers, nothing about the mist that went up from the earth and watered the whole face of the ground; nothing said about making man from dust; nothing about God breathing into his nostrils the breath of life; yet according to the second account, the Garden of Eden was planted, and all the animals were made before Eve was formed. It is impossible to harmonize the two accounts.

So, in the first account, only the word God is used—"God said so and so,—God did so and so." In the second account he is called Lord God,—"the " Lord God formed man,"—"the Lord God caused " it to rain,"—"the Lord God planted a garden." It is now admitted that the book of Genesis is made up of two stories, and it is very easy to take them apart and show exactly how they were put together.

So there are two stories of the flood, differing almost entirely from each other—that is to say, so contradictory that both cannot be true.

There are two accounts of the manner in which Saul was made king, and the accounts are inconsistent with each other.

Scholars now everywhere admit that the copyists made many changes, pieced out fragments, and made additions, interpolations, and meaningless repetitions. It is now generally conceded that the speeches of Elihu, in Job, were interpolated, and most of the prophecies were made by persons whose names even are not known.

The manuscripts of the Old Testament were not alike. The Greek version differed from the Hebrew, and there was no generally received text of the Old Testament until after the beginning of the Christian era. Marks and points to denote vowels were invented probably in the seventh century after Christ; and whether these marks and points were put in the proper places, is still an open question. The Alexandrian version, or what is known as the Septuagint, translated by seventy-two learned Jews assisted by miraculous power, about two hundred years before Christ, could not, it is now said, have been translated from the Hebrew text that we now have. This can only be accounted for by supposing that we have a different Hebrew text. The early Christians adopted the Septuagint and were satisfied for a time ; but so many errors were found, and so many were scanning every word in search of something to assist their peculiar views, that new versions were produced, and the new versions all differed somewhat from the Septuagint as well as from each other. These versions were mostly in Greek. The first Latin Bible was produced in Africa, and no one has ever found out which Latin manuscript was original. Many were produced, and all differed from each other. These Latin versions were compared with each other and with the Hebrew, and a new Latin version was made in the fifth century, and the old ones held their own for about four hundred years, and no one knows which version was right. Besides, there were Ethiopic, Egyptian, Armenian and several other versions, all differing from each other as well as from all others. It was not until the fourteenth century that the Bible was translated into German, and not until the fifteenth that Bibles were printed in the principal languages of Europe ; and most of these Bibles differed from each other, and gave rise to endless disputes and to almost numberless crimes.

No man in the world is learned enough, nor has he time enough, even if he could live a thousand years, to find what books belonged to and constituted the Old Testament. He could not ascertain the authors of the books, nor when they were written, nor what they mean. Until a man has sufficient time to do all this, no one can tell whether he believes the Bible or not. It is sufficient, however, to say that the Old Testament is filled with contradictions as to the number of men slain in battle, as to the number of years certain kings reigned, as to the number of a woman's children, as to dates of events, and as to locations of towns and cities.

Besides all this, many of its laws are contradictory, often commanding and prohibiting the same thing.

The New Testament also is filled with contradictions. The gospels do not even agree upon the terms of salvation. They do not even agree as to the gospel of Christ, as to the mission of Christ. They do not tell the same story regarding the betrayal, the crucifixion, the resurrection or the ascension of Christ. John is the only one that ever heard of being "born again." The evangelists do not give the same account of the same miracles, and the miracles are not given in the same order. They do not agree even in the genealogy of Christ.

Fourth. Is the Bible scientific? In my judgment it is not.

It is unscientific to say that this world was "cre-"ated;" that the universe was produced by an infinite being, who had existed an eternity prior to such "creation." My mind is such that I cannot possibly conceive of a "creation." Neither can I conceive of an infinite being who dwelt in infinite space an infinite length of time.

I do not think it is scientific to say that the universe was made in six days, or that this world is only about six thousand years old, or that man has only been upon the earth for about six thousand years.

If the Bible is true, Adam was the first man. The age of Adam is given, the age of his children, and the time, according to the Bible, was kept and known from Adam, so that if the Bible is true, man has only been in this world about six thousand years. In my judgment, and in the judgment of every scientific man whose judgment is worth having or quoting, man inhabited this earth for thousands of ages prior to the creation of Adam. On one point the Bible is at least certain, and that is, as to the life of Adam. The genealogy is given, the pedigree is there, and it is impossible to escape the conclusion that, according to the Bible, man has only been upon this earth about six thousand years. There is no chance there to say "long periods of time," or "geological ages." There we have the years. And as to the time of the creation of man, the Bible does not tell the truth.

What is generally called "The Fall of Man" is unscientific. God could not have made a moral character for Adam. Even admitting the rest of the story to be true, Adam certainly had to make character for himself.

The idea that there never would have been any disease or death in this world had it not been for the eating of the forbidden fruit is preposterously unscientific. Admitting that Adam was made only six thousand years ago, death was in the world millions of years before that time. The old rocks are filled with remains of what were once living and breathing animals. Continents were built up with the petrified corpses of animals. We know, therefore, that death did not enter the world because of Adam's sin. We know that life and death are but successive links in an eternal chain.

So it is unscientific to say that thorns and brambles were produced by Adam's sin.

It is also unscientific to say that labor was pronounced as a curse upon man. Labor is not a curse. Labor is a blessing. Idleness is a curse.

It is unscientific to say that the sons of God, living, we suppose, in heaven, fell in love with the daughters of men, and that on account of this a flood was sent upon the earth that covered the highest mountains.

The whole story of the flood is unscientific, and no scientific man worthy of the name, believes it.

Neither is the story of the tower of Babel a scientific thing. Does any scientific man believe that God confounded the language of men for fear they would succeed in building a tower high enough to reach to heaven?

It is not scientific to say that angels were in the habit of walking about the earth, eating veal dressed with butter and milk, and making bargains about the destruction of cities.

The story of Lot's wife having been turned into a pillar of salt is extremely unscientific.

It is unscientific to say that people at one time lived to be nearly a thousand years of age. The history of the world shows that human life is lengthening instead of shortening.

It is unscientific to say that the infinite God wrestled with Jacob and got the better of him, putting his thigh out of joint.

It is unscientific to say that God, in the likeness of a flame of fire, inhabited a bush.

It is unscientific to say that a stick could be changed into a living snake. Living snakes can not be made out of sticks. There are not the necessary elements in a stick to make a snake.

It is not scientific to say that God changed water into blood. All the elements of blood are not in water.

It is unscientific to declare that dust was changed into lice.

It is not scientific to say that God caused a thick darkness over the land of Egypt, and yet allowed it to be light in the houses of the Jews.

It is not scientific to say that about seventy people could, in two hundred and fifteen years increase to three millions.

It is not scientific to say that an infinitely good God would destroy innocent people to get revenge upon a king.

It is not scientific to say that slavery was once right, that polygamy was once a virtue, and that extermination was mercy.

It is not scientific to assert that a being of infinite power and goodness went into partnership with insects,—granted letters of marque and reprisal to hornets.

It is unscientific to insist that bread was really rained from heaven.

It is not scientific to suppose that an infinite being spent forty days and nights furnishing Moses with plans and specifications for a tabernacle, an ark, a mercy seat, cherubs of gold, a table, four rings, some dishes, some spoons, one candlestick, several bowls, a few knobs, seven lamps, some snuffers, a pair of tongs, some curtains, a roof for a tent of rams' skins dyed red, a few boards, an altar with horns, ash pans, basins and flesh hooks, shovels and pots and sockets of silver and ouches of gold and pins of brass—for all of which this God brought with him patterns from heaven.

It is not scientific to say that when a man commits a sin, he can settle with God by killing a sheep.

It is not scientific to say that a priest, by laying his hands on the head of a goat, can transfer the sins of a people to the animal.

Was it scientific to endeavor to ascertain whether a woman was virtuous or not, by compelling her to drink water mixed with dirt from the floor of the sanctuary?

Is it scientific to say that a dry stick budded, blossomed, and bore almonds; or that the ashes of a red heifer mixed with water can cleanse us of sin; or that a good being gave cities into the hands of the Jews in consideration of their murdering all the inhabitants?

Is it scientific to say that an animal saw an angel, and conversed with a man?

Is it scientific to imagine that thrusting a spear through the body of a woman ever stayed a plague?

Is it scientific to say that a river cut itself in two and allowed the lower end to run off?

Is it scientific to assert that seven priests blew seven rams' horns loud enough to blow down the walls of a city?

Is it scientific to say that the sun stood still in the midst of heaven, and hasted not to go down for about a whole day, and that the moon also stayed?

Is it scientifically probable that an angel of the Lord devoured unleavened cakes and broth with fire that came out of the end of a stick, as he sat under an oak tree; or that God made known his will by letting dew fall on wool without wetting the ground around it; or that an angel of God appeared to Manoah in the absence of her husband, and that this angel afterwards went up in a flame of fire, and as the result of this visit a child was born whose strength was in his hair?

Is it scientific to say that the muscle of a man depended upon the length of his locks?

Is it unscientific to deny that water gushed from a hollow place in a dry bone?

Is it evidence of a thoroughly scientific mind to believe that one man turned over a house so large that three thousand people were on its roof?

Is it purely scientific to say that a man was once fed by the birds of the air, who brought him bread and meat every morning and evening, and that afterward an angel turned cook and prepared two suppers in one night, for the same prophet, who ate enough to last him forty days and forty nights?

Is it scientific to say that a river divided because the water had been struck with a cloak; or that a man actually went to heaven in a chariot of fire drawn by horses of fire; or that a being of infinite mercy would destroy children for laughing at a bald-headed prophet; or curse children and children's children with leprosy for a father's fault; or that he made iron float in water; or that when one corpse touched another it came to life; or that the sun went backward in heaven so that the shadow on a sundial went back ten degrees, as a sign that a miserable barbarian king would get well?

Is it scientific to say that the earth not only stopped in its rotary motion, but absolutely turned the other way,—that its motion was reversed simply as a sign to a petty king?

Is it scientific to say that Solomon made gold and silver at Jerusalem as plentiful as stones, when we know that there were kings in his day who could have thrown away the value of the whole of Palestine without missing the amount?

Is it scientific to say that Solomon exceeded all the kings of the earth in glory, when his country was barren, without roads, when his people were few, without commerce, without the arts, without the sciences, without education, without luxuries?

According to the Bible, as long as Jehovah attended to the affairs of the Jews, they had nothing but war, pestilence and famine; after Jehovah abandoned them, and the Christians ceased, in a measure, to persecute them, the Jews became the most prosperous of people. Since Jehovah in his anger cast them away, they have produced painters, sculptors, scientists, statesmen, composers, soldiers and philosophers.

It is not scientific to believe that God ever prevented rain, that he ever caused famine, that he ever sent locusts to devour the wheat and corn, that he ever relied on pestilence for the government of mankind; or that he ever killed children to get even with their parents.

It is not scientific to believe that the king of Egypt invaded Palestine with seventy thousand horsemen and twelve hundred chariots of war. There was not, at that time, a road in Palestine over which a chariot could be driven.

It is not scientific to believe that in a battle between Jeroboam and Abijah, the army of Abijah slew in one day five hundred thousand chosen men.

It is not scientific to believe that Zerah, the Ethiopian, invaded Palestine with a million of men who were overthrown and destroyed; or that Jehoshaphat had a standing army of nine hundred and sixty thousand men.

It is unscientific to believe that Jehovah advertised for a liar, as is related in Second Chronicles.

It is not scientific to believe that fire refused to burn, or that water refused to wet.

It is not scientific to believe in dreams, in visions, and in miracles.

It is not scientific to believe that children have been born without fathers, that the dead have ever been raised to life, or that people have bodily ascended to heaven taking their clothes with them.

It is not scientific to believe in the supernatural. Science dwells in the realm of fact, in the realm of demonstration. Science depends upon human experience, upon observation, upon reason.

It is unscientific to say that an innocent man can be punished in place of a criminal, and for a criminal, and that the criminal, on account of such punishment, can be justified.

It is unscientific to say that a finite sin deserves infinite punishment.

It is unscientific to believe that devils can inhabit human beings, or that they can take possession of swine, or that the devil could bodily take a man, or the Son of God, and carry him to the pinnacle of a temple.

In short, the foolish, the unreasonable, the false, the miraculous and the supernatural are unscientific.

Question. Mr. Talmage gives his reason for accepting the New Testament, and says: "You can trace it right out. Jerome and Eusebius in the first century, and Origen in the second century, gave lists of the writers of the New Testament. These lists correspond with our list of the writers of the New Testament, showing that precisely as we have it, they had it in the third and fourth centuries. Where did they get it? From Irenæus. Where did he get it? From Polycarp. Where did Polycarp get it? From Saint John, who was a personal associate of Jesus. The line is just as clear as anything ever was clear." How do you understand this matter, and has Mr. Talmage stated the facts?

Answer. Let us examine first the witnesses produced by Mr. Talmage. We will also call attention to the great principle laid down by Mr. Talmage for the examination of evidence,—that where a witness is found false in one particular, his entire testimony must be thrown away.

Eusebius was born somewhere about two hundred and seventy years after Christ. After many vicissitudes he became, it is said, the friend of Constantine. He made an oration in which he extolled the virtues of this murderer, and had the honor of sitting at the right hand of the man who had shed the blood of his wife and son. In the great controversy with regard to the position that Christ should occupy in the Trinity, he sided with Arius, " and lent himself to the perse-" cution of the orthodox with Athanasius." He insisted that Jesus Christ was not the same as God, and that he was not of equal power and glory. Will Mr. Talmage admit that his witness told the truth in this? " He would not even call the Son co-eternal " with God."

Eusebius must have been an exceedingly truthful man. He declared that the tracks of Pharaoh's chariots were in his day visible upon the shores of the Red Sea; that these tracks had been through all the years miraculously preserved from the action of wind and wave, as a supernatural testimony to the fact that God miraculously overwhelmed Pharaoh and his hosts.

Eusebius also relates that when Joseph and Mary arrived in Eygpt they took up their abode in Hermopolis, a city of Thebæus, in which was the superb temple of Serapis. When Joseph and Mary entered the temple, not only the great idol, but all the lesser idols fell down before him.

"It is believed by the learned Dr. Lardner, that Eusebius was the one guilty of the forgery in the passage found in Josephus concerning Christ. Unblushing falsehoods and literary forgeries of the vilest character darkened the pages of his historical writings." *(Waite's History.)*

From the same authority I learn that Eusebius invented an eclipse, and some earthquakes, to agree with the account of the crucifixion. It is also believed that Eusebius quoted from works that never existed, and that he pretended a work had been written by Porphyry, entitled: "The Philosophy of Oracles," and then quoted from it for the purpose of proving the truth of the Christian religion.

The fact is, Eusebius was utterly destitute of truth. He believed, as many still believe, that he could please God by the fabrication of lies.

Irenæus lived somewhere about the end of the second century. "Very little is known of his early history, and the accounts given in various biographies are for the most part conjectural." The writings of Irenæus are known to us principally through Eusebius, and we know the value of his testimony.

Now, if we are to take the testimony of Irenæus,

why not take it? He says that the ministry of Christ lasted for twenty years, and that Christ was fifty years old at the time of his crucifixion. He also insisted that the "Gospel of Paul" was written by Luke, "a "statement made to give sanction to the gospel of " Luke."

Irenæus insisted that there were four gospels, that there must be, and "he speaks frequently of these " gospels, and argues that they should be four in " number, neither more nor less, because there are " four universal winds, and four quarters of the " world;" and he might have added: because donkeys have four legs.

These facts can be found in "The History of the " Christian Religion to A. D. 200," by Charles B. Waite,—a book that Mr. Talmage ought to read.

According to Mr. Waite, Irenæus, in the thirty-third chapter of his fifth book, *Adversus Hæreses*, cites from Papias the following sayings of Christ: " The days will come in which vines shall grow " which shall have ten thousand branches, and on " each branch ten thousand twigs, and in each twig " ten thousand shoots, and in each shoot ten thousand " clusters, and in every one of the clusters ten " thousand grapes, and every grape when pressed "will give five and twenty metrets of wine." Also that "one thousand million pounds of clear, pure, fine "flour will be produced from one grain of wheat." Irenæus adds that "these things were borne witness "to by Papias the hearer of John and the companion "of Polycarp."

Is it possible that the eternal welfare of a human being depends upon believing the testimony of Polycarp and Irenæus? Are people to be saved or lost on the reputation of Eusebius? Suppose a man is firmly convinced that Polycarp knew nothing about Saint John, and that Saint John knew nothing about Christ,—what then? Suppose he is convinced that Eusebius is utterly unworthy of credit,—what then? Must a man believe statements that he has every reason to think are false?

The question arises as to the witnesses named by Mr. Talmage, whether they were competent to decide as to the truth or falsehood of the gospels. We have the right to inquire into their mental traits for the purpose of giving only due weight to what they have said.

Mr. Bronson C. Keeler is the author of a book called: "A Short History of the Bible." I avail myself of a few of the facts he has there collected. I find in this book, that Irenæus, Clement and Origen believed in the fable of the Phœnix, and insisted that God produced the bird on purpose to prove the probability of the resurrection of the body. Some of the early fathers believed that the hyena changed its sex every year. Others of them gave as a reason why good people should eat only animals with a cloven foot, the fact that righteous people lived not only in this world, but had expectations in the next. They also believed that insane people were possessed by devils; that angels ate manna; that some angels loved the daughters of men and fell; that the pains of women in childbirth, and the fact that serpents crawl on their bellies, were proofs that the account of the fall, as given in Genesis, is true; that the stag renewed its youth by eating poisonous snakes; that eclipses and comets were signs of God's anger; that volcanoes were openings into hell; that demons blighted apples; that a corpse in a cemetery moved to make room for another corpse to be placed beside it. Clement of Alexandria believed that hail storms, tempests and plagues were caused by demons. He also believed, with Mr. Talmage, that the events in the life of Abraham were typical and prophetical of arithmetic and astronomy.

Origen, another of the witnesses of Mr. Talmage, said that the sun, moon and stars were living creatures, endowed with reason and free will, and occasionally inclined to sin. That they had free will, he proved by quoting from Job; that they were rational creatures, he inferred from the fact that they moved. The sun, moon and stars, according to him, were "subject to vanity," and he believed that they prayed to God through his only begotten son.

These intelligent witnesses believed that the blighting of vines and fruit trees, and the disease and destruction that came upon animals and men, were all the work of demons; but that when they had entered into men, the sign of the cross would drive them out. They derided the idea that the earth is round, and one of them said: "About the antipodes also, one " can neither hear nor speak without laughter. It is " asserted as something serious that we should be-" lieve that there are men who have their feet oppo-" site to ours. The ravings of Anaxagoras are more " tolerable, who said that snow was black."

Concerning these early fathers, Professor Davidson, as quoted by Mr. Keeler, uses the following language: "Of the three fathers who contributed " most to the growth of the canon, Irenæus was "credulous and blundering; Tertullian passionate "and one-sided; and Clement of Alexandria, im- "bued with the treasures of Greek wisdom, was "mainly occupied with ecclesiastical ethics. Their "assertions show both ignorance and exaggeration."

These early fathers relied upon by Mr. Talmage, quoted from books now regarded as apocryphal— books that have been thrown away by the church and are no longer considered as of the slightest authority. Upon this subject I again quote Mr. Keeler: " Clement quoted the 'Gospel according to "'the Hebrews,' which is now thrown away by the "church; he also quoted from the Sibylline books "and the Pentateuch in the same sentence. Origen "frequently cited the Gospel of the Hebrews. Jerome "did the same, and Clement believed in the 'Gospel "'according to the Egyptians.' The Shepherd of "Hermas, a book in high repute in the early church, "and one which distinctly claims to have been "inspired, was quoted by Irenæus as Scripture. "Clement of Alexandria said it was a divine revela- "tion. Origen said it was divinely inspired, and "quoted it as Holy Scripture at the same time that "he cited the Psalms and Epistles of Paul. Jerome "quoted the 'Wisdom of Jesus, the Son of Sirach,'

"as divine Scripture. Origen quotes the 'Wisdom
"of Solomon' as the 'Word of God' and 'the
"'words of Christ himself.' Eusebius of Cæsarea
"cites it as a 'Divine Oracle,' and St. Chrysostom
"used it as Scripture. So Eusebius quotes the
"thirteenth chapter of Daniel as Scripture, but as a
"matter of fact, Daniel has not a thirteenth chapter,—
"the church has taken it away. Clement spoke of
"the writer of the fourth book of Esdras as a prophet;
"he thought Baruch as much the word of God as
"any other book, and he quotes it as divine Scripture.
"Clement cites Barnabas as an apostle. Origen
"quotes from the Epistle of Barnabas, calls it 'Holy
"'Scripture,' and places it on a level with the Psalms
"and the Epistles of Paul; and Clement of Alexan-
"dria believed in the 'Epistle of Barnabas,' and the
"'Revelation of Peter,' and wrote comments upon
"these holy books."

Nothing can exceed the credulity of the early fathers, unless it may be their ignorance. They believed everything that was miraculous. They believed everything except the truth. Anything that really happened was considered of no importance by them. They looked for wonders, miracles, and monstrous things, and—generally found them. They revelled in the misshapen and the repulsive. They did not think it wrong to swear falsely in a good cause. They interpolated, forged, and changed the records to suit themselves, for the sake of Christ. They quoted from persons who never wrote. They misrepresented those who had written, and their evidence is absolutely worthless. They were ignorant, credulous, mendacious, fanatical, pious, unreasonable, bigoted, hypocritical, and for the most part, insane. Read the book of Revelation, and you will agree with me that nothing that ever emanated from a madhouse can more than equal it for incoherence. Most of the writings of the early fathers are of the same kind.

As to Saint John, the real truth is, that we know nothing certainly of him. We do not know that he ever lived.

We know nothing certainly of Jesus Christ. We know nothing of his infancy, nothing of his youth, and we are not sure that such a person ever existed.

We know nothing of Polycarp. We do not know where he was born, or where, or how he died. We know nothing for certain about Irenæus. All the names quoted by Mr. Talmage as his witnesses are surrounded by clouds and doubts, by mist and darkness. We only know that many of their statements are false, and do not know that any of them are true.

Question. What do you think of the following statement by Mr. Talmage: "Oh, I have to tell you that no "man ever died for a lie cheerfully and triumphantly"?

Answer. There was a time when men "cheerfully "and triumphantly died" in defence of the doctrine of the "real presence" of God in the wafer and wine. Does Mr. Talmage believe in the doctrine of "tran- "substantiation"? Yet hundreds have died "cheer- "fully and triumphantly" for it. Men have died for the idea that baptism by immersion is the only scriptural baptism. Did they die for a lie? If not, is Mr. Talmage a Baptist?

Giordano Bruno was an atheist, yet he perished at the stake rather than retract his opinions. He did not expect to be welcomed by angels and by God. He did not look for a crown of glory. He expected simply death and eternal extinction. Does the fact that he died for that belief prove its truth?

Thousands upon thousands have died in defence of the religion of Mohammed. Was Mohammed an impostor? Thousands have welcomed death in defence of the doctrines of Buddha. Is Buddhism true?

So I might make a tour of the world, and of all ages of human history, and find that millions and millions have died " cheerfully and triumphantly " in defence of their opinions. There is not the slightest truth in Mr. Talmage's statement.

A little while ago, a man shot at the Czar of Russia. On the day of his execution he was asked if he wished religious consolation. He replied that he believed in no religion. What did that prove? It proved only the man's honesty of opinion. All the martyrs in the world cannot change, never did change, a falsehood into a truth, nor a truth into a falsehood. Martyrdom proves nothing but the sincerity of the martyr and the cruelty and meanness of his murderers. Thousands and thousands of people have imagined that they knew things, that they were certain, and have died rather than retract their honest beliefs.

Mr. Talmage now says that he knows all about the Old Testament, that the prophecies were fulfilled, and yet he does not know when the prophecies were made—whether they were made before or after the fact. He does not know whether the destruction of Babylon was told before it happened, or after. He knows nothing upon the subject. He does not know who made the pretended prophecies. He does not know that Isaiah, or Jeremiah, or Habakkuk, or Hosea ever lived in this world. He does not know who wrote a single book of the Old Testament. He knows nothing on the subject. He believes in the inspiration of the Old Testament because ancient cities finally fell into decay—were overrun and destroyed by enemies, and he accounts for the fact that the Jew does not lose his nationality by saying that the Old Testament is true.

The Jews have been persecuted by the Christians, and they are still persecuted by them; and Mr. Talmage seems to think that this persecution was a part of God's plan, that the Jews might, by persecution, be prevented from mingling with other nationalities, and so might stand, through the instrumentality of perpetual hate and cruelty, the suffering witnesses of the divine truth of the Bible.

The Jews do not testify to the truth of the Bible, but to the barbarism and inhumanity of Christians—to the meanness and hatred of what we are pleased to call the "civilized world." They testify to the fact that nothing so hardens the human heart as religion.

There is no prophecy in the Old Testament foretelling the coming of Jesus Christ. There is not one word in the Old Testament referring to him in any way—not one word. The only way to prove this is to take your Bible, and wherever you find these words: "That it might be fulfilled," and "which was spoken," turn to the Old Testament and find what was written, and you will see that it had not the slightest possible reference to the thing recounted in the New Testament—not the slightest.

Let us take some of the prophecies of the Bible, and see how plain they are, and how beautiful they are. Let us see whether any human being can tell whether they have ever been fulfilled or not.

Here is a vision of Ezekiel: "I looked, and be"hold a whirlwind came out of the north, a great "cloud, and a fire infolding itself, and a brightness "was about it, and out of the midst thereof as the "color of amber, out of the midst of the fire. Also "out of the midst thereof came the likeness of four "living creatures. And this was their appearance; "they had the likeness of a man. And every one "had four faces, and every one had four wings. "And their feet were straight feet; and the sole of "their feet was like the sole of a calf's foot: and they "sparkled like the color of burnished brass. And "they had the hands of a man under their wings on

"' their four sides ; and they four had their faces and
" their wings. Their wings were joined one to
" another ; they turned not when they went ; they
" went every one straight forward. As for the like-
" ness of their faces, they four had the face of a man,
" and the face of a lion, on the right side : and they
" four had the face of an ox on the left side ; they
" four also had the face of an eagle.

" Thus were their faces : and their wings were
" stretched upward ; two wings of every one were
" joined one to another, and two covered their bodies.
" And they went every one straight forward : whither
" the spirit was to go, they went ; and they turned not
" when they went.

" As for the likeness of the living creatures, their
" appearance was like burning coals of fire, and like
" the appearance of lamps : it went up and down
" among the living creatures ; and the fire was bright,
" and out of the fire went forth lightning. And the
" living creatures ran and returned as the appearance
" of a flash of lightning.

" Now as I beheld the living creatures, behold one
" wheel upon the earth by the living creatures, with
" his four faces. The appearance of the wheels and
" their work was like unto the color of a beryl : and

" they four had one likeness : and their appearance
" and their work was as it were a wheel in the middle
" of a wheel. When they went, they went upon
" their four sides : and they turned not when they
" went. As for their rings, they were so high that
" they were dreadful; and their rings were full of
" eyes round about them four. And when the living
" creatures went, the wheels went by them : and
" when the living creatures were lifted up from the
" earth, the wheels were lifted up. Whithersoever
" the spirit was to go, they went, thither was their
" spirit to go; and the wheels were lifted up over
" against them : for the spirit of the living creature
" was in the wheels. When those went, these went;
" and when those stood, these stood ; and when those
" were lifted up from the earth, the wheels were
" lifted up over against them : for the spirit of the
" living creature was in the wheels. And the like-
" ness of the firmament upon the heads of the living
" creature was as the color of the terrible crystal,
" stretched forth over their heads above. And under
" the firmament were their wings straight, the one
" toward the other; every one had two, which
" covered on this side, and every one had two,
" which covered on that side, their bodies."

Is such a vision a prophecy? Is it calculated to convey the slightest information? If so, what?

So, the following vision of the prophet Daniel is exceedingly important and instructive:

"Daniel spake and said: I saw in my vision by night, and behold, the four winds of the heaven strove upon the great sea. And four great beasts came up from the sea, diverse one from another. The first was like a lion, and had eagle's wings: I beheld till the wings thereof were plucked, and it was lifted up from the earth, and made stand upon the feet as a man, and a man's heart was given to it. And behold another beast, a second, like to a bear, and it raised up itself on one side, and it had three ribs in the mouth of it between the teeth of it: and they said thus unto it, Arise, devour much flesh.

"After this I beheld, and lo another, like a leopard, which had upon the back of it four wings of a fowl; the beast had also four heads, and dominion was given to it.

"After this I saw in the night visions, and behold a fourth beast, dreadful and terrible, and strong exceedingly; and it had great iron teeth; it devoured and brake in pieces, and stamped the residue with

"the feet of it; and it was diverse from all the beasts
"that were before it, and it had ten horns. I con-
"sidered the horns, and, behold, there came up
"among them another little horn, before whom
"there were three of the first horns plucked up by
"the roots: and behold, in this horn were eyes like
"the eyes of man, and a mouth speaking great
"things."

I have no doubt that this prophecy has been literally fulfilled, but I am not at present in condition to give the time, place, or circumstances.

A few moments ago, my attention was called to the following extract from *The New York Herald* of the thirteenth of March, instant:

"At the Fifth Avenue Baptist Church, Dr. Armi-
"tage took as his text, 'A wheel in the middle of a
"'wheel'—Ezekiel, i., 16. Here, said the preacher,
"are three distinct visions in one—the living crea-
"tures, the moving wheels and the fiery throne. We
"have time only to stop the wheels of this mystic
"chariot of Jehovah, that we may hold holy converse
"with Him who rides upon the wings of the wind.
"In this vision of the prophet we have a minute and
"amplified account of these magnificent symbols or
"hieroglyphics, this wondrous machinery which de-

"notes immense attributes and agencies and volitions, passing their awful and mysterious course of power and intelligence in revolution after revolution of the emblematical mechanism, in steady and harmonious advancement to the object after which they are reaching. We are compelled to look upon the whole as symbolical of that tender and endearing providence of which Jesus spoke when He said, 'The very hairs of your head are numbered.'"

Certainly, an ordinary person, not having been illuminated by the spirit of prophecy, would never have even dreamed that there was the slightest reference in Ezekiel's vision to anything like counting hairs. As a commentator, the Rev. Dr. Armitage has no equal; and, in my judgment, no rival. He has placed himself beyond the reach of ridicule. It is impossible to say anything about his sermon as laughable as his sermon.

Question. Have you no confidence in any prophecies? Do you take the ground that there never has been a human being who could predict the future?

Answer. I admit that a man of average intelligence knows that a certain course, when pursued long enough, will bring national disaster, and it is perfectly safe to predict the downfall of any and every country in the world. In my judgment, nations, like individuals, have an average life. Every nation is mortal. An immortal nation cannot be constructed of mortal individuals. A nation has a reason for existing, and that reason sustains the same relation to the nation that the acorn does to the oak. The nation will attain its growth—other things being equal. It will reach its manhood and its prime, but it will sink into old age, and at last must die. Probably, in a few thousand years, men will be able to calculate the average life of nations, as they now calculate the average life of persons. There has been no period since the morning of history until now, that men did not know of dead and dying nations. There has always been a national cemetery. Poland is dead, Turkey is dying. In every nation are the seeds of dissolution. Not only nations die, but races of men. A nation is born, becomes powerful, luxurious, at last grows weak, is overcome, dies, and another takes its place, In this way civilization and barbarism, like day and night, alternate through all of history's years.

In every nation there are at least two classes of men : First, the enthusiastic, the patriotic, who believe that the nation will live forever,—that its flag will float while the earth has air ; Second, the owls and ravens and croakers, who are always predicting disaster, defeat, and death. To the last class belong the Jeremiahs, Ezekiels, and Isaiahs of the Jews. They were always predicting the downfall of Jerusalem. They revelled in defeat and captivity. They loved to paint the horrors of famine and war. For the most part, they were envious, hateful, misanthropic and unjust.

There seems to have been a war between church and state. The prophets were endeavoring to preserve the ecclesiastical power. Every king who would listen to them, was chosen of God. He instantly became the model of virtue, and the prophets assured him that he was in the keeping of Jehovah. But if the king had a mind of his own, the prophets immediately called down upon him all the curses of heaven, and predicted the speedy destruction of his kingdom.

If our own country should be divided, if an empire should rise upon the ruins of the Republic, it would be very easy to find that hundreds and thousands of people had foretold that very thing. If you will read the political speeches of the last twenty-two years, you will find prophecies to fit any possible future state of affairs in our country. No matter what happens, you will find that somebody predicted it. If the city of London should lose her trade, if the Parliament house should become the abode of moles and bats, if "the New Zealander should sit upon the "ruins of London Bridge," all these things would be simply the fulfillment of prophecy. The fall of every nation under the sun has been predicted by hundreds and thousands of people.

The prophecies of the Old Testament can be made to fit anything that may happen, or that may not happen. They will apply to the death of a king, or to the destruction of a people,—to the loss of commerce, or the discovery of a continent. Each prophecy is a jugglery of words, of figures, of symbols, so put together, so used, so interpreted, that they can mean anything, everything, or nothing.

Question. Do you see anything "prophetic" in the fate of the Jewish people themselves? Do you think that God made the Jewish people wanderers, so that they might be perpetual witnesses to the truth of the Scriptures?

Answer. I cannot believe that an infinitely good God would make anybody a wanderer. Neither can I believe that he would keep millions of people without country and without home, and allow them to be persecuted for thousands of years, simply that they might be used as witnesses. Nothing could be more absurdly cruel than this.

The Christians justify their treatment of the Jews on the ground that they are simply fulfilling prophecy. The Jews have suffered because of the horrid story that their ancestors crucified the Son of God. Christianity, coming into power, looked with horror upon the Jews, who denied the truth of the gospel. Each Jew was regarded as a dangerous witness against Christianity. The early Christians saw how necessary it was that the people who lived in Jerusalem at the time of Christ should be convinced that he was God, and should testify to the miracles he wrought. Whenever a Jew denied it, the Christian was filled with malignity and hatred, and immediately excited the prejudice of other Christians against the man simply because he was a Jew. They forgot, in their general hatred, that Mary, the mother of Christ, was a Jewess; that Christ himself was of Jewish blood; and with an inconsistency of which, of all religions, Christianity alone could have been guilty, the Jew became an object of especial hatred and aversion.

When we remember that Christianity pretends to be a religion of love and kindness, of charity and forgiveness, must not every intelligent man be shocked by the persecution of the Jews? Even now, in learned and cultivated Germany, the Jew is treated as though he were a wild beast. The reputation of this great people has been stained by a persecution springing only from ignorance and barbarian prejudice. So in Russia, the Christians are anxious to shed every drop of Jewish blood, and thousands are to-day fleeing from their homes to seek a refuge from Christian hate. And Mr. Talmage believes that all these persecutions are kept up by the perpetual intervention of God, in order that the homeless wanderers of the seed of Abraham may testify to the truth of the Old and New Testaments. He thinks that every burning Jewish home sheds light upon the gospel,—that every gash in Jewish flesh cries out in favor of the Bible,—that every violated Jewish maiden shows the interest that God still takes in the preservation of his Holy Word.

I am endeavoring to do away with religious

prejudice. I wish to substitute humanity for superstition, the love of our fellow-men, for the fear of God. In the place of ignorant worship, let us put good deeds. We should be great enough and grand enough to know that the rights of the Jew are precisely the same as our own. We cannot trample upon their rights, without endangering our own; and no man who will take liberty from another, is great enough to enjoy liberty himself.

Day by day Christians are laying the foundation of future persecution. In every Sunday school little children are taught that Jews killed the God of this universe. Their little hearts are filled with hatred against the Jewish people. They are taught as a part of the creed to despise the descendants of the only people with whom God is ever said to have had any conversation whatever.

When we take into consideration what the Jewish people have suffered, it is amazing that every one of them does not hate with all his heart and soul and strength the entire Christian world. But in spite of the persecutions they have endured, they are to-day, where they are permitted to enjoy reasonable liberty, the most prosperous people on the globe. The idea that their condition shows, or tends to show, that upon them abides the wrath of Jehovah, cannot be substantiated by the facts.

The Jews to-day control the commerce of the world. They control the money of the world. It is for them to say whether nations shall or shall not go to war. They are the people of whom nations borrow money. To their offices kings come with their hats in their hands. Emperors beg them to discount their notes. Is all this a consequence of the wrath of God?

We find upon our streets no Jewish beggars. It is a rare sight to find one of these people standing as a criminal before a court. They do not fill our almshouses, nor our penitentiaries, nor our jails. Intellectually and morally they are the equal of any people. They have become illustrious in every department of art and science. The old cry against them is at last perceived to be ignorant. Only a few years ago, Christians would rob a Jew, strip him of his possessions, steal his money, declare him an outcast, and drive him forth. Then they would point to him as a fulfillment of prophecy.

If you wish to see the difference between some Jews and some Christians, compare the addresses of Felix Adler with the sermons of Mr. Talmage.

I cannot convince myself that an infinitely good and wise God holds a Jewish babe in the cradle of to-day responsible for the crimes of Caiaphas the high priest. I hardly think that an infinitely good being would pursue this little babe through all its life simply to get revenge on those who died two thousand years ago. An infinite being ought certainly to know that the child is not to blame; and an infinite being who does not know this, is not entitled to the love or adoration of any honest man.

There is a strange inconsistency in what Mr. Talmage says. For instance, he finds great fault with me because I do not agree with the religious ideas of my father; and he finds fault equally with the Jews who do. The Jews who were true to the religion of their fathers, according to Mr. Talmage, have been made a by-word and a hissing and a reproach among all nations, and only those Jews were fortunate and blest who abandoned the religion of their fathers. The real reason for this inconsistency is this: Mr. Talmage really thinks that a man can believe as he wishes. He imagines that evidence depends simply upon volition; consequently, he holds every one responsible for his belief. Being satisfied that he has the exact truth in this matter, he measures all other people by his standard, and if they fail by that measurement, he holds them personally responsible, and believes that his God does the same. If Mr. Talmage had been born in Turkey, he would in all probability have been a Mohammedan, and would now be denouncing some man who had denied the inspiration of the Koran, as the "champion blas-"phemer" of Constantinople. Certainly he would have been, had his parents been Mohammedans; because, according to his doctrine, he would have been utterly lacking in respect and love for his father and mother had he failed to perpetuate their errors. So, had he been born in Utah, of Mormon parents, he would now have been a defender of polygamy. He would not "run the ploughshare of contempt " through the graves of his parents," by taking the ground that polygamy is wrong.

I presume that all of Mr. Talmage's forefathers were not Presbyterians. There must have been a time when one of his progenitors left the faith of his father, and joined the Presbyterian Church. According to the reasoning of Mr. Talmage, that particular progenitor was an exceedingly bad man; but had it not been for the crime of that bad man, Mr. Talmage might not now have been on the road to heaven.

I hardly think that all the inventors, the thinkers, the philosophers, the discoverers, dishonored their parents. Fathers and mothers have been made immortal by such sons. And yet these sons demonstrated the errors of their parents. A good father wishes to be excelled by his children.

SIXTH INTERVIEW.

SIXTH INTERVIEW.

It is a contradiction in terms and ideas to call anything a revelation that comes to us at second-hand, either verbally or in writing. Revelation is necessarily limited to the first communication—after this, it is only an account of something which that person says was a revelation made to him; and though he may find himself obliged to believe it, it cannot be incumbent on me to believe it in the same manner; for it was not a revelation made to ME, *and I have only his word for it that it was made to him.*—THOMAS PAINE.

Question. What do you think of the arguments presented by Mr. Talmage in favor of the inspiration of the Bible?

Answer. Mr. Talmage takes the ground that there are more copies of the Bible than of any other book, and that consequently it must be inspired.

It seems to me that this kind of reasoning proves entirely too much. If the Bible is the inspired word of God, it was certainly just as true when there was only one copy, as it is to-day; and the facts contained in it were just as true before they were written, as afterwards. We all know that it is a fact in human nature, that a man can tell a falsehood so often that he finally believes it himself; but I never suspected, until now, that a mistake could be printed enough times to make it true.

There may have been a time, and probably there was, when there were more copies of the Koran than of the Bible. When most Christians were utterly ignorant, thousands of Moors were educated; and it is well known that the arts and sciences flourished in Mohammedan countries in a far greater degree than in Christian. Now, at that time, it may be that there were more copies of the Koran than of the Bible. If some enterprising Mohammedan had only seen the force of such a fact, he might have established the inspiration of the Koran beyond a doubt; or, if it had been found by actual count that the Koran was a little behind, a few years of industry spent in the multiplication of copies, might have furnished the evidence of its inspiration.

Is it not simply amazing that a doctor of divinity, a Presbyterian clergyman, in this day and age, should seriously rely upon the number of copies of the Bible to substantiate the inspiration of that book? Is it possible to conceive of anything more fig-leaflessly absurd? If there is anything at all in this argument, it is, that all books are true in proportion to the number of copies that exist. Of course, the same rule will work with newspapers; so that the newspaper having the largest circulation can consistently claim infallibility. Suppose that an exceedingly absurd statement should appear in *The New York Herald*, and some one should denounce it as utterly without any foundation in fact or probability; what would Mr. Talmage think if the editor of the *Herald*, as an evidence of the truth of the statement, should rely on the fact that his paper had the largest circulation of any in the city? One would think that the whole church had acted upon the theory that a falsehood repeated often enough was as good as the truth.

Another evidence brought forward by the reverend gentleman to prove the inspiration of the Scriptures, is the assertion that if Congress should undertake to pass a law to take the Bible from the people, thirty millions would rise in defence of that book.

This argument also seems to me to prove too much, and as a consequence, to prove nothing. If Congress should pass a law prohibiting the reading of Shakespeare, every American would rise in defence of his right to read the works of the greatest man this world has known. Still, that would not even tend to show that Shakespeare was inspired. The fact is, the American people would not allow Congress to pass a law preventing them from reading any good book. Such action would not prove the book to be inspired; it would prove that the American people believe in liberty.

There are millions of people in Turkey who would peril their lives in defence of the Koran. A fact like this does not prove the truth of the Koran; it simply proves what Mohammedans think of that book, and what they are willing to do for its preservation.

It can not be too often repeated, that martyrdom does not prove the truth of the thing for which the martyr dies; it only proves the sincerity of the martyr and the cruelty of his murderers. No matter how many people regard the Bible as inspired,—that fact furnishes no evidence that it is inspired. Just as many people have regarded other books as inspired; just as many millions have been deluded about the inspiration of books ages and ages before Christianity was born.

The simple *belief* of one man, or of millions of men, is no *evidence* to another. Evidence must be based, not upon the belief of other people, but upon *facts*. A believer may state the facts upon which his belief is founded, and the person to whom he states them gives them the weight that according to the construction and constitution of his mind he must. But simple, bare belief is not testimony. We should build upon facts, not upon beliefs of others, nor upon the shifting sands of public opinion. So much for this argument.

The next point made by the reverend gentleman is, that an infidel cannot be elected to any office in the United States, in any county, precinct, or ward.

For the sake of the argument, let us admit that this is true. What does it prove? There was a time when no Protestant could have been elected to any office. What did that prove? There was a time when no Presbyterian could have been chosen to fill any public station. What did that prove? The same may be said of the members of each religious denomination. What does that prove?

Mr. Talmage says that Christianity must be true, because an infidel cannot be elected to office. Now, suppose that enough infidels should happen to settle in one precinct to elect one of their own number to office; would that prove that Christianity was not true in that precinct? There was a time when no man could have been elected to any office, who insisted on the rotundity of the earth; what did that prove? There was a time when no man who denied the existence of witches, wizards, spooks and devils, could hold any position of honor; what did that prove? There was a time when an abolitionist could not be elected to office in any State in this Union; what did that prove? There was a time when they were not allowed to express their honest thoughts; what does that prove? There was a time when a Quaker could not have been elected to any office; there was a time in the history of this country when but few of them were allowed to live; what does that prove? Is it necessary, in order to ascertain the truth of Christianity, to look over the election returns? Is "inspiration" a question to be settled by the ballot? I admit that it was once, in the first place, settled that way. I admit that books were voted in and voted out, and that the Bible was finally formed in accordance with a vote; but does Mr. Talmage insist that the question is not still open? Does he not know, that a fact cannot by any possibility be affected by opinion? We make laws for the whole people, by the whole people. We agree that a majority shall rule, but nobody ever pretended that a question of taste could be settled by an appeal to majorities, or that a question of logic could be affected by numbers. In the world of thought, each man is an absolute monarch, each brain is a kingdom, that cannot be invaded even by the tyranny of majorities.

No man can avoid the intellectual responsibility of deciding for himself.

Suppose that the Christian religion had been put to vote in Jerusalem? Suppose that the doctrine of the "fall" had been settled in Athens, by an appeal to the people, would Mr. Talmage have been willing to abide by their decision? If he settles the inspiration of the Bible by a popular vote, he must settle the meaning of the Bible by the same means. There are more Methodists than Presbyterians—why does the gentleman remain a Presbyterian? There are more Buddhists than Christians—why does he vote against majorities? He will remember that Christianity was once settled by a popular vote—that the divinity of Christ was submitted to the people, and the people said: "Crucify him!"

The next, and about the strongest, argument Mr. Talmage makes is, that I am an infidel because I was defeated for Governor of Illinois.

When put in plain English, his statement is this:

that I was defeated because I was an infidel, and that I am an infidel because I was defeated. This, I believe, is called reasoning in a circle. The truth is, that a good many people did object to me because I was an infidel, and the probability is, that if I had denied being an infidel, I might have obtained an office. The wonderful part is, that any Christian should deride me because I preferred honor to political success. He who dishonors himself for the sake of being honored by others, will find that two mistakes have been made—one by himself, and the other, by the people.

I presume that Mr. Talmage really thinks that I was extremely foolish to avow my real opinions. After all, men are apt to judge others somewhat by themselves. According to him, I made the mistake of preserving my manhood and losing an office. Now, if I had in fact been an infidel, and had denied it, for the sake of position, then I admit that every Christian might have pointed at me the finger of contempt. But I was an infidel, and admitted it. Surely, I should not be held in contempt by Christians for having made the admission. I was not a believer in the Bible, and I said so. I was not a Christian, and I said so. I was not willing to receive the support of any man under a false impression. I thought it better to be honestly beaten, than to dishonestly succeed. According to the ethics of Mr. Talmage I made a mistake, and this mistake is brought forward as another evidence of the inspiration of the Scriptures. If I had only been elected Governor of Illinois,—that is to say, if I had been a successful hypocrite, I might now be basking in the sunshine of this gentleman's respect. I preferred to tell the truth—to be an honest man,—and I have never regretted the course I pursued.

There are many men now in office who, had they pursued a nobler course, would be private citizens. Nominally, they are Christians; actually, they are nothing; and this is the combination that generally insures political success.

Mr. Talmage is exceedingly proud of the fact that Christians will not vote for infidels. In other words, he does not believe that in our Government the church has been absolutely divorced from the state. He believes that it is still the Christian's duty to make the religious test. Probably he wishes to get his God into the Constitution. My position is this:

Religion is an individual matter—a something for each individual to settle for himself, and with which no other human being has any concern, provided the religion of each human being allows liberty to every other. When called upon to vote for men to fill the offices of this country, I do not inquire as to the religion of the candidates. It is none of my business. I ask the questions asked by Jefferson: "Is he " honest; is he capable?" It makes no difference to me, if he is willing that others should be free, what creed he may profess. The moment I inquire into his religious belief, I found a little inquisition of my own; I repeat, in a small way, the errors of the past, and reproduce, in so far as I am capable, the infamy of the ignorant orthodox years.

Mr. Talmage will accept my thanks for his frankness. I now know what controls a Presbyterian when he casts his vote. He cares nothing for the capacity, nothing for the fitness, of the candidate to discharge the duties of the office to which he aspires; he simply asks: Is he a Presbyterian, is he a Protestant, does he believe our creed? and then, no matter how ignorant he may be, how utterly unfit, he receives the Presbyterian vote. According to Mr. Talmage, he would vote for a Catholic who, if he had the power, would destroy all liberty of conscience, rather than vote for an infidel who, had he the power, would destroy all the religious tyranny of the world, and allow every human being to think for himself, and to worship God, or not, as and how he pleased.

Mr. Talmage makes the serious mistake of placing the Bible above the laws and Constitution of his country. He places Jehovah above humanity. Such men are not entirely safe citizens of any republic. And yet, I am in favor of giving to such men all the liberty I ask for myself, trusting to education and the spirit of progress to overcome any injury they may do, or seek to do.

When this country was founded, when the Constitution was adopted, the churches agreed to let the State alone. They agreed that all citizens should have equal civil rights. Nothing could be more dangerous to the existence of this Republic than to introduce religion into politics. The American theory is, that governments are founded, not by gods, but by men, and that the right to govern does not come from God, but "from the consent of the governed." Our fathers concluded that the people were sufficiently intelligent to take care of themselves—to make good laws and to execute them. Prior to that time, all authority was supposed to come from the clouds. Kings were set upon thrones by God, and it was the business of the people simply to submit. In all really civilized countries, that doctrine has been abandoned. The source of political power is *here*, not in heaven. We are willing that those in heaven should control affairs there; we are willing that the angels should have a government to suit themselves; but while we live here, and while our interests are upon this earth, we propose to make and execute our own laws.

If the doctrine of Mr. Talmage is the true doctrine, if no man should be voted for unless he is a Christian, then no man should vote unless he is a Christian. It will not do to say that sinners may vote, that an infidel may be the repository of political power, but must not be voted for. A decent Christian who is not willing that an infidel should be elected to an office, would not be willing to be elected to an office by infidel votes. If infidels are too bad to be voted for, they are certainly not good enough to vote, and no Christian should be willing to represent such an infamous constituency.

If the political theory of Mr. Talmage is carried out, of course the question will arise in a little while, What is a Christian? It will then be necessary to write a creed to be subscribed by every person before he is fit to vote or to be voted for. This of course must be done by the State, and must be settled, under our form of government, by a majority vote. Is Mr. Talmage willing that the question, What is Christianity? should be so settled? Will he pledge himself in advance to subscribe to such a creed? Of course he will not. He will insist that he has the right to read the Bible for himself, and that he must be bound by his own conscience. In this he would be right. If he has the right to read the Bible for himself, so have I. If he is to be bound by his conscience, so am I. If he honestly believes the Bible to be true, he must say so, in order to preserve his manhood; and if I honestly believe it to be uninspired,— filled with mistakes,—I must say so, or lose my manhood. How infamous I would be should I endeavor to deprive him of his vote, or of his right to be voted for, because he had been true to his conscience! And how infamous he is to try to deprive me of the right to vote, or to be voted for, because I am true to my conscience!

When we were engaged in civil war, did Mr. Talmage object to any man's enlisting in the ranks who was not a Christian? Was he willing, at that time, that sinners should vote to keep our flag in heaven? Was he willing that the "unconverted" should cover the fields of victory with their corpses, that this nation might not die? At the same time, Mr. Talmage knew that every "unconverted" soldier killed, went down to eternal fire. Does Mr. Talmage believe that it is the duty of a man to fight for a government in which he has no rights? Is the man who shoulders his musket in the defence of human freedom good enough to cast a ballot? There is in the heart of this priest the same hatred of real liberty that drew the sword of persecution, that built dungeons, that forged chains and made instruments of torture.

Nobody, with the exception of priests, would be willing to trust the liberties of this country in the hands of any church. In order to show the political estimation in which the clergy are held, in order to show the confidence the people at large have in the sincerity and wisdom of the clergy, it is sufficient to state, that no priest, no bishop, could by any possibility be elected President of the United States. No party could carry that load. A fear would fall upon the mind and heart of every honest man that this country was about to drift back to the Middle Ages, and that the old battles were to be refought. If the bishop running for President was of the Methodist Church, every other church would oppose him. If he was a Catholic, the Protestants would as a body combine against him. Why? The churches have no confidence in each other. Why? Because they are acquainted with each other.

As a matter of fact, the infidel has a thousand times more reason to vote against the Christian, than the Christian has to vote against the infidel. The Christian believes in a book superior to the Constitution—superior to all Constitutions and all laws. The infidel believes that the Constitution and laws are superior to any book. He is not controlled by any power beyond the seas or above the clouds. He does not receive his orders from Rome, or Sinai. He receives them from his fellow-citizens, legally and constitutionally expressed. The Christian believes in a power greater than man, to which, upon the peril of eternal pain, he must bow. His allegiance, to say the best of it, is divided. The Christian puts the fortune of his own soul over and above the temporal welfare of the entire world; the infidel puts the good of mankind here and now, beyond and over all.

There was a time in New England when only church members were allowed to vote, and it may be instructive to state the fact that during that time Quakers were hanged, women were stripped, tied to carts, and whipped from town to town, and their babes sold into slavery, or exchanged for rum. Now in that same country, thousands and thousands of infidels vote, and yet the laws are nearer just, women are not whipped and children are not sold.

If all the convicts in all the penitentiaries of the United States could be transported to some island in the sea, and there allowed to make a government for themselves, they would pass better laws than John Calvin did in Geneva. They would have clearer and better views of the rights of men, than unconvicted Christians used to have. I do not say that these convicts are better people, but I do say that, in my judgment, they would make better laws. They certainly could not make worse.

If these convicts were taken from the prisons of the United States, they would not dream of uniting church and state. They would have no religious test. They would allow every man to vote and to be voted for, no matter what his religious views might be. They would not dream of whipping Quakers, of burning Unitarians, of imprisoning or burning Universalists or infidels. They would allow all the people to guess for themselves. Some of these convicts, of course, would believe in the old ideas, and would insist upon the suppression of free thought. Those coming from Delaware would probably repeat with great gusto the opinions of Justice Comegys, and insist that the whipping-post was the handmaid of Christianity.

It would be hard to conceive of a much worse government than that founded by the Puritans. They took the Bible for the foundation of their political structure. They copied the laws given to Moses from Sinai, and the result was one of the worst governments that ever disgraced this world. They believed the Old Testament to be inspired. They believed that Jehovah made laws for all people and for all time. They had not learned the hypocrisy that believes and avoids. They did not say: This law was once just, but is now unjust; it was once good, but now it is infamous; it was given by God once, but now it can only be obeyed by the devil. They had not reached the height of biblical exegesis on which we find the modern theologian perched, and who tells us that Jehovah has reformed. The Puritans were consistent. They did what people must do who honestly believe in the inspiration of the Old Testament. If God gave laws from Sinai what right have we to repeal them?

As people have gained confidence in each other, they have lost confidence in the sacred Scriptures. We know now that the Bible can not be used as the foundation of government. It is capable of too many meanings. Nobody can find out exactly what it upholds, what it permits, what it denounces, what it denies. These things depend upon what part you read. If it is all true, it upholds everything bad and denounces everything good, and it also denounces the bad and upholds the good. Then there are passages where the good is denounced and the bad commanded; so that any one can go to the Bible and find some text, some passage, to uphold anything he may desire. If he wishes to enslave his fellow-men, he will find hundreds of passages in his favor. If he wishes to be a polygamist, he can find his authority there. If he wishes to make war, to exterminate his neighbors, there his warrant can be found. If, on the other hand, he is oppressed himself, and wishes to make war upon his king, he can find a battle-cry. And if the king wishes to put him down, he can find text for text on the other side. So, too, upon all questions of reform. The teetotaler goes there to get his verse, and the moderate drinker finds within the sacred lids his best excuse.

INTERVIEWS. 313

Most intelligent people are now convinced that the bible is not a guide; that in reading it you must exercise your reason; that you can neither safely reject nor accept all; that he who takes one passage for a staff, trips upon another; that while one text is a light, another blows it out; that it is such a mingling of rocks and quicksands, such a labyrinth of clews and snares—so few flowers among so many nettles and thorns, that it misleads rather than directs, and taken altogether, is a hindrance and not a help.

Another important point made by Mr. Talmage is, that if the Bible is thrown away, we will have nothing left to swear witnesses on, and that consequently the administration of justice will become impossible.

There was a time when the Bible did not exist, and if Mr. Talmage is correct, of course justice was impossible then, and truth must have been a stranger to human lips. How can we depend upon the testimony of those who wrote the Bible, as there was no Bible in existence while they were writing, and consequently there was no way to take their testimony, and we have no account of their having been sworn on the Bible after they got it finished. It is extremely sad to think that all the nations of antiquity were left entirely without the means of eliciting truth. No wonder that Justice was painted blindfolded.

What perfect fetichism it is, to imagine that a man will tell the truth simply because he has kissed an old piece of sheepskin stained with the saliva of all classes. A farce of this kind adds nothing to the testimony of an honest man; it simply allows a rogue to give weight to his false testimony. This is really the only result that can be accomplished by kissing the Bible. A desperate villain, for the purpose of getting revenge, or making money, will gladly go through the ceremony, and ignorant juries and superstitious judges will be imposed upon. The whole system of oaths is false, and does harm instead of good. Let every man walk into court and tell his story, and let the truth of the story be judged by its reasonableness, taking into consideration the character of the witness, the interest he has, and the position he occupies in the controversy, and then let it be the business of the jury to ascertain the real truth —to throw away the unreasonable and the impossible, and make up their verdict only upon what they believe to be reasonable and true. An honest man does not need the oath, and a rascal uses it simply to accomplish his purpose. If the history of courts proved that every man, after kissing the Bible, told the truth, and that those who failed to kiss it sometimes lied, I should be in favor of swearing all people on the Bible ; but the experience of every lawyer is, that kissing the Bible is not always the preface of a true story. It is often the ceremonial embroidery of a falsehood.

If there is an infinite God who attends to the affairs of men, it seems to me almost a sacrilege to publicly appeal to him in every petty trial. If one will go into any court, and notice the manner in which oaths are administered,—the utter lack of solemnity—the matter-of-course air with which the whole thing is done, he will be convinced that it is a form of no importance. Mr. Talmage would probably agree with the judge of whom the following story is told :

A witness was being sworn. The judge noticed that he was not holding up his hand. He said to the clerk : "Let the witness hold up his right hand." "His right arm was shot off," replied the clerk. "Let "him hold up his left, then." "That was shot off, too, "your honor." "Well, then, let him raise one foot; "no man can be sworn in this court without holding "something up."

My own opinion is, that if every copy of the Bible in the world were destroyed, there would be some way to ascertain the truth in judicial proceedings; and any other book would do just as well to swear witnesses upon, or a block in the shape of a book covered with some kind of calfskin could do equally well, or just the calfskin would do. Nothing is more laughable than the performance of this ceremony, and I have never seen in court one calf kissing the skin of another, that I did not feel humiliated that such things were done in the name of Justice.

Mr. Talmage has still another argument in favor of the preservation of the Bible. He wants to know what book could take its place on the centre-table.

I admit that there is much force in this. Suppose we all admitted the Bible to be an uninspired book, it could still be kept on the centre-table. It would be just as true then as it is now. Inspiration can not add anything to a fact; neither can inspiration make the immoral moral, the unjust just, or the cruel merciful. If it is a fact that God established human slavery, that does not prove slavery to be right; it simply shows that God was wrong. If I have the right to use my reason in determining whether the Bible is inspired or not, and if in accordance with my reason I conclude that it is inspired, I have still the right to use my reason in determining whether the commandments of God are good or bad. Now, suppose we take from the Bible every word upholding slavery, every passage in favor of polygamy, every verse commanding soldiers to kill women and children, it would be just as fit for the centre-table as now. Suppose every impure word was taken from it; suppose that the history of Tamar was left out, the biography of Lot, and all other barbarous accounts of a barbarous people, it would look just as well upon the centre-table as now.

Suppose that we should become convinced that the writers of the New Testament were mistaken as to the eternity of punishment, or that all the passages now relied upon to prove the existence of perdition were shown to be interpolations, and were thereupon expunged, would not the book be dearer still to every human being with a heart? I would like to see every good passage in the Bible preserved. I would like to see, with all these passages from the Bible, the loftiest sentiments from all other books that have ever been uttered by men in all ages and of all races, bound in one volume, and to see that volume, filled with the greatest, the purest and the best, become the household book.

The average Bible, on the average centre-table, is about as much used as though it were a solid block. It is scarcely ever opened, and people who see its covers every day are unfamiliar with its every page.

I admit that some things have happened somewhat hard to explain, and tending to show that the Bible is no ordinary book. I heard a story, not long ago, bearing upon this very subject.

A man was a member of the church, but after a time, having had bad luck in business affairs, became somewhat discouraged. Not feeling able to contribute his share to the support of the church, he ceased going to meeting, and finally became an average sinner. His bad luck pursued him until he found himself and his family without even a crust to eat. At this point, his wife told him that she believed they were suffering from a visitation of God, and begged him to restore family worship, and see if God would not do something for them. Feeling that he could not possibly make matters worse, he took the Bible from its resting place on a shelf where it had quietly slumbered and collected the dust of many months, and gathered his family about him.

He opened the sacred volume, and to his utter astonishment, there, between the divine leaves, was a ten-dollar bill. He immediately dropped on his knees. His wife dropped on hers, and the children on theirs, and with streaming eyes they returned thanks to God. He rushed to the butcher's and bought some steak, to the baker's and bought some bread, to the grocer's and got some eggs and butter and tea, and joyfully hastened home. The supper was cooked, it was on the table, grace was said, and every face was radiant with joy. Just at that happy moment a knock was heard, the door was opened, and a policeman entered and arrested the father for passing counterfeit money.

Mr. Talmage is also convinced that the Bible is inspired and should be preserved because there is no other book that a mother could give her son as he leaves the old home to make his way in the world.

Thousands and thousands of mothers have presented their sons with Bibles without knowing really what the book contains. They simply followed the custom, and the sons as a rule honored the Bible, not because they knew anything of it, but because it was a gift from mother. But surely, if all the passages upholding polygamy were out, the mother would give the book to her son just as readily, and he would receive it just as joyfully. If there were not one word in it tending to degrade the mother, the gift would certainly be as appropriate. The fact that mothers have presented Bibles to their sons does not prove that the book is inspired. The most that can be proved by this fact is that the mothers believed it to be inspired. It does not even tend to show what the book is, neither does it tend to establish the truth of one miracle recorded upon its pages. We cannot believe that fire refused to burn, simply because the statement happens to be in a book presented to a son by his mother, and if all the mothers of the entire world should give Bibles to all their children, this would not prove that it was once right to murder mothers, or to enslave mothers, or to sell their babes.

The inspiration of the Bible is not a question of natural affection. It can not be decided by the love a mother bears her son. It is a question of fact, to be substantiated like other facts. If the Turkish mother should give a copy of the Koran to her son, I would still have my doubts about the inspiration of that book; and if some Turkish soldier saved his life by having in his pocket a copy of the Koran that accidentally stopped a bullet just opposite his heart, I should still deny that Mohammed was a prophet of God.

Nothing can be more childish than to ascribe mysterious powers to inanimate objects. To imagine that old rags made into pulp, manufactured into paper, covered with words, and bound with the skin of a calf or a sheep, can have any virtues when thus put together that did not belong to the articles out of which the book was constructed, is of course infinitely absurd.

In the days of slavery, negroes used to buy dried roots of other negroes, and put these roots in their pockets, so that a whipping would not give them pain. Kings have bought diamonds to give them luck. Crosses and scapularies are still worn for the purpose of affecting the inevitable march of events. People still imagine that a verse in the Bible can step in between a cause and its effect; really believe that an amulet, a charm, the bone of some saint, a piece of a cross, a little image of the Virgin, a picture of a priest, will affect the weather, will delay frost, will prevent disease, will insure safety at sea, and in some cases prevent hanging. The banditti of Italy have great confidence in these things, and whenever they start upon an expedition of theft and plunder, they take images and pictures of saints with them, such as have been blest by a priest or pope. They pray sincerely to the Virgin, to give them luck, and see not the slightest inconsistency in appealing to all the saints in the calendar to assist them in robbing honest people.

Edmund Abôut tells a story that illustrates the belief of the modern Italian. A young man was gambling. Fortune was against him. In the room was a little picture representing the Virgin and her child. Before this picture he crossed himself, and asked the assistance of the child. Again he put down his money and again lost. Returning to the picture, he told the child that he had lost all but one piece, that he was about to hazard that, and made a very urgent request that he would favor him with divine assistance. He put down the last piece. He lost. Going to the picture and shaking his fist at the child, he cried out: "Miserable bambino, I am glad they crucified you!"

The confidence that one has in an image, in a relic, in a book, comes from the same source,—fetichism. To ascribe supernatural virtues to the skin of a snake, to a picture, or to a bound volume, is intellectually the same.

Mr. Talmage has still another argument in favor

of the inspiration of the Scriptures. He takes the ground that the Bible must be inspired, because so many people believe it.

Mr. Talmage should remember that a scientific fact does not depend upon the vote of numbers;— it depends simply upon demonstration; it depends upon intelligence and investigation, not upon an ignorant multitude; it appeals to the highest, instead of to the lowest. Nothing can be settled by popular prejudice.

According to Mr. Talmage, there are about three hundred million Christians in the world. Is this true? In all countries claiming to be Christian—including all of civilized Europe, Russia in Asia, and every country on the Western hemisphere, we have nearly four hundred millions of people. Mr. Talmage claims that three hundred millions are Christians. I suppose he means by this, that if all should perish to-night, about three hundred millions would wake up in heaven—having lived and died good and consistent Christians.

There are in Russia about eighty millions of people —how many Christians? I admit that they have recently given more evidence of orthodox Christianity than formerly. They have been murdering old men;

they have thrust daggers into the breasts of women; they have violated maidens—because they were Jews. Thousands and thousands are sent each year to the mines of Siberia, by the Christian government of Russia. Girls eighteen years of age, for having expressed a word in favor of human liberty, are to-day working like beasts of burden, with chains upon their limbs and with the marks of whips upon their backs. Russia, of course, is considered by Mr. Talmage as a Christian country—a country utterly destitute of liberty—without freedom of the press, without freedom of speech, where every mouth is locked and every tongue a prisoner—a country filled with victims, soldiers, spies, thieves and executioners. What would Russia be, in the opinion of Mr. Talmage, but for Christianity? How could it be worse, when assassins are among the best people in it? The truth is, that the people in Russia, to-day, who are in favor of human liberty, are not Christians. The men willing to sacrifice their lives for the good of others, are not believers in the Christian religion. The men who wish to break chains are infidels; the men who make chains are Christians. Every good and sincere Catholic of the Greek Church is a bad citizen, an enemy of progress, a foe of human liberty. Yet Mr. Talmage regards Russia as a Christian country.

The sixteen millions of people in Spain are claimed as Christians. Spain, that for centuries was the assassin of human rights; Spain, that endeavored to spread Christianity by flame and fagot; Spain, the soil where the Inquisition flourished, where bigotry grew, and where cruelty was worship,—where murder was prayer. I admit that Spain is a Christian nation. I admit that infidelity has gained no foothold beyond the Pyrenees. The Spaniards are orthodox. They believe in the inspiration of the Old and New Testaments. They have no doubts about miracles—no doubts about heaven, no doubts about hell. I admit that the priests, the highwaymen, the bishops and thieves, are equally true believers. The man who takes your purse on the highway, and the priest who forgives the robber, are alike orthodox.

It gives me pleasure, however, to say that even in Spain there is a dawn. Some great men, some men of genius, are protesting against the tyranny of Catholicism. Some men have lost confidence in the cathedral, and are beginning to ask the State to erect the schoolhouse. They are beginning to suspect that priests are for the most part impostors and plunderers.

According to Mr. Talmage, the twenty-eight millions in Italy are Christians. There the Christian Church was early established, and the popes are to-day the successors of St. Peter. For hundreds and hundreds of years, Italy was the beggar of the world, and to her, from every land, flowed streams of gold and silver. The country was covered with convents, and monasteries, and churches, and cathedrals filled with monks and nuns. Its roads were crowded with pilgrims, and its dust was on the feet of the world. What has Christianity done for Italy—Italy, its soil a blessing, its sky a smile—Italy, with memories great enough to kindle the fires of enthusiasm in any human breast?

Had it not been for a few Freethinkers, for a few infidels, for such men as Garibaldi and Mazzini, the heaven of Italy would still have been without a star.

I admit that Italy, with its popes and bandits, with its superstition and ignorance, with its sanctified beggars, is a Christian nation; but in a little while,—in a few days,—when according to the prophecy of Garibaldi priests, with spades in their hands, will dig ditches to drain the Pontine marshes; in a little while, when the pope leaves the Vatican, and seeks the protection of a nation he has denounced,—asking alms of intended victims; when the nuns shall marry, and the monasteries shall become factories, and the whirl of wheels shall take the place of drowsy prayers —then, and not until then, will Italy be,—not a Christian nation, but great, prosperous, and free.

In Italy, Giordano Bruno was burned. Some day, his monument will rise above the cross of Rome.

We have in our day one example,—and so far as I know, history records no other,—of the resurrection of a nation. Italy has been called from the grave of superstition. She is "the first fruits of them that " slept."

I admit with Mr. Talmage that Portugal is a Christian country—that she engaged for hundreds of years in the slave trade, and that she justified the infamous traffic by passages in the Old Testament. I admit, also, that she persecuted the Jews in accordance with the same divine volume. I admit that all the crime, ignorance, destitution, and superstition in that country were produced by the Catholic Church. I also admit that Portugal would be better if it were Protestant.

Every Catholic is in favor of education enough to

change a barbarian into a Catholic; every Protestant is in favor of education enough to change a Catholic into a Protestant; but Protestants and Catholics alike are opposed to education that will lead to any real philosophy and science. I admit that Portugal is what it is, on account of the preaching of the gospel. I admit that Portugal can point with pride to the triumphs of what she calls civilization within her borders, and truthfully ascribe the glory to the church. But in a little while, when more railroads are built, when telegraphs connect her people with the civilized world, a spirit of doubt, of investigation, will manifest itself in Portugal.

When the people stop counting beads, and go to the study of mathematics; when they think more of plows than of prayers for agricultural purposes; when they find that one fact gives more light to the mind than a thousand tapers, and that nothing can by any possibility be more useless than a priest,—then Portugal will begin to cease to be what is called a Christian nation.

I admit that Austria, with her thirty-seven millions, is a Christian nation—including her Croats, Hungarians, Servians, and Gypsies. Austria was one of the assassins of Poland. When we remember that John

Sobieski drove the Mohammedans from the gates of Vienna, and rescued from the hand of the "infidel" the beleagured city, the propriety of calling Austria a Christian nation becomes still more apparent. If one wishes to know exactly how "Christian" Austria is, let him read the history of Hungary, let him read the speeches of Kossuth. There is one good thing about Austria : slowly but surely she is undermining the church by education. Education is the enemy of superstition. Universal education does away with the classes born of the tyranny of ecclesiasticism — classes founded upon cunning, greed, and brute strength. Education also tends to do away with intellectual cowardice. The educated man is his own priest, his own pope, his own church.

When cunning collects tolls from fear, the church prospers.

Germany is another Christian nation. Bismarck is celebrated for his Christian virtues.

Only a little while ago, Bismarck, when a bill was under consideration for ameliorating the condition of the Jews, stated publicly that Germany was a Christian nation, that her business was to extend and protect the religion of Jesus Christ, and that being a Christian nation, no laws should be passed ameliorating the condition of the Jews. Certainly a remark like this could not have been made in any other than a Christian nation. There is no freedom of the press, there is no freedom of speech, in Germany. The Chancellor has gone so far as to declare that the king is not responsible to the people. Germany must be a Christian nation. The king gets his right to govern, not from his subjects, but from God. He relies upon the New Testament. He is satisfied that "the powers that be in Germany are ordained " of God." He is satisfied that treason against the German throne is treason against Jehovah. There are millions of Freethinkers in Germany. They are not in the majority, otherwise there would be more liberty in that country. Germany is not an infidel nation, or speech would be free, and every man would be allowed to express his honest thoughts.

Wherever I see Liberty in chains, wherever the expression of opinion is a crime, I know that that country is not infidel; I know that the people are not ruled by reason. I also know that the greatest men of Germany—her Freethinkers, her scientists, her writers, her philosophers, are, for the most part, infidel. Yet Germany is called a Christian nation, and ought to be so called until her citizens are free.

France is also claimed as a Christian country. This is not entirely true. France once was thoroughly Catholic, completely Christian. At the time of the massacre of Saint Bartholomew, the French were Christians. Christian France made exiles of the Huguenots. Christian France for years and years was the property of the Jesuits. Christian France was ignorant, cruel, orthodox and infamous. When France was Christian, witnesses were cross-examined with instruments of torture.

Now France is not entirely under Catholic control, and yet she is by far the most prosperous nation in Europe. I saw, only the other day, a letter from a Protestant bishop, in which he states that there are only about a million Protestants in France, and only four or five millions of Catholics, and admits, in a very melancholy way, that thirty-four or thirty-five millions are Freethinkers. The bishop is probably mistaken in his figures, but France is the best housed, the best fed, the best clad country in Europe.

Only a little while ago, France was overrun, trampled into the very earth, by the victorious hosts of Germany, and France purchased her peace with the savings of centuries. And yet France is now rich and prosperous and free, and Germany poor, discontent and enslaved. Hundreds and thousands of Germans, unable to find liberty at home, are coming to the United States.

I admit that England is a Christian country. Any doubts upon this point can be dispelled by reading her history—her career in India, what she has done in China, her treatment of Ireland, of the American Colonies, her attitude during our Civil war; all these things show conclusively that England is a Christian nation.

Religion has filled Great Britain with war. The history of the Catholics, of the Episcopalians, of Cromwell—all the burnings, the maimings, the brandings, the imprisonments, the confiscations, the civil wars, the bigotry, the crime—show conclusively that Great Britain has enjoyed to the full the blessings of "our most holy religion."

Of course, Mr. Talmage claims the United States as a Christian country. The truth is, our country is not as Christian as it once was. When heretics were hanged in New England, when the laws of Virginia and Maryland provided that the tongue of any man who denied the doctrine of the Trinity should be bored with hot iron, and that for the second offence he should suffer death, I admit that this country was

Christian. When we engaged in the slave trade, when our flag protected piracy and murder in every sea, there is not the slightest doubt that the United States was a Christian country. When we believed in slavery, and when we deliberately stole the labor of four millions of people; when we sold women and babes, and when the people of the North enacted a law by virtue of which every Northern man was bound to turn hound and pursue a human being who was endeavoring to regain his liberty, I admit that the United States was a Christian nation. I admit that all these things were upheld by the Bible —that the slave trader was justified by the Old Testament, that the bloodhound was a kind of missionary in disguise, that the auction block was an altar, the slave pen a kind of church, and that the whipping-post was considered almost as sacred as the cross. At that time, our country was a Christian nation.

I heard Frederick Douglass say that he lectured against slavery for twenty years before the doors of a single church were opened to him. In New England, hundreds of ministers were driven from their pulpits because they preached against the crime of human slavery. At that time, this country was a Christian nation.

Only a few years ago, any man speaking in favor of the rights of man, endeavoring to break a chain from a human limb, was in danger of being mobbed by the Christians of this country. I admit that Delaware is still a Christian State. I heard a story about that State the other day.

About fifty years ago, an old Revolutionary soldier applied for a pension. He was asked his age, and he replied that he was fifty years old. He was told that if that was his age, he could not have been in the Revolutionary War, and consequently was not entitled to any pension. He insisted, however, that he was only fifty years old. Again they told him that there must be some mistake. He was so wrinkled, so bowed, had so many marks of age, that he must certainly be more than fifty years old. "Well," said the old man, "if I must explain, I will: I lived forty " years in Delaware; but I never counted that time, " and I hope God won't."

The fact is, we have grown less and less Christian every year from 1620 until now, and the fact is that we have grown more and more civilized, more and more charitable, nearer and nearer just.

Mr. Talmage speaks as though all the people in what he calls the civilized world were Christians. Admitting this to be true, I find that in these countries millions of men are educated, trained and drilled to kill their fellow Christians. I find Europe covered with forts to protect Christians from Christians, and the seas filled with men-of-war for the purpose of ravaging the coasts and destroying the cities of Christian nations. These countries are filled with prisons, with workhouses, with jails and with toiling, ignorant and suffering millions. I find that Christians have invented most of the instruments of death, that Christians are the greatest soldiers, fighters, destroyers. I find that every Christian country is taxed to its utmost to support these soldiers; that every Christian nation is now groaning beneath the grievous burden of monstrous debt, and that nearly all these debts were contracted in waging war. These bonds, these millions, these almost incalculable amounts, were given to pay for shot and shell, for rifle and torpedo, for men-of-war, for forts and arsenals, and all the devilish enginery of death. I find that each of these nations prays to God to assist it as against all others; and when one nation has overrun, ravaged and pillaged another, it immediately returns thanks to the Almighty, and the ravaged and pillaged kneel and thank God that it is no worse.

Mr. Talmage is welcome to all the evidence he can find in the history of what he is pleased to call the civilized nations of the world, tending to show the inspiration of the Bible.

And right here it may be well enough to say again, that the question of inspiration can not be settled by the votes of the superstitious millions. It can not be affected by numbers. It must be decided by each human being for himself. If every man in this world, with one exception, believed the Bible to be the inspired word of God, the man who was the exception could not lose his right to think, to investigate, and to judge for himself.

Question. You do not think, then, that any of the arguments brought forward by Mr. Talmage for the purpose of establishing the inspiration of the Bible, are of any weight whatever?

Answer. I do not. I do not see how it is possible to make poorer, weaker, or better arguments than he has made.

Of course, there can be no "evidence" of the inspiration of the Scriptures. What is "inspiration"? Did God use the prophets simply as instruments? Did he put his thoughts in their minds, and use their hands to make a record? Probably few Christians will agree as to what they mean by "inspiration." The general idea is, that the minds of the writers of the books of the Bible were controlled by the divine will in such a way that they expressed, independently of their own opinions, the thought of God. I believe it is admitted that God did not choose the exact words, and is not responsible for the punctuation or syntax. It is hard to give any reason for claiming more for the Bible than is claimed by those who wrote it. There is no claim of "inspiration" made by the writer of First and Second Kings. Not one word about the author having been "inspired" is found in the book of Job, or in Ruth, or in Chronicles, or in the Psalms, or Ecclesiastes, or in Solomon's Song, and nothing is said about the author of the book of Esther having been "inspired." Christians now say that Matthew, Mark, Luke and John were "inspired" to write the four gospels, and yet neither Mark, nor Luke, nor John, nor Matthew claims to have been "inspired." If they were "inspired," certainly they should have stated that fact. The very first thing stated in each of the gospels should have been a declaration by the writer that he had been "inspired," and that he was about to write the book under the guidance of God, and at the conclusion of each gospel there should have been a solemn statement that the writer had put down nothing of himself, but had in all things followed the direction and guidance of the divine will. The church now endeavors to establish the inspiration of the Bible by force, by social ostracism, and by attacking the reputation of every man who denies or doubts. In all Christian countries, they begin with the child in the cradle. Each infant is told by its mother, by its father, or by some of its relatives, that "the Bible is an inspired book." This pretended fact, by repetition "in season and out of " season," is finally burned and branded into the brain to such a degree that the child of average intelligence never outgrows the conviction that the Bible is, in some peculiar sense, an "inspired" book. The question has to be settled for each generation. The evidence is not sufficient, and the foundation of Christianity is perpetually insecure. Beneath this great religious fabric there is no rock. For eighteen centuries, hundreds and thousands and millions of people have been endeavoring to establish the fact that the Scriptures are inspired, and since the dawn of science, since the first star appeared in the night of the Middle Ages, until this moment, the number of people who have doubted the fact of inspiration has steadily increased. These doubts have not been born of ignorance, they have not been suggested by the unthinking. They have forced themselves upon the thoughtful, upon the educated, and now the verdict of the intellectual world is, that the Bible is not inspired. Notwithstanding the fact that the church has taken advantage of infancy, has endeavored to control education, has filled all primers and spelling-books and readers and text books with superstition—feeding all minds with the miraculous and supernatural, the growth toward a belief in the natural and toward the rejection of the miraculous has been steady and sturdy since the sixteenth century. There has been, too, a moral growth, until many passages in the Bible have become barbarous, inhuman and infamous. The Bible has remained the same, while the world has changed. In the light of physical and moral discovery, "the inspired volume" seems in many respects absurd. If the same progress is made in the next, as in the last, century, it is very easy to predict the place that will then be occupied by the Bible. By comparing long periods of time, it is easy to measure the advance of the human race. Compare the average sermon of to-day with the average sermon of one hundred years ago. Compare what ministers teach to-day with the creeds they profess to believe, and you will see the immense distance that even the church has traveled in the last century.

The Christians tell us that scientific men have made mistakes, and that there is very little certainty in the domain of human knowledge. This I admit. The man who thought the world was flat, and who had a way of accounting for the movement of the heavenly bodies, had what he was pleased to call a philosophy. He was, in his way, a geologist and an astronomer. We admit that he was mistaken; but if we claimed that the first geologist and the first astronomer were inspired, it would not do for us to admit that any advance had been made, or that any errors of theirs had been corrected. We do not claim that the first scientists were inspired. We do not claim that the last are inspired. We admit that all scientific men are fallible. We admit that they do not know everything. We insist that they know but little, and that even in that little which they are supposed to know, there is the possibility of error. The first geologist said: "The earth is flat." Suppose that the geologists of to-day should insist that that man was inspired, and then endeavor to show that the word "flat," in the "Hebrew," did not mean *quite* flat, but just a little rounded; what would we think of their honesty? The first astronomer insisted that the sun and moon and stars revolved around this earth—that this little earth was the centre of the entire system. Suppose that the astronomers of to-day should insist that that astronomer was inspired, and should try to explain, and say that he simply used the language of the common people, and when he stated that the sun and moon and stars revolved around the earth, he merely meant that they "apparently revolved," and that the earth, in fact, turned over, would we consider them honest men? You might as well say that the first painter was inspired, or that the first sculptor had the assistance of God, as to say that the first writer, or the first bookmaker, was divinely inspired. It is more probable that the modern geologist is inspired than that the ancient one was, because the modern geologist is nearer right. It is more probable that William Lloyd Garrison was inspired upon the question of slavery than that Moses was. It is more probable that the author of the Declaration of Independence spoke by divine authority than that the author of the Pentateuch did. In other words, if there can be any evidence of "inspiration," it must lie in the fact of doing or saying the best possible thing that could have been done or said at that time or upon that subject.

To make myself clear: The only possible evidence of "inspiration" would be perfection—a perfection excelling anything that man unaided had ever attained. An "inspired" book should excel all other books; an inspired statue should be the best in this world; an inspired painting should be beyond all others. If the Bible has been improved in any particular, it was not, in that particular, "inspired." If slavery is wrong, the Bible is not inspired. If polygamy is vile and loathsome, the Bible is not inspired. If wars of extermination are cruel and heartless, the Bible is not "inspired." If there is within that book a contradiction of any natural fact; if there is one ignorant falsehood, if there is one mistake, then it is not "inspired." I do not mean mistakes that have grown out of translations; but if there was in the original manuscript one mistake, then it is not "inspired." I do not demand a miracle; I do not demand a knowledge of the future; I simply demand an absolute knowledge of the past. I demand an absolute knowledge of the then present; I demand a knowledge of the constitution of the human mind—of the facts in nature, and that is all I demand.

Question. If I understand you, you think that all political power should come from the people; do you not believe in any "special providence," and do you take the ground that God does not interest himself in the affairs of nations and individuals?

Answer. The Christian idea is that God made the world, and made certain laws for the government of matter and mind, and that he never interferes except upon special occasions, when the ordinary laws fail to work out the desired end. Their notion is, that the Lord now and then stops the horses simply to show that he is driving. It seems to me that if an infinitely wise being made the world, he must have made it the best possible; and that if he made laws for the government of matter and mind, he must have made the best possible laws. If this is true, not one of these laws can be violated without producing a positive injury. It does not seem probable that infinite wisdom would violate a law that infinite wisdom had made.

Most ministers insist that God now and then interferes in the affairs of this world; that he has not interfered as much lately as he did formerly. When the world was comparatively new, it required altogether more tinkering and fixing than at present.

Things are at last in a reasonably good condition, and consequently a great amount of interference is not necessary. In old times it was found necessary frequently to raise the dead, to change the nature of fire and water, to punish people with plagues and famine, to destroy cities by storms of fire and brimstone, to change women into salt, to cast hailstones upon heathen, to interfere with the movements of our planetary system, to stop the earth not only, but sometimes to make it turn the other way, to arrest the moon, and to make water stand up like a wall. Now and then, rivers were divided by striking them with a coat, and people were taken to heaven in chariots of fire. These miracles, in addition to curing the sick, the halt, the deaf and blind, were in former times found necessary, but since the "apostolic age," nothing of the kind has been resorted to except in Catholic countries. Since the death of the last apostle, God has appeared only to members of the Catholic Church, and all modern miracles have been performed for the benefit of Catholicism. There is no authentic account of the Virgin Mary having ever appeared to a Protestant. The bones of Protestant saints have never cured a solitary disease. Protestants now say that the testimony of the Catholics can not be relied upon, and yet, the authenticity of every book in the New Testament was established by Catholic testimony. Some few miracles were performed in Scotland, and in fact in England and the United States, but they were so small that they are hardly worth mentioning. Now and then, a man was struck dead for taking the name of the Lord in vain. Now and then, people were drowned who were found in boats on Sunday. Whenever anybody was about to commit murder, God has not interfered—the reason being that he gave man free-will, and expects to hold him accountable in another world, and there is no exception to this free-will doctrine, but in cases where men swear or violate the Sabbath. They are allowed to commit all other crimes without any interference on the part of the Lord.

My own opinion is, that the clergy found it necessary to preserve the Sabbath for their own uses, and for that reason endeavored to impress the people with the enormity of its violation, and for that purpose gave instances of people being drowned and suddenly struck dead for working or amusing themselves on that day. The clergy have objected to any other places of amusement except their own, being opened on that day. They wished to compel people either to go to church or stay at home. They have also known that profanity tended to do away with the feelings of awe they wished to cultivate, and for that reason they have insisted that swearing was one of the most terrible of crimes, exciting above all others the wrath of God.

There was a time when people fell dead for having spoken disrespectfully to a priest. The priest at that time pretended to be the visible representative of God, and as such, entitled to a degree of reverence amounting almost to worship. Several cases are given in the ecclesiastical history of Scotland where men were deprived of speech for having spoken rudely to a parson.

These stories were calculated to increase the importance of the clergy and to convince people that they were under the special care of the Deity. The story about the bears devouring the little children was told in the first place, and has been repeated since, simply to protect ministers from the laughter of children. There ought to be carved on each side of every pulpit a bear with fragments of children in its mouth, as this animal has done so much to protect the dignity of the clergy.

Besides the protection of ministers, the drowning

of breakers of the Sabbath, and striking a few people dead for using profane language, I think there is no evidence of any providential interference in the affairs of this world in what may be called modern times. Ministers have endeavored to show that great calamities have been brought upon nations and cities as a punishment for the wickedness of the people. They have insisted that some countries have been visited with earthquakes because the people had failed to discharge their religious duties; but as earthquakes happened in uninhabited countries, and often at sea, where no one is hurt, most people have concluded that they are not sent as punishments. They have insisted that cities have been burned as a punishment, and to show the indignation of the Lord, but at the same time they have admitted that if the streets had been wider, the fire departments better organized, and wooden buildings fewer, the design of the Lord would have been frustrated.

After reading the history of the world, it is somewhat difficult to find which side the Lord is really on. He has allowed Catholics to overwhelm and destroy Protestants, and then he has allowed Protestants to overwhelm and destroy Catholics. He has allowed Christianity to triumph over Paganism, and he allowed

Mohammedans to drive back the hosts of the cross from the sepulchre of his son. It is curious that this God would allow the slave trade to go on, and yet punish the violators of the Sabbath. It is simply wonderful that he would allow kings to wage cruel and remorseless war, to sacrifice millions upon the altar of heartless ambition, and at the same time strike a man dead for taking his name in vain. It is wonderful that he allowed slavery to exist for centuries in the United States; that he allows polygamy now in Utah; that he cares nothing for liberty in Russia, nothing for free speech in Germany, nothing for the sorrows of the overworked, underpaid millions of the world; that he cares nothing for the innocent languishing in prisons, nothing for the patriots condemned to death, nothing for the heart-broken widows and orphans, nothing for the starving, and yet has ample time to note a sparrow's fall. If he would only strike dead the would-be murderers; if he would only palsy the hands of husbands uplifted to strike their wives; if he would render speechless the cursers of children, he could afford to overlook the swearers and breakers of his Sabbath.

For one, I am not satisfied with the government of this world, and I am going to do what little I can to make it better. I want more thought and less fear, more manhood and less superstition, less prayer and more help, more education, more reason, more intellectual hospitality, and above all, and over all, more liberty and kindness.

Question. Do you think that God, if there be one, when he saves or damns a man, will take into consideration all the circumstances of the man's life?

Answer. Suppose that two orphan boys, James and John, are given homes. James is taken into a Christian family and John into an infidel. James becomes a Christian, and dies in the faith. John becomes an infidel, and dies without faith in Christ. According to the Christian religion, as commonly preached, James will go to heaven, and John to hell.

Now, suppose that God knew that if James had been raised by the infidel family, he would have died an infidel, and that if John had been raised by the Christian family, he would have died a Christian. What then? Recollect that the boys did not choose the families in which they were placed.

Suppose that a child, cast away upon an island in which he found plenty of food, grew to manhood; and suppose that after he had reached mature years, the island was visited by a missionary who taught a false religion; and suppose that this islander was convinced that he ought to worship a wooden idol; and suppose, further, that the worship consisted in sacrificing animals; and suppose the islander, actuated only by what he conceived to be his duty and by thankfulness, sacrificed a toad every night and every morning upon the altar of his wooden god; that when the sky looked black and threatening he sacrificed two toads; that when feeling unwell he sacrificed three; and suppose that in all this he was honest, that he really believed that the shedding of toad-blood would soften the heart of his god toward him? And suppose that after he had become fully convinced of the truth of his religion, a missionary of the " true religion " should visit the island, and tell the history of the Jews—unfold the whole scheme of salvation? And suppose that the islander should honestly reject the true religion? Suppose he should say that he had " internal evidence " not only, but that many miracles had been performed by his god, in his behalf; that often when the sky was black with storm, he had sacrificed a toad, and in a few moments the sun was again visible, the heavens blue, and without a cloud; that on several occasions, having forgotten at evening to sacrifice his toad, he found himself unable to sleep—that his conscience smote him, he had risen, made the sacrifice, returned to his bed, and in a few moments sunk into a serene and happy slumber? And suppose, further, that the man honestly believed that the efficacy of the sacrifice depended largely on the size of the toad? Now suppose that in this belief the man had died,—what then?

It must be remembered that God knew when the missionary of the false religion went to the island; and knew that the islander would be convinced of the truth of the false religion; and he also knew that the missionary of the true religion could not, by any possibility, convince the islander of the error of his way; what then?

If God is infinite, we cannot speak of him as making efforts, as being tired. We cannot consistently say that one thing is easy to him, and another thing is hard, providing both are possible. This being so, why did not God reveal himself to every human being? Instead of having an inspired book, why did he not make inspired folks? Instead of having his commandments put on tables of stone, why did he not write them on each human brain?

Why was not the mind of each man so made that every religious truth necessary to his salvation was an axiom?

Do we not know absolutely that man is greatly influenced by his surroundings? If Mr. Talmage had been born in Turkey, is it not probable that he would now be a whirling Dervish? If he had first seen the light in Central Africa, he might now have been prostrate before some enormous serpent; if in India, he might have been a Brahmin, running a prayer-machine; if in Spain, he would probably have been a priest, with his beads and holy water. Had he been born among the North American Indians, he would speak of the "Great Spirit," and solemnly smoke the the pipe of peace.

Mr. Talmage teaches that it is the duty of children to perpetuate the errors of their parents; consequently, the religion of his parents determined his theology. It is with him not a question of reason, but of parents; not a question of argument, but of filial affection. He does not wish to be a philosopher, but an obedient son. Suppose his father had been a Catholic, and his mother a Protestant,—what then? Would he show contempt for his mother by following the path of his father; or would he show disrespect for his father, by accepting the religion of his mother; or would he have become a Protestant with Catholic proclivities, or a Catholic with Protestant leanings? Suppose his parents had both been infidels—what then?

Is it not better for each one to decide honestly for himself? Admitting that your parents were good and kind; admitting that they were honest in their views, why not have the courage to say, that in your opinion, father and mother were both mistaken? No one can honor his parents by being a hypocrite, or an intellectual coward. Whoever is absolutely true to himself, is true to his parents, and true to the whole world. Whoever is untrue to himself, is false to all mankind. Religion must be an individual matter. If there is a God, and if there is a day of judgment, the church that a man belongs to will not be tried, but the man will be tried.

It is a fact that the religion of most people was made for them by others; that they have accepted certain dogmas, not because they have examined them, but because they were told that they were true. Most of the people in the United States, had they been born in Turkey, would now be Mohammedans, and most of the Turks, had they been born in Spain, would now be Catholics.

It is almost, if not quite, impossible for a man to rise entirely above the ideas, views, doctrines and religions of his tribe or country. No one expects to find philosophers in Central Africa, or scientists among the Fejees. No one expects to find philosophers or scientists in any country where the church has absolute control.

If there is an infinitely good and wise God, of course he will take into consideration the surroundings of every human being. He understands the philosophy of environment, and of heredity. He knows exactly the influence of the mother, of all associates, of all associations. He will also take into consideration the amount, quality and form of each brain, and whether the brain was healthy or diseased. He will take into consideration the strength of the passions, the weakness of the judgment. He will know exactly the force of all temptation—what was resisted. He will take an account of every effort made in the right direction, and will understand all the winds and waves and quicksands and shores and shallows in, upon and around the sea of every life.

My own opinion is, that if such a being exists, and all these things are taken into consideration, we will be absolutely amazed to see how small the difference is between the "good" and the "bad." Certainly there is no such difference as would justify a being of infinite wisdom and benevolence in rewarding one with eternal joy and punishing the other with eternal pain.

Question. What are the principal reasons that have satisfied you that the Bible is not an inspired book?

Answer. The great evils that have afflicted this world are:

First. Human slavery—where men have bought and sold their fellow-men—sold babes from mothers, and have practiced every conceivable cruelty upon the helpless.

Second. Polygamy—an institution that destroys the home, that treats woman as a simple chattel, that does away with the sanctity of marriage, and with all that is sacred in love.

Third. Wars of conquest and extermination—by which nations have been made the food of the sword.

Fourth. The idea entertained by each nation that all other nations are destitute of rights—in other words, patriotism founded upon egotism, prejudice, and love of plunder.

Fifth. Religious persecution.

Sixth. The divine right of kings—an idea that rests upon the inequality of human rights, and insists that people should be governed without their consent; that the right of one man to govern another comes from God, and not from the consent of the governed. This is caste—one of the most odious forms of slavery.

Seventh. A belief in malicious supernatural beings—devils, witches, and wizards.

Eighth. A belief in an infinite being who ordered, commanded, established and approved all these evils.

Ninth. The idea that one man can be good for another, or bad for another—that is to say, that one can be rewarded for the goodness of another, or justly punished for the sins of another.

Tenth. The dogma that a finite being can commit an infinite sin, and thereby incur the eternal displeasure of an infinitely good being, and be justly subjected to eternal torment.

My principal objection to the Bible is that it sustains all of these ten evils—that it is the advocate of human slavery, the friend of polygamy; that within its pages I find the command to wage wars of extermination; that I find also that the Jews were taught to hate foreigners—to consider all human beings as inferior to themselves; I also find persecution commanded as a religious duty; that kings were seated upon their thrones by the direct act of God, and that to rebel against a king was rebellion against God. I object to the Bible also because I find within its pages the infamous spirit of caste—I see the sons of Levi set apart as the perpetual beggars and governors of a people; because I find the air filled with demons seeking to injure and betray the sons of men; because this book is the fountain of modern superstition, the bulwark of tyranny and the fortress of caste. This book also subverts the idea of justice by threatening infinite punishment for the sins of a finite being.

At the same time, I admit—as I always have admitted—that there are good passages in the Bible—good laws, good teachings, with now and then a true line of history. But when it is asserted that every word was written by inspiration—that a being of infinite wisdom and goodness is its author,—then I raise the standard of revolt.

Question. What do you think of the declaration of Mr. Talmage that the Bible will be read in heaven throughout all the endless ages of eternity?

Answer. Of course I know but very little as to what is or will be done in heaven. My knowledge of that country is somewhat limited, and it may be possible that the angels will spend most of their time in turning over the sacred leaves of the Old Testament. I can not positively deny the statement of the Reverend Mr. Talmage as I have but very little idea as to how the angels manage to kill time.

The Reverend Mr. Spurgeon stated in a sermon that some people wondered what they would do through all eternity in heaven. He said that, as for himself, for the first hundred thousand years he would look at the wound in one of the Savior's feet, and for the next hundred thousand years he would look at the wound in his other foot, and for the next hundred thousand years he would look at the wound in one of his hands, and for the next hundred thousand years he would look at the wound in the other hand, and for the next hundred thousand years he would look at the wound in his side.

Surely, nothing could be more delightful than this

A man capable of being happy in such employment, could of course take great delight in reading even the genealogies of the Old Testament. It is very easy to see what a glow of joy would naturally overspread the face of an angel while reading the history of the Jewish wars, how the seraphim and cherubim would clasp their rosy palms in ecstasy over the fate of Korah and his company, and what laughter would wake the echoes of the New Jerusalem as some one told again the story of the children and the bears; and what happy groups, with folded pinions, would smilingly listen to the 109th Psalm.

An orthodox "state of mind"

THE
TALMAGIAN CATECHISM.

THE TALMAGIAN CATECHISM.

As Mr. Talmage delivered the series of sermons referred to in these interviews, for the purpose of furnishing arguments to the young, so that they might not be misled by the sophistry of modern infidelity, I have thought it best to set forth, for use in Sunday schools, the pith and marrow of what he has been pleased to say, in the form of

A SHORTER CATECHISM.

Question. Who made you?

Answer. Jehovah, the original Presbyterian.

Question. What else did he make?

Answer. He made the world and all things.

Question. Did he make the world out of nothing?

Answer. No.

Question. What did he make it out of?

Answer. Out of his "omnipotence." Many infidels have pretended that if God made the universe, and if there was nothing until he did make it, he had nothing to make it out of. Of course this is perfectly absurd when we remember that he always had his "omnipotence;" and that is, undoubtedly, the material used.

Question. Did he create his own "omnipotence"?

Answer. Certainly not, he was always omnipotent.

Question. Then if he always had "omnipotence," he did not "create" the material of which the universe is made; he simply took a portion of his "omnipotence" and changed it to "universe"?

Answer. Certainly, that is the way I understand it.

Question. Is he still omnipotent, and has he as much "omnipotence" now as he ever had?

Answer. Well, I suppose he has.

Question. How long did it take God to make the universe?

Answer. Six "good-whiles."

Question. How long is a "good-while"?

Answer. That will depend upon the future discoveries of geologists. "Good-whiles" are of such a nature that they can be pulled out, or pushed up; and it is utterly impossible for any infidel, or scientific geologist, to make any period that a "good-while" won't fit.

Question. What do you understand by "the "morning and evening" of a "good-while"?

Answer. Of course the words "morning and

"evening" are used figuratively, and mean simply the beginning and the ending, of each "good-while."

Question. On what day did God make vegetation?

Answer. On the third day.

Question. Was that before the sun was made?

Answer. Yes; a "good-while" before.

Question. How did vegetation grow without sunlight?

Answer. My own opinion is, that it was either " nourished by the glare of volcanoes in the moon;" or "it may have gotten sufficient light from rivers " of molten granite;" or, "sufficient light might have " been emitted by the crystallization of rocks." It has been suggested that light might have been furnished by fire-flies and phosphorescent bugs and worms, but this I regard as going too far.

Question. Do you think that light emitted by rocks would be sufficient to produce trees?

Answer. Yes, with the assistance of the " Aurora " Borealis, or even the Aurora Australis;" but with both, most assuredly.

Question. If the light of which you speak was sufficient, why was the sun made?

Answer. To keep time with.

Question. What did God make man of?

Answer. He made man of dust and "omnipo-" tence."

Question. Did he make a woman at the same time that he made a man?

Answer. No; he thought at one time to avoid the necessity of making a woman, and he caused all the animals to pass before Adam, to see what he would call them, and to see whether a fit companion could be found for him. Among them all, not one suited Adam, and Jehovah immediately saw that he would have to make an help-meet on purpose.

Question. What was woman made of?

Answer. She was made out of "man's side, out of his right side," and some more "omnipotence." Infidels say that she was made out of a rib, or a bone, but that is because they do not understand Hebrew.

Question. What was the object of making woman out of man's side?

Answer. So that a young man would think more of a neighbor's girl than of his own uncle or grandfather.

Question. What did God do with Adam and Eve after he got them done?

Answer. He put them into a garden to see what they would do.

Question. Do we know where the Garden of Eden was, and have we ever found any place where a "river parted and became into four heads"?

Answer. We are not certain where this garden was, and the river that parted into four heads cannot at present be found. Infidels have had a great deal to say about these four rivers, but they will wish they had even one, one of these days.

Question. What happened to Adam and Eve in the garden?

Answer. They were tempted by a snake who was an exceedingly good talker, and who probably came in walking on the end of his tail. This supposition is based upon the fact that, as a punishment, he was condemned to crawl on his belly. Before that time, of course. he walked upright.

Question. What happened then?

Answer. Our first parents gave way, ate of the forbidden fruit, and in consequence, disease and death entered the world. Had it not been for this, there would have been no death and no disease. Suicide would have been impossible, and a man could have been blown into a thousand atoms by dynamite, and the pieces would immediately have come together again. Fire would have refused to burn and water to drown; there could have been no hunger, no thirst; all things would have been equally healthy.

Question. Do you mean to say that there would have been no death in the world, either of animals, insects, or persons?

Answer. Of course.

Question. Do you also think that all briers and thorns sprang from the same source, and that had the apple not been eaten, no bush in the world would have had a thorn, and brambles and thistles would have been unknown?

Answer. Certainly.

Question. Would there have been no poisonous plants, no poisonous reptiles?

Answer. No, sir; there would have been none; there would have been no evil in the world if Adam and Eve had not partaken of the forbidden fruit.

Question. Was the snake who tempted them to eat, evil?

Answer. Certainly.

Question. Was he in the world before the forbidden fruit was eaten?

Answer. Of course he was; he tempted them to eat it.

Question. How, then, do you account for the fact that, before the forbidden fruit was eaten, an evil serpent was in the world?

Answer. Perhaps apples had been eaten in other worlds.

Question. Is it not wonderful that such awful consequences flowed from so small an act?

Answer. It is not for you to reason about it; you should simply remember that God is omnipotent. There is but one way to answer these things, and that is to admit their truth. Nothing so puts the Infinite out of temper as to see a human being impudent enough to rely upon his reason. The moment we rely upon our reason, we abandon God, and try to take care of ourselves. Whoever relies entirely upon God, has no need of reason, and reason has no need of him.

Question. Were our first parents under the immediate protection of an infinite God?

Answer. They were.

Question. Why did he not protect them? Why did he not warn them of this snake? Why did he not put them on their guard? Why did he not make them so sharp, intellectually, that they could not be deceived? Why did he not destroy that snake; or how did he come to make him; what did he make him for?

Answer. You must remember that, although God made Adam and Eve perfectly good, still he was very anxious to test them. He also gave them the power of choice, knowing at the same time exactly what they would choose, and knowing that he had made them so that they must choose in a certain way. A being of infinite wisdom tries experiments. Knowing exactly what will happen, he wishes to see if it will.

Question. What punishment did God inflict upon Adam and Eve for the sin of having eaten the forbidden fruit?

Answer. He pronounced a curse upon the woman, saying that in sorrow she should bring forth children, and that her husband should rule over her; that she, having tempted her husband, was made his slave; and through her, all married women have been deprived of their natural liberty. On account of the sin of Adam and Eve, God cursed the ground, saying that it should bring forth thorns and thistles, and that man should eat his bread in sorrow, and that he should eat the herb of the field.

Question. Did he turn them out of the garden because of their sin?

Answer. No. The reason God gave for turning them out of the garden was: "Behold the man is "become as one of us, to know good and evil; and "now, lest he put forth his hand and take of the "tree of life and eat and live forever, therefore, the "Lord God sent him forth from the Garden of Eden "to till the ground from whence he was taken."

Question. If the man had eaten of the tree of life, would he have lived forever?

Answer. Certainly.

Question. Was he turned out to prevent his eating?

Answer. He was.

Question. Then the Old Testament tells us how we lost immortality, not that we are immortal, does it?

Answer. Yes; it tells us how we lost it.

Question. Was God afraid that Adam and Eve might get back into the garden, and eat of the fruit of the tree of life?

Answer. I suppose he was, as he placed "cher-"ubim and a flaming sword which turned every "way to guard the tree of life."

Question. Has any one ever seen any of these cherubim?

Answer. Not that I know of.

Question. Where is the flaming sword now?

Answer. Some angel has it in heaven.

Question. Do you understand that God made coats of skins, and clothed Adam and Eve when he turned them out of the garden?

Answer. Yes, sir.

Question. Do you really believe that the infinite God killed some animals, took their skins from them, cut out and sewed up clothes for Adam and Eve?

Answer. The Bible says so; we know that he had patterns for clothes, because he showed some to Moses on Mount Sinai.

Question. About how long did God continue to pay particular attention to his children in this world?

Answer. For about fifteen hundred years; and some of the people lived to be nearly a thousand years of age.

Question. Did this God establish any schools or institutions of learning? Did he establish any church? Did he ordain any ministers, or did he have any revivals?

Answer. No; he allowed the world to go on pretty much in its own way. He did not even keep his own boys at home. They came down and made love to the daughters of men, and finally the world got exceedingly bad.

Question. What did God do then?

Answer. He made up his mind that he would drown them. You see they were all totally depraved,—in every joint and sinew of their bodies, in every drop of their blood, and in every thought of their brains.

Question. Did he drown them all?

Answer. No, he saved eight, to start with again.

Question. Were these eight persons totally depraved?

Answer. Yes.

Question. Why did he not kill them, and start over again with a perfect pair? Would it not have been better to have had his flood at first, before he made anybody, and drowned the snake?

Answer. "God's way are not our ways;" and besides, you must remember that " a thousand years " are as one day " with God.

Question. How did God destroy the people?

Answer. By water; it rained forty days and forty nights, and "the fountains of the great deep were " broken up."

Question. How deep was the water?

Answer. About five miles.

Question. How much did it rain each day?

Answer. About eight hundred feet; though the better opinion now is, that it was a local flood. Infidels have raised objections and pressed them to that degree that most orthodox people admit that the flood was rather local.

Question. If it was a local flood, why did they put birds of the air into the ark? Certainly, birds could have avoided a local flood?

Answer. If you take this away from us, what do you propose to give us in its place? Some of the best people of the world have believed this story. Kind husbands, loving mothers, and earnest patriots have believed it, and that is sufficient.

Question. At the time God made these people, did he know that he would have to drown them all?

Answer. Of course he did.

Question. Did he know when he made them that they would all be failures?

Answer. Of course.

Question. Why, then, did he make them?

Answer. He made them for his own glory, and no man should disgrace his parents by denying it.

Question. Were the people after the flood just as bad as they were before?

Answer. About the same.

Question. Did they try to circumvent God?

Answer. They did.

Question. How?

Answer. They got together for the purpose of building a tower, the top of which should reach to heaven, so that they could laugh at any future floods, and go to heaven at any time they desired.

Question. Did God hear about this?

Answer. He did.

Question. What did he say?

Answer. He said: " Go to ; let us go down," and see what the people are doing ; I am satisfied they will succeed.

Question. How were the people prevented from succeeding?

Answer. God confounded their language, so that the mason on top could not cry "mort'!" to the hod-carrier below ; he could not think of the word to use, to save his life, and the building stopped.

Question. If it had not been for the confusion of tongues at Babel, do you really think that all the people in the world would have spoken just the same language, and would have pronounced every word precisely the same?

Answer. Of course.

Question. If it had not been, then, for the confusion of languages, spelling books, grammars and dictionaries would have been useless?

Answer. I suppose so.

Question. Do any two people in the whole world speak the same language, now?

Answer. Of course they don't, and this is one of the great evidences that God introduced confusion into the languages. Every error in grammar, every mistake in spelling, every blunder in pronunciation, proves the truth of the Babel story.

Question. This being so, this miracle is the best attested of all?

Answer. I suppose it is.

Question. Do you not think that a confusion of tongues would bring men together instead of separating them? Would not a man unable to converse with his fellow feel weak instead of strong; and would not people whose language had been confounded cling together for mutual support?

Answer. According to nature, yes; according to theology, no; and these questions must be answered according to theology. And right here, it may be well enough to state, that in theology the unnatural is the probable, and the impossible is what has always happened. If theology were simply natural, anybody could be a theologian.

Question. Did God ever make any other special efforts to convert the people, or to reform the world?

Answer. Yes, he destroyed the cities of Sodom and Gomorrah with a storm of fire and brimstone.

Question. Do you suppose it was really brimstone?

Answer. Undoubtedly.

Question. Do you think this brimstone came from the clouds?

Answer. Let me tell you that you have no right to examine the Bible in the light of what people are pleased to call "science." The natural has nothing to do with the supernatural. Naturally there would be no brimstone in the clouds, but supernaturally there might be. God could make brimstone out of his "omnipotence." We do not know really what brimstone is, and nobody knows exactly how brimstone is made. As a matter of fact, all the brimstone in the world might have fallen at that time.

Question. Do you think that Lot's wife was changed into salt?

Answer. Of course she was. A miracle was performed. A few centuries ago, the statue of salt made by changing Lot's wife into that article, was standing. Christian travelers have seen it.

Question. Why do you think she was changed into salt?

Answer. For the purpose of keeping the event fresh in the minds of men.

Question. God having failed to keep people innocent in a garden; having failed to govern them outside of a garden; having failed to reform them by water; having failed to produce any good result by a confusion of tongues; having failed to reform them with fire and brimstone, what did he then do?

Answer. He concluded that he had no time to waste on them all, but that he would have to select one tribe, and turn his entire attention to just a few folks.

Question. Whom did he select?

Answer. A man by the name of Abram.

Question. What kind of man was Abram?

Answer. If you wish to know, read the twelfth chapter of Genesis; and if you still have any doubts as to his character, read the twentieth chapter of the same book, and you will see that he was a man who made merchandise of his wife's body. He had had such good fortune in Egypt, that he tried the experiment again on Abimelech.

Question. Did Abraham show any gratitude?

Answer. Yes; he offered to sacrifice his son, to show his confidence in Jehovah.

Question. What became of Abraham and his people?

Answer. God took such care of them, that in about two hundred and fifteen years they were all slaves in the land of Egypt.

Question. How long did they remain in slavery?

Answer. Two hundred and fifteen years.

Question. Were they the same people that God had promised to take care of?

Answer. They were.

Question. Was God, at that time, in favor of slavery?

Answer. Not at that time. He was angry at the Egyptians for enslaving the Jews, but he afterwards authorized the Jews to enslave other people.

Question. What means did he take to liberate the Jews?

Answer. He sent his agents to Pharaoh, and demanded their freedom; and upon Pharaoh's refusing, he afflicted the people, who had nothing to do with it, with various plagues,—killed children, and tormented and tortured beasts.

Question. Was such conduct Godlike?

Answer. Certainly. If you have anything against your neighbor, it is perfectly proper to torture his horse, or torment his dog. Nothing can be nobler than this. You see it is much better to injure his animals than to injure him. To punish animals for the sins of their owners must be just, or God would not have done it. Pharaoh insisted on keeping the people in slavery, and therefore God covered the bodies of oxen and cows with boils. He also bruised them to death with hailstones. From this we infer, that "the loving kindness of God is over all his works."

Question. Do you consider such treatment of animals consistent with divine mercy?

Answer. Certainly. You know that under the Mosaic dispensation, when a man did a wrong, he could settle with God by killing an ox, or a sheep, or some doves. If the man failed to kill them, of course God would kill them. It was upon this principle that he destroyed the animals of the Egyptians. They had sinned, and he merely took his pay.

Question. How was it possible, under the old dispensation, to please a being of infinite kindness?

Answer. All you had to do was to take an innocent animal, bring it to the altar, cut its throat, and sprinkle the altar with its blood. Certain parts of it were to be given to the butcher as his share, and the rest was to be burnt on the altar. When God saw an animal thus butchered, and smelt the warm blood mingled with the odor of burning flesh, he was pacified, and the smile of forgiveness shed its light upon his face. Of course, infidels laugh at these things; but what can you expect of men who have not been " born " again " ? " The carnal mind is enmity with God."

Question. What else did God do in order to induce Pharaoh to liberate the Jews?

Answer. He had his agents throw down a cane in the presence of Pharaoh and thereupon Jehovah changed this cane into a serpent.

Question. Did this convince Pharaoh?

Answer. No; he sent for his own magicians.

Question. What did they do?

Answer. They threw down some canes and they also were changed into serpents.

Question. Did Jehovah change the canes of the Egyptian magicians into snakes?

Answer. I suppose he did, as he is the only one capable of performing such a miracle.

Question. If the rod of Aaron was changed into a serpent in order to convince Pharaoh that God had sent Aaron and Moses, why did God change the sticks of the Egyptian magicians into serpents—why did he discredit his own agents, and render worthless their only credentials?

Answer. Well, we cannot explain the conduct of Jehovah; we are perfectly satisfied that it was for the best. Even in this age of the world God allows infidels to overwhelm his chosen people with arguments; he allows them to discover facts that his ministers can not answer, and yet we are satisfied that in the end God will give the victory to us. All these things are tests of faith. It is upon this principle that God allows geology to laugh at Genesis, that he permits astronomy apparently to contradict his holy word.

Question. What did God do with these people after Pharaoh allowed them to go?

Answer. Finding that they were not fit to settle a new country, owing to the fact that when hungry they longed for food, and sometimes when their lips were cracked with thirst insisted on having water, God in his infinite mercy had them marched round and round, back and forth, through a barren wilderness, until all, with the exception of two persons, died.

Question. Why did he do this?

Answer. Because he had promised these people that he would take them "to a land flowing with "milk and honey."

Question. Was God always patient and kind and merciful toward his children while they were in the wilderness?

Answer. Yes, he always was merciful and kind and patient. Infidels have taken the ground that he visited them with plagues and disease and famine; that he had them bitten by serpents, and now and then allowed the ground to swallow a few thousands of them, and in other ways saw to it that they were kept as comfortable and happy as was consistent with good government; but all these things were for their good; and the fact is, infidels have no real sense of justice.

Question. How did God happen to treat the Israelites in this way, when he had promised Abraham that he would take care of his progeny, and when he had promised the same to the poor wretches while they were slaves in Egypt?

Answer. Because God is unchangeable in his nature, and wished to convince them that every being should be perfectly faithful to his promise.

Question. Was God driven to madness by the conduct of his chosen people?

Answer. Almost.

Question. Did he know exactly what they would do when he chose them?

Answer. Exactly.

Question. Were the Jews guilty of idolatry?

Answer. They were. They worshiped other gods—gods made of wood and stone.

Question. Is it not wonderful that they were not convinced of the power of God, by the many miracles wrought in Egypt and in the wilderness?

Answer. Yes, it is very wonderful; but the Jews, who must have seen bread rained from heaven; who saw water gush from the rocks and follow them up hill and down; who noticed that their clothes did not wear out, and did not even get shiny at the knees, while the elbows defied the ravages of time, and their shoes remained perfect for forty years; it *is* wonderful that when they saw the ground open and swallow their comrades; when they saw God talking face to face with Moses as a man talks with his friend; after they saw the cloud by day and the pillar of fire by night,—it is absolutely astonishing that they had more faith in a golden calf that they made themselves, than in Jehovah.

Question. How is it that the Jews had no confidence in these miracles?

Answer. Because they were there and saw them.

Question. Do you think that it is necessary for us to believe all the miracles of the Old Testament in order to be saved?

Answer. The Old Testament is the foundation of the New. If the Old Testament is not inspired, then the New is of no value. If the Old Testament is inspired, all the miracles are true, and we cannot believe that God would allow any errors, or false statements, to creep into an inspired volume, and to be perpetuated through all these years.

Question. Should we believe the miracles, whether they are reasonable or not?

Answer. Certainly; if they were reasonable, they would not be miracles. It is their unreasonableness that appeals to our credulity and our faith. It is impossible to have theological faith in anything that can be demonstrated. It is the office of faith to believe, not only without evidence, but in spite of evidence. It is impossible for the carnal mind to believe that Samson's muscle depended upon the length of his hair. "God has made the wisdom of "this world foolishness." Neither can the unconverted believe that Elijah stopped at a hotel kept by ravens. Neither can they believe that a barrel would in and of itself produce meal, or that an earthen pot could create oil. But to a Christian, in order that a widow might feed a preacher, the truth of these stories is perfectly apparent.

Question. How should we regard the wonderful stories of the Old Testament?

Answer. They should be looked upon as "types" and "symbols." They all have a spiritual significance. The reason I believe the story of Jonah is, that Jonah is a type of Christ.

Question. Do you believe the story of Jonah to be a true account of a literal fact?

Answer. Certainly. You must remember that Jonah was not swallowed by a whale. God "pre-"pared a great fish" for that occasion. Neither is it by any means certain that Jonah was in the belly of this whale. "He probably stayed in his mouth." Even if he was in his stomach, it was very easy for him to defy the ordinary action of gastric juice by rapidly walking up and down.

Question. Do you think that Jonah was really in the whale's stomach?

Answer. My own opinion is that he stayed in his mouth. The only objection to this theory is, that it is more reasonable than the other and requires less faith. Nothing could be easier than for God to make a fish large enough to furnish ample room for one passenger in his mouth. I throw out this suggestion simply that you may be able to answer the objections of infidels who are always laughing at this story.

Question. Do you really believe that Elijah went to heaven in a chariot of fire, drawn by horses of fire?

Answer. Of course he did.

Question. What was this miracle performed for?

Answer. To convince the people of the power of God.

Question. Who saw the miracle?

Answer. Nobody but Elisha.

Question. Was he convinced before that time?

Answer. Oh yes; he was one of God's prophets.

Question. Suppose that in these days two men should leave a town together, and after a while one of them should come back having on the clothes of the other, and should account for the fact that he had his friend's clothes by saying that while they were going along the road together a chariot of fire came down from heaven drawn by fiery steeds, and thereupon his friend got into the carriage, threw him his clothes, and departed,—would you believe it?

Answer. Of course things like that don't happen in these days; God does not have to rely on wonders now.

Question. Do you mean that he performs no miracles at the present day?

Answer. We cannot say that he does not perform miracles now, but we are not in position to call attention to any particular one. Of course he supervises the affairs of nations and men and does whatever in his judgment is necessary.

Question. Do you think that Samson's strength depended on the length of his hair?

Answer. The Bible so states, and **the Bible is true. A physiologist might say that a man could not use the muscle in his hair for lifting purposes, but these same physiologists could not tell you how you move a finger, nor how you lift a feather; still, actuated by the pride of intellect, they insist that the length of a man's hair could not determine his strength. God says it did; the physiologist says that it did not; we can not hesitate whom to believe. For the purpose of avoiding eternal agony I am willing to believe anything; I am willing to say that strength depends upon the length of hair, or faith upon the length of ears. I am perfectly willing to believe that a man caught three hundred foxes, and put fire brands between their tails; that he slew thousands with a bone, and that he made a bee hive out of a lion. I will believe, if necessary, that when this man's hair was short he hardly had strength enough to stand, and that when it was long, he could carry away the gates of a city, or overthrow a temple filled with people. If the infidel is right, I will lose nothing by believing, but if he is wrong, I shall gain an eternity of joy. If God did not intend that we should believe these stories, he never would have told them, and why should a man put his soul in peril by trying to disprove one of the statements of the Lord?

Question. Suppose it should turn out that some of these miracles depend upon mistranslations of the original Hebrew, should we still believe them?

Answer. The safe side is the best side. It is far better to err on the side of belief, than on the side of infidelity. God does not threaten anybody with eternal punishment for believing too much.

Danger lies on the side of investigation, on the side of thought. The perfectly idiotic are absolutely safe. As they diverge from that point,—as they rise in the intellectual scale, as the brain develops, as the faculties enlarge, the danger increases. I know that some biblical students now take the ground that Samson caught no foxes,—that he only took sheaves of wheat that had been already cut and bound, set them on fire, and threw them into the grain still standing. If this is what he did, of course there is nothing miraculous about it, and the value of the story is lost. So, others contend that Elijah was not fed by the ravens, but by the Arabs. They tell us that the Hebrew word standing for "Arab" also stands for "bird," and that the word really means " migratory—going from place to place—homeless." But I prefer the old version. It certainly will do no harm to believe that ravens brought bread and flesh to a prophet of God. Where they got their bread and flesh is none of my business; how they knew where the prophet was, and recognized him; or how God talks to ravens, or how he gave them directions, I have no right to inquire. I leave these questions to the scientists, the blasphemers, and thinkers. There are many people in the church anxious to get the miracles out of the Bible, and thousands, I have no doubt, would be greatly gratified to learn that there is, in fact, nothing miraculous in Scripture; but when you take away the miraculous, you take away the supernatural; when you take away the supernatural, you destroy the ministry; and when you take away the ministry, hundreds of thousands of men will be left without employment.

Question. Is it not wonderful that the Egyptians were not converted by the miracles wrought in their country?

Answer. Yes, they all would have been, if God had not purposely hardened their hearts to prevent it. Jehovah always took great delight in furnishing the evidence, and then hardening the man's heart so that he would not believe it. After all the miracles that had been performed in Egypt,—the most wonderful that were ever done in any country, the Egyptians were as unbelieving as at first; they pursued the Israelites, knowing that they were protected by an infinite God, and failing to overwhelm them, came back and worshiped their own false gods just as firmly as before. All of which shows the unreasonableness of a Pagan, and the natural depravity of human nature.

Question. How did it happen that the Canaanites were never convinced that the Jews were assisted by Jehovah?

Answer. They must have been an exceedingly brave people to contend so many years with the chosen people of God. Notwithstanding all their cities were burned time and time again; notwithstanding all the men, women and children were put to the edge of the sword; notwithstanding the taking of all their cattle and sheep, they went right on fighting just as valiantly and desperately as ever. Each one lost his life many times, and was just as ready for the next conflict. My own opinion is, that God kept them alive by raising them from the dead after each battle, for the purpose of punishing the Jews. God used his enemies as instruments for the civilization of the Jewish people. He did not wish to convert them, because they would give him much more trouble as Jews than they did as Canaanites. He had all the Jews he could conveniently take care of. He found it much easier to kill a hundred Canaanites than to civilize one Jew.

Question. How do you account for the fact that the heathen were not surprised at the stopping of the sun and moon?

Answer. They were so ignorant that they had not the slightest conception of the real cause of the phenomenon. Had they known the size of the earth, and the relation it sustained to the other heavenly bodies; had they known the magnitude of the sun, and the motion of the moon, they would, in all probability, have been as greatly astonished as the Jews were; but being densely ignorant of astronomy, it must have produced upon them not the slightest impression. But we must remember that the sun and moon were not stopped for the purpose of converting these people, but to give Joshua more time to kill them. As soon as we see clearly the purpose of Jehovah, we instantly perceive how admirable were the means adopted.

Question. Do you not consider the treatment of the Canaanites to have been cruel and ferocious?

Answer. To a totally depraved man, it does look cruel; to a being without any good in him,—to one who has inherited the rascality of many generations, the murder of innocent women and little children does seem horrible; to one who is " contaminated in " all his parts," by original sin,—who was " conceived " in sin, and brought forth in iniquity," the assassination of men, and the violation of captive maidens, do not seem consistent with infinite goodness. But when one has been "born again," when "the love "of God has been shed abroad in his heart," when he loves all mankind, when he "overcomes evil with "good," when he "prays for those who despite-"fully use him and persecute him,"—to such a man, the extermination of the Canaanites, the violation of women, the slaughter of babes, and the destruction of countless thousands, is the highest evidence of the goodness, the mercy, and the long-suffering of God. When a man has been "born again," all the passages of the Old Testament that appear so horrible and so unjust to one in his natural state, become the dearest, the most consoling, and the most beautiful of truths. The real Christian reads the accounts of these ancient battles with the greatest possible satisfaction. To one who really loves his enemies, the groans of men, the shrieks of women, and the cries of babes, make music sweeter than the zephyr's breath.

Question. In your judgment, why did God destroy the Canaanites?

Answer. To prevent their contaminating his chosen people. He knew that if the Jews were allowed to live with such neighbors, they would finally become as bad as the Canaanites themselves. He wished to civilize his chosen people, and it was therefore necessary for him to destroy the heathen.

Question. Did God succeed in civilizing the Jews after he had "removed" the Canaanites?

Answer. Well, not entirely. He had to allow the heathen he had not destroyed to overrun the whole land and make captives of the Jews. This was done for the good of his chosen people.

Question. Did he then succeed in civilizing them?

Answer. Not quite.

Question. Did he *ever* quite succeed in civilizing them?

Answer. Well, we must admit that the experiment never was a conspicuous success. The Jews were chosen by the Almighty 430 years before he appeared to Moses on Mount Sinai. He was their direct Governor. He attended personally to their religion and politics, and gave up a great part of his valuable time for about two thousand years, to the management of their affairs; and yet, such was the condition of the Jewish people, after they had had all these advantages, that when there arose among them a perfectly kind, just, generous and honest man, these people, with whom God had been laboring for so many centuries, deliberately put to death that good and loving man.

Question. Do you think that God really endeavored to civilize the Jews?

Answer. This is an exceedingly hard question. If he had really tried to do it, of course he could have done it. We must not think of limiting the power of the infinite. But you must remember that if he had succeeded in civilizing the Jews, if he had educated them up to the plane of intellectual liberty, and made them just and kind and merciful, like himself, they would not have crucified Christ, and you can see at once the awful condition in which we would all be to-day. No atonement could have been made; and if no atonement had been made, then, according to the Christian system, the whole world would have been lost. We must admit that there was no time in the history of the Jews from Sinai to Jerusalem, that they would not have put a man like Christ to death.

Question. So you think that, after all, it was not God's intention that the Jews should become civilized?

Answer. We do not know. We can only say that "God's ways are not our ways." It may be that God took them in his special charge, for the purpose of keeping them bad enough to make the necessary sacrifice. That may have been the divine plan. In any event, it is safer to believe the explanation that is the most unreasonable.

Question. Do you think that Christ knew the Jews would crucify him?

Answer. Certainly.

Question. Do you think that when he chose Judas he knew that he would betray him?

Answer. Certainly.

Question. Did he know when Judas went to the chief priest and made the bargain for the delivery of Christ?

Answer. Certainly.

Question. Why did he allow himself to be betrayed, if he knew the plot?

Answer. Infidelity is a very good doctrine to live by, but you should read the last words of Paine and Voltaire.

Question. If Christ knew that Judas would betray him, why did he choose him?

Answer. Nothing can exceed the atrocities of the French Revolution—when they carried a woman through the streets and worshiped her as the goddess of Reason.

Question. Would not the mission of Christ have been a failure had no one betrayed him?

Answer. Thomas Paine was a drunkard, and recanted on his death-bed, and died a blaspheming infidel besides.

Question. Is it not clear that an atonement was necessary; and is it not equally clear that the atonement could not have been made unless somebody had betrayed Christ; and unless the Jews had been wicked and orthodox enough to crucify him?

Answer. Of course the atonement had to be made. It was a part of the "divine plan" that Christ should be betrayed, and that the Jews should be wicked enough to kill him. Otherwise, the world would have been lost.

Question. Suppose Judas had understood the divine plan, what ought he to have done? Should he have betrayed Christ, or let somebody else do it; or should he have allowed the world to perish, including his own soul?

Answer. If you take the Bible away from the world, "how would it be possible to have witnesses "sworn in courts;" how would it be possible to administer justice?

Question. If Christ had not been betrayed and

crucified, is it true that his own mother would be in perdition to-day?

Answer. Most assuredly. There was but one way by which she could be saved, and that was by the death of her son—through the blood of the atonement. She was totally depraved through the sin of Adam, and deserved eternal death. Even her love for the infant Christ was, in the sight of God,— that is to say, of her babe,—wickedness. It can not be repeated too often that there is only one way to be saved, and that is, to believe in the Lord Jesus Christ.

Question. Could Christ have prevented the Jews from crucifying him?

Answer. He could.

Question. If he could have saved his life and did not, was he not guilty of suicide?

Answer. No one can understand these questions who has not read the prophecies of Daniel, and has not a clear conception of what is meant by "the full-"ness of time."

Question. What became of all the Canaanites, the Egyptians, the Hindus, the Greeks and Romans and Chinese? What became of the billions who died before the promise was made to Abraham; of the billions and billions who never heard of the Bible, who never heard the name, even, of Jesus Christ—never knew of "the scheme of salvation"? What became of the millions and billions who lived in this hemisphere, and of whose existence Jehovah himself seemed perfectly ignorant?

Answer. They were undoubtedly lost. God having made them, had a right to do with them as he pleased. They are probably all in hell to-day, and the fact that they are damned, only adds to the joy of the redeemed. It is by contrast that we are able to perceive the infinite kindness with which God has treated us.

Question. Is it not possible that something can be done for a human soul in another world as well as in this?

Answer. No; this is the only world in which God even attempts to reform anybody. In the other world, nothing is done for the purpose of making anybody better. Here in this world, where man lives but a few days, is the only opportunity for moral improvement. A minister can do a thousand times more for a soul than its creator; and this country is much better adapted to moral growth than heaven itself. A person who lived on this earth a few years, and died without having been converted, has no hope in another world. The moment he arrives at the judgment seat, nothing remains but to damn him. Neither God, nor the Holy Ghost, nor Jesus Christ, can have the least possible influence with him there.

Question. When God created each human being, did he know exactly what would be his eternal fate?

Answer. Most assuredly he did.

Question. Did he know that hundreds and millions and billions would suffer eternal pain?

Answer. Certainly. But he gave them freedom of choice between good and evil.

Question. Did he know exactly how they would use that freedom?

Answer. Yes.

Question. Did he know that billions would use it wrong?

Answer. Yes.

Question. Was it optional with him whether he should make such people or not?

Answer. Certainly.

Question. Had these people any option as to whether they would be made or not?

Answer. No.

Question. Would it not have been far better to leave them unconscious dust?

Answer. These questions show how foolish it is to judge God according to a human standard. What to us seems just and merciful, God may regard in an exactly opposite light; and we may hereafter be developed to such a degree that we will regard the agonies of the damned as the highest possible evidence of the goodness and mercy of God.

Question. How do you account for the fact that God did not make himself known except to Abraham and his descendants? Why did he fail to reveal himself to the other nations—nations that, compared with the Jews, were learned, cultivated and powerful? Would you regard a revelation now made to the Esquimaux as intended for us; and would it be a revelation of which we would be obliged to take notice?

Answer. Of course, God could have revealed himself, not only to all the great nations, but to each individual. He could have had the Ten Commandments engraved on every heart and brain; or he could have raised up prophets in every land; but he chose, rather, to allow countless millions of his children to wander in the darkness and blackness of

Nature; chose, rather, that they should redden their hands in each other's blood; chose, rather, that they should live without light, and die without hope; chose, rather, that they should suffer, not only in this world, but forever in the next. Of course we have no right to find fault with the choice of God.

Question. Now you can tell a sinner to "believe "on the Lord Jesus Christ;" what could a sinner have been told in Egypt, three thousand years ago; and in what language would you have addressed a Hindu in the days of Buddha—the "divine scheme" at that time being a secret in the divine breast?

Answer. It is not for us to think upon these questions. The moment we examine the Christian system, we begin to doubt. In a little while, we shall be infidels, and shall lose the respect of those who refuse to think. It is better to go with the majority. These doctrines are too sacred to be touched. You should be satisfied with the religion of your father and your mother. "You want some book on the "centre-table," in the parlor; it is extremely handy to have a Family Record; and what book, other than the Bible, could a mother give a son as he leaves the old homestead?

Question. Is it not wonderful that all the writers

of the four gospels do not give an account of the ascension of Jesus Christ?

Answer. This question has been answered long ago, time and time again.

Question. Perhaps it has, but would it not be well enough to answer it once more? Some may not have seen the answer?

Answer. Show me the hospitals that infidels have built; show me the asylums that infidels have founded.

Question. I know you have given the usual answer; but after all, is it not singular that a miracle so wonderful as the bodily ascension of a man, should not have been mentioned by all the writers of that man's life? Is it not wonderful that some of them said that he did ascend, and others that he agreed to stay with his disciples always?

Answer. People unacquainted with the Hebrew, can have no conception of these things. A story in plain English, does not sound as it does in Hebrew. Miracles seem altogether more credible, when told in a dead language.

Question. What, in your judgment, became of the dead who were raised by Christ? Is it not singular that they were never mentioned afterward?

Would not a man who had been raised from the dead naturally be an object of considerable interest, especially to his friends and acquaintances? And is it not also wonderful that Christ, after having wrought so many miracles, cured so many lame and halt and blind, fed so many thousands miraculously, and after having entered Jerusalem in triumph as a conqueror and king, had to be pointed out by one of his own disciples who was bribed for the purpose?

Answer. Of course, all these things are exceedingly wonderful, and if found in any other book, would be absolutely incredible; but we have no right to apply the same kind of reasoning to the Bible that we apply to the Koran or to the sacred books of the Hindus. For the ordinary affairs of this world, God has given us reason; but in the examination of religious questions, we should depend upon credulity and faith.

Question. If Christ came to offer himself a sacrifice, for the purpose of making atonement for the sins of such as might believe on him, why did he not make this fact known to all of his disciples?

Answer. He did. This was, and is, the gospel.

Question. How is it that Matthew says nothing about "salvation by faith," but simply says that God will be merciful to the merciful, that he will forgive the forgiving, and says not one word about the necessity of believing anything?

Answer. But you will remember that Mark says, in the last chapter of his gospel, that "whoso be-"lieveth not shall be damned."

Question. Do you admit that Matthew says nothing on the subject?

Answer. Yes, I suppose I must.

Question. Is not that passage in Mark generally admitted to be an interpolation?

Answer. Some biblical scholars say that it is.

Question. Is that portion of the last chapter of Mark found in the Syriac version of the Bible?

Answer. It is not.

Question. If it was necessary to believe on Jesus Christ, in order to be saved, how is it that Matthew failed to say so?

Answer. "There are more copies of the Bible "printed to-day, than of any other book in the world, "and it is printed in more languages than any other "book."

Question. Do you consider it necessary to be " regenerated "—to be " born again "—in order to be saved?

Answer. Certainly.

Question. Did Matthew say anything on the subject of "regeneration"?

Answer. No.

Question. Did Mark?

Answer. No.

Question. Did Luke?

Answer. No.

Question. Is Saint John the only one who speaks of the necessity of being "born again"?

Answer. He is.

Question. Do you think that Matthew, Mark and Luke knew anything about the necessity of "regen-"eration"?

Answer. Of course they did.

Question. Why did they fail to speak of it?

Answer. There is no civilization without the Bible. The moment you throw away the sacred Scriptures, you are all at sea—you are without an anchor and without a compass.

Question. You will remember that, according to Mark, Christ said to his disciples: "Go ye into all "the world, and preach the gospel to every creature." Did he refer to the gospel set forth by Mark?

Answer. Of course he did.

Question. Well, in the gospel set forth by Mark, there is not a word about "regeneration," and no word about the necessity of believing anything—except in an interpolated passage. Would it not seem from this, that "regeneration" and a "belief in the "Lord Jesus Christ," are no part of the gospel?

Answer. Nothing can exceed in horror the last moments of the infidel; nothing can be more terrible than the death of the doubter. When the glories of this world fade from the vision; when ambition becomes an empty name; when wealth turns to dust in the palsied hand of death, of what use is philosophy then? Who cares then for the pride of intellect? In that dread moment, man needs something to rely on, whether it is true or not.

Question. Would it not have been more convincing if Christ, after his resurrection, had shown himself to his enemies as well as to his friends? Would it not have greatly strengthened the evidence in the case, if he had visited Pilate; had presented himself before Caiaphas, the high priest; if he had again entered the temple, and again walked the streets of Jerusalem?

Answer. If the evidence had been complete and overwhelming, there would have been no praiseworthiness in belief; even publicans and sinners would have believed, if the evidence had been sufficient. The amount of evidence required is the test of the true Christian spirit.

Question. Would it not also have been better had the ascension taken place in the presence of unbelieving thousands; it seems such a pity to have wasted such a demonstration upon those already convinced?

Answer. These questions are the natural fruit of the carnal mind, and can be accounted for only by the doctrine of total depravity. Nothing has given the church more trouble than just such questions. Unholy curiosity, a disposition to pry into the divine mysteries, a desire to know, to investigate, to explain —in short, to understand, are all evidences of a reprobate mind.

Question. How can we account for the fact that Matthew alone speaks of the wise men of the East coming with gifts to the infant Christ; that he alone speaks of the little babes being killed by Herod? Is it possible that the other writers never heard of these things?

Answer. Nobody can get any good out of the Bible by reading it in a critical spirit. The contradictions and discrepancies are only apparent, and melt away before the light of faith. That which in other books would be absolute and palpable contradiction, is, in the Bible, when spiritually discerned, a perfect and beautiful harmony. My own opinion is, that seeming contradictions are in the Bible for the purpose of testing and strengthening the faith of Christians, and for the further purpose of ensnaring infidels, "that they might believe a lie and be damned."

Question. Is it possible that a good God would take pains to deceive his children?

Answer. The Bible is filled with instances of that kind, and all orthodox ministers now know that fossil animals—that is, representations of animals in stone, were placed in the rocks on purpose to mislead men like Darwin and Humboldt, Huxley and Tyndall. It is also now known that God, for the purpose of misleading the so-called men of science, had hairy elephants preserved in ice, made stomachs for them, and allowed twigs of trees to be found in these stomachs, when, as a matter of fact, no such elephants ever lived or ever died. These men who are endeavoring to overturn the Scriptures with the lever of science will find that they have been deceived. Through all eternity they will regret their philosophy. They will wish, in the next world, that they had thrown away geology and physiology and all other "ologies" except theology. The time is coming when Jehovah will "mock at their fears and " laugh at their calamity."

Question. If Joseph was not the father of Christ, why was his genealogy given to show that Christ was of the blood of David; why would not the genealogy of any other Jew have done as well?

Answer. That objection was raised and answered hundreds of years ago.

Question. If they wanted to show that Christ was of the blood of David, why did they not give the genealogy of his mother if Joseph was not his father?

Answer. That objection was answered hundreds of years ago.

Question. How was it answered?

Answer. When Voltaire was dying, he sent for a priest.

Question. How does it happen that the two genealogies given do not agree?

Answer. Perhaps they were written by different persons.

Question. Were both these persons inspired by the same God?

Answer. Of course.

Question. Why were the miracles recorded in the New Testament performed?

Answer. The miracles were the evidence relied on to prove the supernatural origin and the divine mission of Jesus Christ.

Question. Aside from the miracles, is there any evidence to show the supernatural origin or character of Jesus Christ?

Answer. Some have considered that his moral precepts are sufficient, of themselves, to show that he was divine.

Question. Had all of his moral precepts been taught before he lived?

Answer. The same things had been said, but they did not have the same meaning.

Question. Does the fact that Buddha taught the same tend to show that he was of divine origin?

Answer. Certainly not. The rules of evidence applicable to the Bible are not applicable to other books. We examine other books in the light of reason; the Bible is the only exception. So, we should not judge of Christ as we do of any other man.

Question. Do you think that Christ wrought

many of his miracles because he was good, charitable, and filled with pity?

Answer. Certainly

Question. Has he as much power now as he had when on earth?

Answer. Most assuredly.

Question. Is he as charitable and pitiful now, as he was then?

Answer. Yes.

Question. Why does he not now cure the lame and the halt and the blind?

Answer. It is well known that, when Julian the Apostate was dying, catching some of his own blood in his hand and throwing it into the air he exclaimed: "Galileean, thou hast conquered!"

Question. Do you consider it our duty to love our neighbor?

Answer. Certainly.

Question. Is virtue the same in all worlds?

Answer. Most assuredly.

Question. Are we under obligation to render good for evil, and to "pray for those who despitefully use us"?

Answer. Yes.

Question. Will Christians in heaven love their neighbors?

Answer. Yes; if their neighbors are not in hell.

Question. Do good Christians pity sinners in this world?

Answer. Yes.

Question. Why?

Answer. Because they regard them as being in great danger of the eternal wrath of God.

Question. After these sinners have died, and been sent to hell, will the Christians in heaven then pity them?

Answer. No. Angels have no pity.

Question. If we are under obligation to love our enemies, is not God under obligation to love his? If we forgive our enemies, ought not God to forgive his? If we forgive those who injure us, ought not God to forgive those who have not injured him?

Answer. God made us, and he has therefore the right to do with us as he pleases. Justice demands that he should damn all of us, and the few that he will save will be saved through mercy and without the slightest respect to anything they may have done themselves. Such is the justice of God, that those in hell will have no right to complain, and those in heaven will have no right to be there. **Hell is justice, and salvation is charity.**

Question. Do you consider it possible for a law to be justly satisfied by the punishment of an innocent person?

Answer. Such is the scheme of the atonement. As man is held responsible for the sin of Adam, so he will be credited with the virtues of Christ; and you can readily see that one is exactly as reasonable as the other.

Question. Suppose a man honestly reads the New Testament, and honestly concludes that it is not an inspired book; suppose he honestly makes up his mind that the miracles are not true; that the devil never really carried Christ to the pinnacle of the temple; that devils were really never cast out of a man and allowed to take refuge in swine;—I say, suppose that he is honestly convinced that these things are not true, what ought he to say?

Answer. He ought to say nothing.

Question. Suppose that the same man should read the Koran, and come to the conclusion that it is not an inspired book; what ought he to say?

Answer. He ought to say that it is not inspired; his fellow-men are entitled to his honest opinion, and it is his duty to do what he can do to destroy a pernicious superstition.

Question. Suppose then, that a reader of the Bible, having become convinced that it is not inspired—honestly convinced—says nothing—keeps his conclusion absolutely to himself, and suppose he dies in that belief, can he be saved?

Answer. Certainly not.

Question. Has the honesty of his belief anything to do with his future condition?

Answer. Nothing whatever.

Question. Suppose that he tried to believe, that he hated to disagree with his friends, and with his parents, but that in spite of himself he was forced to the conclusion that the Bible is not the inspired word of God, would he then deserve eternal punishment?

Answer. Certainly he would.

Question. Can a man control his belief?

Answer. He cannot—except as to the Bible.

Question. Do you consider it just in God to create a man who cannot believe the Bible, and then damn him because he does not?

Answer. Such is my belief.

Question. Is it your candid opinion that a man who does not believe the Bible should keep his belief a secret from his fellow-men?

Answer. It is.

Question. How do I know that you believe the Bible? You have told me that if you did not believe it, you would not tell me?

Answer. There is no way for you to ascertain, except by taking my word for it.

Question. What will be the fate of a man who does not believe it, and yet pretends to believe it?

Answer. He will be damned.

Question. Then hypocrisy will not save him?

Answer. No.

Question. And if he does not believe it, and admits that he does not believe it, then his honesty will not save him?

Answer. No. Honesty on the wrong side is no better than hypocrisy on the right side.

Question. Do we know who wrote the gospels?

Answer. Yes; we do.

Question. Are we absolutely sure who wrote them?

Answer. Of course; we have the evidence as it has come to us through the Catholic Church.

Question. Can we rely upon the Catholic Church now?

Answer. No; assuredly no! But we have the testimony of Polycarp and Irenæus and Clement, and others of the early fathers, together with that of the Christian historian, Eusebius.

Question. What do we really know about Polycarp?

Answer. We know that he suffered martyrdom under Marcus Aurelius, and that for quite a time the fire refused to burn his body, the flames arching over him, leaving him in a kind of fiery tent; and we also know that from his body came a fragrance like frankincense, and that the Pagans were so exasperated at seeing the miracle, that one of them thrust a sword through the body of Polycarp; that the blood flowed out and extinguished the flames and that out of the wound flew the soul of the martyr in the form of a dove.

Question. Is that all we know about Polycarp?

Answer. Yes, with the exception of a few more like incidents.

Question. Do we know that Polycarp ever met St. John?

Answer. Yes; Eusebius says so.

Question. Are we absolutely certain that he ever lived?

Answer. Yes, or Eusebius could not have written about him.

Question. Do we know anything of the character of Eusebius?

Answer. Yes; we know that he was untruthful only when he wished to do good. But God can use even the dishonest. Other books have to be substantiated by truthful men, but such is the power of God, that he can establish the inspiration of the Bible by the most untruthful witnesses. If God's witnesses were honest, anybody could believe, and what becomes of faith, one of the greatest virtues?

Question. Is the New Testament now the same as it was in the days of the early fathers?

Answer. Certainly not. Many books now thrown out, and not esteemed of divine origin, were esteemed divine by Polycarp and Irenæus and Clement and many of the early churches. These books are now called "apocryphal."

Question. Have you not the same witnesses in favor of their authenticity, that you have in favor of the gospels?

Answer. Precisely the same. Except that they were thrown out.

Question. Why were they thrown out?

Answer. Because the Catholic Church did not esteem them inspired.

Question. Did the Catholics decide for us which are the true gospels and which are the true epistles?

Answer. Yes. The Catholic Church was then the only church, and consequently must have been the true church.

Question. How did the Catholic Church select the true books?

Answer. Councils were called, and votes were taken, very much as we now pass resolutions in political meetings.

Question. Was the Catholic Church infallible then?

Answer. It was then, but it is not now.

Question. If the Catholic Church at that time had thrown out the book of Revelation, would it now be our duty to believe that book to have been inspired?

Answer. No, I suppose not.

Question. Is it not true that some of these books were adopted by exceedingly small majorities?

Answer. It is.

Question. If the Epistle to the Hebrews and to the Romans, and the book of Revelation had been thrown out, could a man now be saved who honestly believes the rest of the books?

Answer. This is doubtful.

Question. Were the men who picked out the inspired books inspired?

Answer. We cannot tell, but the probability is that they were.

Question. Do we know that they picked out the right ones?

Answer. Well, not exactly, but we believe that they did.

Question. Are we certain that some of the books that were thrown out were not inspired?

Answer. Well, the only way to tell is to read them carefully.

Question. If upon reading these apocryphal books a man concludes that they are not inspired, will he be damned for that reason?

Answer. No. Certainly not.

Question. If he concludes that some of them are inspired, and believes them, will he then be damned for that belief?

Answer. Oh, no! Nobody is ever damned for believing too much.

Question. Does the fact that the books now comprising the New Testament were picked out by the Catholic Church prevent their being examined now by an honest man, as they were examined at the time they were picked out?

Answer. No; not if the man comes to the conclusion that they are inspired.

Question. Does the fact that the Catholic Church picked them out and declared them to be inspired, render it a crime to examine them precisely as you would examine the books that the Catholic Church threw out and declared were not inspired?

Answer. I think it does.

Question. At the time the council was held in which it was determined which of the books of the New Testament are inspired, a respectable minority voted against some that were finally decided to be inspired. If they were honest in the vote they gave, and died without changing their opinions, are they now in hell?

Answer. Well, they ought to be.

Question. If those who voted to leave the book of Revelation out of the canon, and the gospel of Saint John out of the canon, believed honestly that these were not inspired books, how should they have voted?

Answer. Well, I suppose a man ought to vote as he honestly believes—except in matters of religion.

Question. If the Catholic Church was not infallible, is the question still open as to what books are, and what are not, inspired?

Answer. I suppose the question is still open—but it would be dangerous to decide it.

Question. If, then, I examine all the books again, and come to the conclusion that some that were thrown out were inspired, and some that were accepted were not inspired, ought I to say so?

Answer. Not if it is contrary to the faith of your father, or calculated to interfere with your own political prospects.

Question. Is it as great a sin to admit into the Bible books that are uninspired as to reject those that are inspired?

Answer. Well, it is a crime to reject an inspired book, no matter how unsatisfactory the evidence is for its inspiration, but it is not a crime to receive an uninspired book. God damns nobody for believing too much. An excess of credulity is simply to err in the direction of salvation.

Question. Suppose a man disbelieves in the inspiration of the New Testament—believes it to be entirely the work of uninspired men; and suppose he also believes—but not from any evidence obtained in the New Testament—that Jesus Christ was the son of God, and that he made atonement for his soul, can he then be saved without a belief in the inspiration of the Bible?

Answer. This has not yet been decided by our church, and I do not wish to venture an opinion.

Question. Suppose a man denies the inspiration of the Scriptures; suppose that he also denies the divinity of Jesus Christ; and suppose, further, that he acts precisely as Christ is said to have acted; suppose he loves his enemies, prays for those who despitefully use him, and does all the good he possibly can, is it your opinion that such a man will be saved?

Answer. No, sir. There is "none other name "given under heaven and among men," whereby a sinner can be saved but the name of Christ.

Question. Then it is your opinion that God would save a murderer who believed in Christ, and would damn another man, exactly like Christ, who failed to believe in him?

Answer. Yes; because we have the blessed promise that, out of Christ, "our God is a consuming "fire."

Question. Suppose a man read the Bible carefully and honestly, and was not quite convinced that it was true, and that while examining the subject, he died: what then?

Answer. I do not believe that God would allow him to examine the matter in another world, or to make up his mind in heaven. Of course, he would eternally perish.

Question. Could Christ now furnish evidence enough to convince every human being of the truth of the Bible?

Answer. Of course he could, because he is infinite.

Question. Are any miracles performed now?

Answer. Oh, no!

Question. Have we any testimony, except human testimony, to substantiate any miracle?

Answer. Only human testimony.

Question. Do all men give the same force to the same evidence?

Answer. By no means.

Question. Have all honest men who have examined the Bible believed it to be inspired?

Answer. Of course they have. Infidels are not honest.

Question. Could any additional evidence have been furnished?

Answer. With perfect ease.

Question. Would God allow a soul to suffer

eternal agony rather than furnish evidence of the truth of his Bible?

Answer. God has furnished plenty of evidence, and altogether more than was really necessary. We should read the Bible in a believing spirit.

Question. Are all parts of the inspired books equally true?

Answer. Necessarily.

Question. According to Saint Matthew, God promises to forgive all who will forgive others; not one word is said about believing in Christ, or believing in the miracles, or in any Bible; did Matthew tell the truth?

Answer. The Bible must be taken as a whole; and if other conditions are added somewhere else, then you must comply with those other conditions. Matthew may not have stated all the conditions.

Question. I find in another part of the New Testament, that a young man came to Christ and asked him what was necessary for him to do in order that he might inherit eternal life. Christ did not tell him that he must believe the Bible, or that he must believe in him, or that he must keep the Sabbath-day; was Christ honest with that young man?

Answer. Well, I suppose he was.

Question. You will also recollect that Zaccheus said to Christ, that where he had wronged any man he had made restitution, and further, that half his goods he had given to the poor; and you will remember that Christ said to Zaccheus: "This day " hath salvation come to thy house." Why did not Christ tell Zaccheus that he " must be born again ;" that he must " believe on the Lord Jesus Christ"?

Answer. Of course there are mysteries in our holy religion that only those who have been " born "again" can understand. You must remember that " the carnal mind is enmity with God."

Question. Is it not strange that Christ, in his Sermon on the Mount, did not speak of " regeneration," or of the "scheme of salvation"?

Answer. Well, it may be.

Question. Can a man be saved now by living exactly in accordance with the Sermon on the Mount?

Answer. He can not.

Question. Would then a man, by following the course of conduct prescribed by Christ in the Sermon on the Mount, lose his soul?

Answer. He most certainly would, because there is not one word in the Sermon on the Mount about believing on the Lord Jesus Christ; not one word about believing in the Bible; not one word about the "atonement;" not one word about "regeneration." So that, if the Presbyterian Church is right, it is absolutely certain that a man might follow the teachings of the Sermon on the Mount, and live in accordance with its every word, and yet deserve and receive the eternal condemnation of God. But we must remember that the Sermon on the Mount was preached before Christianity existed. Christ was talking to Jews.

Question. Did Christ write anything himself, in the New Testament?

Answer. Not a word.

Question. Did he tell any of his disciples to write any of his words?

Answer. There is no account of it, if he did.

Question. Do we know whether any of the disciples wrote anything?

Answer. Of course they did.

Question. How do you know?

Answer. Because the gospels bear their names.

Question. Are you satisfied that Christ was absolutely God?

Answer. Of course he was. We believe that Christ and God and the Holy Ghost are all the same, that the three form one, and that each one is three.

Question. Was Christ the God of the universe at the time of his birth?

Answer. He certainly was.

Question. Was he the infinite God, creator and controller of the entire universe, before he was born?

Answer. Of course he was. This is the mystery of "God manifest in the flesh." The infidels have pretended that he was like any other child, and was in fact supported by Nature instead of being the supporter of Nature. They have insisted that like other children, he had to be cared for by his mother. Of course he *appeared* to be cared for by his mother. It was a part of the plan that in all respects he should *appear* to be like other children.

Question. Did he know just as much before he was born as after?

Answer. If he was God of course he did.

Question. How do you account for the fact that Saint Luke tells us, in the last verse of the second chapter of his gospel, that "Jesus increased in wis-" dom and stature"?

Answer. That I presume is a figure of speech; because, if he was God, he certainly could not have increased in wisdom. The physical part of him could increase in stature, but the intellectual part must have been infinite all the time.

Question. Do you think that Luke was mistaken?

Answer. No; I believe what Luke said. If it appears untrue, or impossible, then I know that it is figurative or symbolical.

Question. Did I understand you to say that Christ was actually God?

Answer. Of course he was.

Question. Then why did Luke say in the same verse of the same chapter that "Jesus increased in " favor with God"?

Answer. I dare you to go into a room by yourself and read the fourteenth chapter of Saint John!

Question. Is it necessary to understand the Bible in order to be saved?

Answer. Certainly not; it is only necessary that you believe it.

Question. Is it necessary to believe all the miracles?

Answer. It may not be necessary, but as it is impossible to tell which ones can safely be left out, you had better believe them all.

Question. Then you regard belief as the safe way?

Answer. Of course it is better to be fooled in this world than to be damned in the next.

Question. Do you think that there are any cruelties on God's part recorded in the Bible?

Answer. At first flush, many things done by God himself, as well as by his prophets, appear to be cruel; but if we examine them closely, we will find them to be exactly the opposite.

Question. How do you explain the story of Elisha and the children,—where the two she-bears destroyed forty-two children on account of their impudence?

Answer. This miracle, in my judgment, establishes two things: 1. That children should be polite to ministers, and 2. That God is kind to animals—" giving them their meat in due season." These bears have been great educators—they are the foundation of the respect entertained by the young for theologians. No child ever sees a minister now without thinking of a bear.

Question. What do you think of the story of Daniel—you no doubt remember it? Some men told the king that Daniel was praying contrary to law, and thereupon Daniel was cast into a den of lions; but the lions could not touch him, their mouths having been shut by angels. The next morning, the king, finding that Daniel was still intact, had him taken out; and then, for the purpose of gratifying Daniel's God, the king had all the men who had made the complaint against Daniel, and their wives and their little children, brought and cast into the lions' den. According to the account, the lions were so hungry that they caught these wives and children as they dropped, and broke all their bones in pieces before they had even touched the ground. Is it not wonderful that God failed to protect these innocent wives and children?

Answer. These wives and children were heathen; they were totally depraved. And besides, they were used as witnesses. The fact that they were devoured with such quickness shows that the lions were hungry. Had it not been for this, infidels would have accounted for the safety of Daniel by saying that the lions had been fed.

Question. Do you believe that Shadrach, Meshach and Abednego were cast "into a burning fiery furnace "heated one seven times hotter than it was wont to "be heated," and that they had on "their coats, their "hosen and their hats," and that when they came out "not a hair of their heads was singed, nor was "the smell of fire upon their garments"?

Answer. The evidence of this miracle is exceedingly satisfactory. It resulted in the conversion of Nebuchadnezzar.

Question. How do you know he was converted?

Answer. Because immediately after the miracle the king issued a decree that "every people, nation "and language that spoke anything amiss against "the God of Shadrach and Company, should be cut "in pieces." This decree shows that he had become a true disciple and worshiper of Jehovah.

Question. If God in those days preserved from the fury of the fire men who were true to him and would not deny his name, why is it that he has failed to protect thousands of martyrs since that time?

Answer. This is one of the divine mysteries. God has in many instances allowed his enemies to kill his friends. I suppose this was allowed for the good of his enemies, that the heroism of the martyrs might convert them.

Question. Do you believe all the miracles?

Answer. I believe them all, because I believe the Bible to be inspired.

Question. What makes you think it is inspired?

Answer. I have never seen anybody who knew it was not; besides, my father and mother believed it.

Question. Have you any other reasons for believing it to be inspired?

Answer. Yes; there are more copies of the Bible printed than of any other book; and it is printed in more languages. And besides, it would be impossible to get along without it.

Question. Why could we not get along without it?

Answer. We would have nothing to swear witnesses by; no book in which to keep the family record; nothing for the centre-table, and nothing for a mother to give her son. No nation can be civilized without the Bible.

Question. Did God always know that a Bible was necessary to civilize a country?

Answer. Certainly he did.

Question. Why did he not give a Bible to the Egyptians, the Hindus, the Greeks and the Romans?

Answer. It is astonishing what perfect fools infidels are.

Question. Why do you call infidels "fools"?

Answer. Because I find in the fifth chapter of the gospel according to Matthew the following: "Who-"soever shall say 'Thou fool!' shall be in danger of "hell fire."

Question. Have I the right to read the Bible?

Answer. Yes. You not only have the right, but it is your duty.

Question. In reading the Bible the words make certain impressions on my mind. These impressions depend upon my brain,—upon my intelligence. Is not this true?

Answer. Of course, when you read the Bible, impressions are made upon your mind.

Question. Can I control these impressions?

Answer. I do not think you can, as long as you remain in a sinful state.

Question. How am I to get out of this sinful state?

Answer. You must believe on the Lord Jesus Christ, and you must read the Bible in a prayerful spirit and with a believing heart.

Question. Suppose that doubts force themselves upon my mind?

Answer. Then you will know that you are a sinner, and that you are depraved.

Question. If I have the right to read the Bible, have I the right to try to understand it?

Answer. Most assuredly.

Question. Do you admit that I have the right to reason about it and to investigate it?

Answer. Yes; I admit that. Of course you cannot help reasoning about what you read.

Question. Does the right to read a book include the right to give your opinion as to the truth of what the book contains?

Answer. Of course,—if the book is not inspired. Infidels hate the Bible because it is inspired, and Christians know that it is inspired because infidels say that it is not.

Question. Have I the right to decide for myself whether or not the book is inspired?

Answer. You have no right to deny the truth of God's Holy Word.

Question. Is God the author of all books?

Answer. Certainly not.

Question. Have I the right to say that God did not write the Koran?

Answer. Yes.

Question. Why?

Answer. Because the Koran was written by an impostor.

Question. How do you know?

Answer. My reason tells me so.

Question. Have you the right to be guided by your reason?

Answer. I must be.

Question. Have you the same right to follow your reason after reading the Bible?

Answer. No. The Bible is the standard of reason. The Bible is not to be judged or corrected by your reason. Your reason is to be weighed and measured by the Bible. The Bible is different from other books and must not be read in the same critical spirit, nor judged by the same standard.

Question. What did God give us reason for?

Answer. So that we might investigate other religions, and examine other so-called sacred books.

Question. If a man honestly thinks that the Bible is not inspired, what should he say?

Answer. He should admit that he is mistaken.

Question. When he thinks he is right?

Answer. Yes. The Bible is different from other books. It is the master of reason. You read the Bible, not to see if that is wrong, but to see whether your reason is right. It is the only book about which a man has no right to reason. He must believe. The Bible is addressed, not to the reason, but to the ears: " He that hath ears to hear, let " him hear."

Question. Do you think we have the right to tell

what the Bible means—what ideas God intended to convey, or has conveyed to us, through the medium of the Bible?

Answer. Well, I suppose you have that right. Yes, that must be your duty. You certainly ought to tell others what God has said to you.

Question. Do all men get the same ideas from the Bible?

Answer. No.

Question. How do you account for that?

Answer. Because all men are not alike; they differ in intellect, in education, and in experience.

Question. Who has the right to decide as to the real ideas that God intended to convey?

Answer. I am a Protestant, and believe in the right of private judgment. Whoever does not is a Catholic. Each man must be his own judge, but God will hold him responsible.

Question. Does God believe in the right of private judgment?

Answer. Of course he does.

Question. Is he willing that I should exercise my judgment in deciding whether the Bible is inspired or not?

Answer. No. He believes in the exercise of

private judgment only in the examination and rejection of other books than the Bible.

Question. Is he a Catholic?

Answer. I cannot answer blasphemy! Let me tell you that God will "laugh at your calamity, and " will mock when your fear cometh." You will be accursed.

Question. Why do you curse infidels?

Answer. Because I am a Christian.

Question. Did not Christ say that we ought to " bless those who curse us," and that we should " love our enemies"?

Answer. Yes, but he cursed the Pharisees and called them " hypocrites" and " vipers."

Question. How do you account for that?

Answer. It simply shows the difference between theory and practice.

Question. What do you consider the best way to answer infidels.

Answer. The old way is the best. You should say that their arguments are ancient, and have been answered over and over again. If this does not satisfy your hearers, then you should attack the character of the infidel—then that of his parents—then that of his children.

Question. Suppose that the infidel is a good man, how will you answer him then?

Answer. But an infidel cannot be a good man. Even if he is, it is better that he should lose his reputation, than that thousands should lose their souls. We know that all infidels are vile and infamous. We may not have the evidence, but we know that it exists.

Question. How should infidels be treated? Should Christians try to convert them?

Answer. Christians should have nothing to do with infidels. It is not safe even to converse with them. They are always talking about reason, and facts, and experience. They are filled with sophistry and should be avoided.

Question. Should Christians pray for the conversion of infidels?

Answer. Yes; but such prayers should be made in public and the name of the infidel should be given and his vile and hideous heart portrayed so that the young may be warned.

Question. Whom do you regard as infidels?

Answer. The scientists—the geologists, the astronomers, the naturalists, the philosophers. No one can overestimate the evil that has been wrought by Laplace, Humboldt, Darwin, Huxley, Haeckel, Renan, Emerson, Strauss, Büchner, Tyndall, and their wretched followers. These men pretended to know more than Moses and the prophets. They were "dogs baying at the moon." They were "wolves" and "fools." They tried to "assassinate "God," and worse than all, they actually laughed at the clergy,

Question. Do you think they did, and are doing great harm?

Answer. Certainly. Of what use are all the sciences, if you lose your own soul? People in hell will care nothing about education. The rich man said nothing about science, he wanted water. Neither will they care about books and theories in heaven. If a man is perfectly happy, it makes no difference how ignorant he is.

Question. But how can he answer these scientists?

Answer. Well, my advice is to let their arguments alone. Of course, you will deny all their facts; but the most effective way is to attack their character.

Question. But suppose they are good men,— what then?

Answer. The better they are, the worse they are.

We cannot admit that the infidel is really good. He may appear to be good, and it is our duty to strip the mask of appearance from the face of unbelief. If a man is not a Christian, he is totally depraved, and why should we hesitate to make a misstatement about a man whom God is going to make miserable forever?

Question. Are we not commanded to love our enemies?

Answer. Yes, but not the enemies of God.

Question. Do you fear the final triumph of infidelity?

Answer. No. We have no fear. We believe that the Bible can be revised often enough to agree with anything that may really be necessary to the preservation of the church. We can always rely upon revision. Let me tell you that the Bible is the most peculiar of books. At the time God inspired his holy prophets to write it, he knew exactly what the discoveries and demonstrations of the future would be, and he wrote his Bible in such a way that the words could always be interpreted in accordance with the intelligence of each age, and so that the words used are capable of several meanings, so that, no matter what may hereafter be discovered, the Bible will be found to agree with it,—for the reason that the knowledge of Hebrew will grow in the exact proportion that discoveries are made in other departments of knowledge. You will therefore see, that all efforts of infidelity to destroy the Bible will simply result in giving a better translation.

Question. What do you consider is the strongest argument in favor of the inspiration of the Scriptures?

Answer. The dying words of Christians.

Question. What do you consider the strongest argument against the truth of infidelity?

Answer. The dying words of infidels. You know how terrible were the death-bed scenes of Hume, Voltaire, Paine and Hobbes, as described by hundreds of persons who were not present; while all Christians have died with the utmost serenity, and with their last words have testified to the sustaining power of faith in the goodness of God.

Question. What were the last words of Jesus Christ?

Answer. " My God, my God, why hast thou for- " saken me?"

A VINDICATION OF THOMAS PAINE.

VINDICATION OF THOMAS PAINE.

"To argue with a man who has renounced the use and authority of reason, is like administering medicine to the dead."—THOMAS PAINE.

PEORIA, October 8, 1877.

To the Editor of the N. Y. Observer:

SIR: Last June in San Francisco, I offered a thousand dollars in gold—not as a wager, but as a gift—to any one who would substantiate the absurd story that Thomas Paine died in agony and fear, frightened by the clanking chains of devils. I also offered the same amount to any minister who would prove that Voltaire did not pass away as serenely as the coming of the dawn. Afterward I was informed that you had accepted the offer, and had called upon me to deposit the money. Acting upon this information, I sent you the following letter:

PEORIA, ILL., August 31st, 1877.

To the Editor of the New York Observer:

I have been informed that you accepted, in your paper, an offer made by me to any clergyman in San Francisco. That offer was, that I would pay one thousand dollars in gold to any minister in that city who would prove that Thomas Paine died in terror because of religious opinions he had expressed, or that Voltaire did not pass away serenely as the coming of the dawn.

For many years religious journals and ministers have been circulating certain pretended accounts of the frightful agonies endured by Paine and Voltaire when dying; that these great men at the moment of death were terrified because they had given their honest opinions upon the subject of religion to their fellow-men. The imagination of the religious world has been taxed to the utmost in inventing absurd and infamous accounts of the last moments of these intellectual giants. Every Sunday school paper, thousands of idiotic tracts, and countless stupidities called sermons, have been filled with these calumnies.

Paine and Voltaire both believed in God—both hoped for immortality—both believed in special providence. But both denied the inspiration of the Scriptures—both denied the divinity of Jesus Christ. While theologians most cheerfully admit that most murderers die without fear, they deny the possibility of any man who has expressed his disbelief in the inspiration of the Bible dying except in an agony of terror. These stories are used in revivals and in

Sunday schools, and have long been considered of great value.

I am anxious that these slanders shall cease. I am desirous of seeing justice done, even at this late day, to the dead.

For the purpose of ascertaining the evidence upon which these death-bed accounts really rest, I make to you the following proposition:—

First.—AS TO THOMAS PAINE: I will deposit with the First National Bank of Peoria, Illinois, one thousand dollars in gold, upon the following conditions: This money shall be subject to your order when you shall, in the manner hereinafter provided, substantiate that Thomas Paine admitted the Bible to be an inspired book, or that he recanted his Infidel opinions—or that he died regretting that he had disbelieved the Bible—or that he died calling upon Jesus Christ in any religious sense whatever.

In order that a tribunal may be created to try this question, you may select one man, I will select another, and the two thus chosen shall select a third, and any two of the three may decide the matter.

As there will be certain costs and expenditures on both sides, such costs and expenditures shall be paid by the defeated party.

In addition to the one thousand dollars in gold, I

will deposit a bond with good and sufficient security in the sum of two thousand dollars, conditioned for the payment of all costs in case I am defeated. I shall require of you a like bond.

From the date of accepting this offer you may have ninety days to collect and present your testimony, giving me notice of time and place of taking depositions. I shall have a like time to take evidence upon my side, giving you like notice, and you shall then have thirty days to take further testimony in reply to what I may offer. The case shall then be argued before the persons chosen; and their decisions shall be final as to us.

If the arbitrator chosen by me shall die, I shall have the right to choose another. You shall have the same right. If the third one, chosen by our two, shall die, the two shall choose another; and all vacancies, from whatever cause, shall be filled upon the same principle.

The arbitrators shall sit when and where a majority shall determine, and shall have full power to pass upon all questions arising as to competency of evidence, and upon all subjects.

Second.—AS TO VOLTAIRE: I make the same proposition, if you will substantiate that Voltaire died expressing remorse or showing in any way that he was in mental agony because he had attacked Catholicism—or because he had denied the inspiration of the Bible—or because he had denied the divinity of Christ.

I make these propositions because I want you to stop slandering the dead.

If the propositions do not suit you in any particular, please state your objections, and I will modify them in any way consistent with the object in view.

If Paine and Voltaire died filled with childish and silly fear, I want to know it, and I want the world to know it. On the other hand, if the believers in superstition have made and circulated these cruel slanders concerning the mighty dead, I want the world to know that.

As soon as you notify me of the acceptance of these propositions I will send you the certificate of the bank that the money has been deposited upon the foregoing conditions, together with copies of bonds for costs.   Yours truly,

R. G. INGERSOLL.

In your paper of September 27, 1877, you acknowledge the receipt of the foregoing letter, and after giving an outline of its contents, say: "As not one of the affirmations, in the form stated in this letter, was contained in the offer we made, we have no occasion to substantiate them. But we are prepared to produce the evidence of the truth of our own statement, and even to go further; to show not only that Tom Paine 'died a drunken, cowardly, and beastly death,' but that for many years previous, and up to that event he lived a drunken and beastly life."

In order to refresh your memory as to what you had published, I call your attention to the following, which appeared in the *N. Y. Observer*, July 19, 1877:

"Put Down the Money.

"Col. Bob Ingersoll, in a speech full of ribaldry and blasphemy, made in San Francisco recently, said:

"I will give $1,000 in gold coin to any clergyman who can substantiate that the death of Voltaire was not as peaceful as the dawn; and of Tom Paine whom they assert died in fear and agony, frightened by the clanking chains of devils—in fact frightened to death by God. I will give $1,000 likewise to any one who can substantiate this 'absurd story'—a story without a word of truth in it."

"We have published the testimony, and the witnesses are on hand to prove that Tom Paine died a drunken, cowardly and beastly death. *Let the Colonel deposit the money with any honest man, and the absurd story, as he terms it, shall be shown to be an ower true tale. But he won't do it. His talk is Infidel 'buncombe' and nothing more.*"

On the 31st of August I sent you my letter, and on the 27th of September you say in your paper: "As not one of the affirmations in the form stated in this letter was contained in the offer we made, we have no occasion to substantiate them."

What were the affirmations contained in the offer you made? I had offered a thousand dollars in gold to any one who would substantiate "*the absurd story* *that Thomas Paine died in fear and agony, frightened by the clanking chains of devils—in fact, frightened to death by God.*

In response to this offer you said: "Let the Colonel deposit the money with an honest man and the 'absurd story' as he terms it, shall be shown to be an 'ower true tale.' But he won't do it. His talk is infidel 'buncombe' and nothing more."

Did you not offer to prove that Paine died in fear and agony, frightened by the clanking chains of devils? Did you not ask me to deposit the money that you might prove the "absurd story" to be an "ower true tale" and obtain the money? Did you not in your paper of the twenty-seventh of September in effect deny that you had offered to prove this "absurd story"? As soon as I offered to deposit the gold and give bonds besides to cover costs, did you not publish a falsehood?

You have eaten your own words, and, for my part, I would rather have dined with Ezekiel than with you.

You have not met the issue. You have knowingly avoided it. The question was not as to the personal habits of Paine. The real question was and is, whether Paine was filled with fear and horror at the time of his death on account of his religious opinions. That is the question. You avoid this. In effect, you abandon that charge and make others.

To you belongs the honor of having made the most cruel and infamous charges against Thomas Paine that have ever been made. Of what you have said you cannot prove the truth of one word.

You say that Thomas Paine died a drunken, cowardly and beastly death.

I pronounce this charge to be a cowardly and beastly falsehood.

Have you any evidence that he was in a drunken condition when he died?

What did he say or do of a *cowardly* character just before, or at about the time of his death?

In what way was his death cowardly? You must answer these questions, and give your proof, or all honest men will hold you in abhorrence. You have made these charges. The man against whom you make them is dead. He cannot answer you. I can. He cannot compel you to produce your testimony, or admit by your silence that you have cruelly slandered the defenceless dead. I can and I will. You say that his death was cowardly. In what respect? Was it cowardly in him to hold the Thirty-Nine Articles in contempt? Was it cowardly *not* to call on your Lord? Was it cowardly not to be afraid? You say that his death was beastly. Again I ask, in what respect? Was it beastly to submit to the inevitable with tranquillity? Was it beastly to look with composure upon the approach of death? Was it beastly to die without a complaint, without a murmur—to pass from life without a fear?

DID THOMAS PAINE RECANT?

Mr. Paine had prophesied that fanatics would crawl and cringe around him during his last moments. He believed that they would put a lie in the mouth of Death.

When the shadow of the coming dissolution was upon him, two clergymen, Messrs. Milledollar and Cunningham, called to annoy the dying man. Mr. Cunningham had the politeness to say, "You have now a full view of death—you cannot live long, and whosoever does not believe in the Lord Jesus Christ will asuredly be damned." Mr. Paine replied, " Let me have none of your popish stuff. Get away with you. Good morning."

On another occasion a Methodist minister obtruded himself when Willet Hicks was present. This minister declared to Mr. Paine "that unless he repented of his unbelief he would be damned." Paine, although at the door of death, rose in his bed and indignantly requested the clergyman to leave his room. On another occasion, two brothers by the name of Pigott, sought to convert him. He was displeased and requested their departure. Afterward Thomas Nixon and Captain Daniel Pelton visited him for the express purpose of ascertaining whether he had, in any manner, changed his religious opinions. They were assured by the dying man that he still held the principles he had expressed in his writings.

Afterward, these gentlemen hearing that William Cobbett was about to write a life of Paine, sent him the following note:

NEW YORK, April 24, 1818.

"SIR : We have been informed that you have a design to write a history of the life and writings of Thomas Paine. If you have been furnished with materials in respect to his religious opinions, or rather of his recantation of his former opinions before his death, all you have heard of his recanting is false. Being aware that such reports would be raised after his death by fanatics who infested his house at the time it was expected he would die, we, the subscribers, intimate acquaintances of Thomas Paine since the year 1776, went to his house. He was sitting up in a chair, and apparently in full vigor and use of all his mental faculties. We interrogated him upon his religious opinions, and if he had changed his mind, or repented of anything he had said or wrote on that subject. He answered, "Not at all," and appeared rather offended at our supposition that any change should take place in his mind. We took down in writing the questions put to him and his answers thereto before a number of persons then in his room, among whom were his doctor, Mrs. Bonneville, &c. This paper is mislaid and cannot be found at present, but the above is the substance which can be attested by many living witnesses."

THOMAS NIXON.
DANIEL PELTON.

Mr. Jarvis, the artist, saw Mr. Paine one or two days before his death. To Mr. Jarvis he expressed his belief in his written opinions upon the subject of religion. B. F. Haskin, an attorney of the city of

New York, also visited him and inquired as to his religious opinions. Paine was then upon the threshold of death, but he did not tremble. He was not a coward. He expressed his firm and unshaken belief in the religious ideas he had given to the world.

Dr. Manley was with him when he spoke his last words. Dr. Manley asked the dying man if he did not wish to believe that Jesus was the Son of God, and the dying philosopher answered: "I have no wish to believe on that subject." Amasa Woodsworth sat up with Thomas Paine the night before his death. In 1839 Gilbert Vale hearing that Mr. Woodsworth was living in or near Boston, visited him for the purpose of getting his statement. The statement was published in the *Beacon* of June 5, 1839, while thousands who had been acquainted with Mr. Paine were living.

The following is the article referred to.

"We have just returned from Boston. One object of our visit to that city, was to see a Mr. Amasa Woodsworth, an engineer, now retired in a handsome cottage and garden at East Cambridge, Boston. This gentleman owned the house occupied by Paine at his death—while he lived next door. As an act of kindness Mr. Woodsworth visited Mr. Paine every day for six weeks before his death. He frequently sat up with him, and did so on the last two nights of his life. He was always there with Dr. Manley, the physician, and assisted in removing Mr. Paine while his bed was prepared. He was present when Dr. Manley asked Mr. Paine "if he wished to believe that Jesus Christ was the Son of God," and he describes Mr. Paine's answer as animated. He says that lying on his back he used some action and with much emphasis, replied, " I have no wish to believe on that subject." He lived some time after this, but was not known to speak, for he died tranquilly. He accounts for the insinuating style of Dr. Manley's letter, by stating that that gentleman just after its publication joined a church. He informs us that he has openly reproved the doctor for the falsity contained in the spirit of that letter, boldly declaring before Dr. Manley, who is yet living, that nothing which he saw justified the insinuations. Mr. Woodsworth assures us that he neither heard nor saw anything to justify the belief of any mental change in the opinions of Mr. Paine previous to his death; but that being very ill and in pain chiefly arising from the skin being removed in some parts by long lying, he was generally too uneasy to enjoy conversation on abstract subjects. This, then, is the best evidence that can be procured on this subject, and we publish it while the contravening parties are yet alive, and with the authority of Mr. Woodsworth.

GILBERT VALE.

A few weeks ago I received the following letter which confirms the statement of Mr. Vale:

> NEAR STOCKTON, CAL., GREEN-
> WOOD COTTAGE, July 9, 1877.

COL. INGERSOLL: In 1842 I talked with a gentleman in Boston. I have forgotten his name; but he was then an engineer of the Charleston navy yard. I am thus particular so that you can find his name on the books. He told me that he nursed Thomas Paine in his last illness, and closed his eyes when dead. I asked him if he recanted and called upon God to save him. He replied, "No. He died as he had taught. He had a sore upon his side and when we turned him it was very painful and he would cry out 'O God!' or something like that." "But," said the narrator, "that was nothing, for he believed in a God." I told him that I had often heard it asserted from the pulpit that Mr. Paine had recanted in his last moments. The gentleman said that it was not true, and he appeared to be an intelligent, truthful man. With respect, I remain, &c.,

PHILIP GRAVES, M.D.

The next witness is Willet Hicks, a Quaker preacher. He says that during the last illness of Mr. Paine he visited him almost daily, and that Paine died firmly convinced of the truth of the religious opinions he had given to his fellow-men. It was to this same Willet Hicks that Paine applied for permission to be buried in the cemetery of the Quakers. Permission was refused. This refusal settles the question of recantation. If he had recanted, of course there could have been no objection to his body being buried by the side of the best hypocrites on the earth.

If Paine recanted why should he be denied "a little earth for charity"? Had he recanted, it would have been regarded as a vast and splendid triumph for the gospel. It would with much noise and pomp and ostentation have been heralded about the world.

I received the following letter to-day. The writer is well know in this city, and is a man of high character:

PEORIA, Oct. 8th, 1877.

ROBERT G. INGERSOLL, *Esteemed Friend:* My parents were Friends (Quakers). My father died when I was very young. The elderly and middle-aged Friends visited at my mother's house. We lived in the city of New York. Among the number I distinctly remember Elias Hicks, Willet Hicks, and a Mr.—— Day, who was a bookseller in Pearl street. There were many others, whose names I do not now remember. The subject of the recantation by Thomas Paine of his views about the Bible in his last illness, or at any other time, was discussed by them in my presence at different times. I learned from them that some of them had attended upon Thomas Paine in his last sickness and ministered to his wants up to the time of his death. And upon the question of whether he did recant there was but one expression. They all said that he did not recant in any manner. I often heard them say they wished he had recanted. In fact, according to them, the nearer he approached death the more positive he appeared to be in his convictions.

These conversations were from 1820 to 1822. I was at that time from ten to twelve years old, but these conversations impressed themselves upon me because many thoughtless people then blamed the Society of Friends for their kindness to that "arch Infidel," Thomas Paine.

Truly yours,
A. C. HANKINSON.

A few days ago I received the following letter:

ALBANY, NEW YORK, Sept. 27, 1877.

Dear Sir: It is over twenty years ago that professionally I made the acqaintance of John Hogeboom, a Justice of the Peace of the county of Rensselaer, New York. He was then over seventy years of age and had the reputation of being a man of candor and integrity. He was a great admirer of Paine. He told me that he was personally acquainted with him, and used to see him frequently during the last years of his life in the city of New York, where Hogeboom then resided. I asked him if there was any truth in the charge that Paine was in the habit of getting drunk. He said that it was utterly false; that he never heard of such a thing during the life-time of Mr. Paine, and did not believe any one else did. I asked him about the recantation of his religious opinions on his death-bed, and the revolting death-bed scenes that the world had heard so much about. He said there was no truth in them, that he had received his information from persons who attended Paine in his last illness, "and that he passed peacefully away, as we may say, in the sunshine of a great soul." . . .

Yours truly,

W. J. HILTON.

The witnesses by whom I substantiate the fact that Thomas Paine did not recant, and that he died holding the religious opinions he had published, are:

First—Thomas Nixon, Captain Daniel Pelton, B. F. Haskin. These gentlemen visited him during his last illness for the purpose of ascertaining whether he had in any respect changed his views upon religion. He told them that he had not.

Second—James Cheetham. This man was the most malicious enemy Mr. Paine had, and yet he admits that "Thomas Paine died placidly, and almost without a struggle." (See Life of Thomas Paine, by James Cheetham).

Third—The ministers, Milledollar and Cunningham. These gentlemen told Mr. Paine that if he died without believing in the Lord Jesus Christ he would be damned, and Paine replied, "Let me have none of your popish stuff. Good morning." (See Sherwin's Life of Paine, p. 220).

Fourth—Mrs. Hedden. She told these same preachers when they attempted to obtrude themselves upon Mr. Paine again, that the attempt to convert Mr. Paine was useless—"that if God did not change his mind no human power could."

Fifth—Andrew A. Dean. This man lived upon Paine's farm at New Rochelle, and corresponded with him upon religious subjects. (See Paine's Theological Works, p. 308.)

Sixth—Mr. Jarvis, the artist with whom Paine lived. He gives an account of an old lady coming to Paine and telling him that God Almighty had sent her to tell him that unless he repented and believed in the blessed Savior, he would be damned. Paine replied that God would not send such a foolish old woman with such an impertinent message. (See Clio Rickman's Life of Paine.)

Seventh—Wm. Carver, with whom Paine boarded. Mr. Carver said again and again that Paine did not recant. He knew him well, and had every opportunity of knowing. (See Life of Paine by Gilbert Vale.)

Eighth—Dr. Manley, who attended him in his last sickness, and to whom Paine spoke his last words. Dr. Manley asked him if he did not wish to believe in Jesus Christ, and he replied, "I have no wish to believe on that subject."

Ninth—Willet Hicks and Elias Hicks, who were with him frequently during his last sickness, and both of whom tried to persuade him to recant. According to their testimony, Mr. Paine died as he had lived—a believer in God, and a friend of man. Willet Hicks was offered money to say something false against Thomas Paine. He was even offered money to remain silent and allow others to slander the dead. Mr. Hicks, speaking of Thomas Paine, said: "He was a good man—an honest man." (Vale's Life of Paine.)

Tenth—Amasa Woodsworth, who was with him every day for some six weeks immediately preceding his death, and sat up with him the last two nights of his life. This man declares that Paine did not recant and that he died tranquilly. The evidence of Mr. Woodsworth is conclusive.

Eleventh—Thomas Paine himself. The will of Thomas Paine, written by himself, commences as follows:

"The last will and testament of me, the subscriber, Thomas Paine, reposing confidence in my creator God, and in no other being, for I know of no other, nor believe in any other;" and closes in these words; "I have lived an honest and useful life to mankind; my time has been spent in doing good, and I die in perfect composure and resignation to the will of my creator God."

Twelfth—If Thomas Paine recanted, why do you pursue him? If he recanted, he died substantially in your belief, for what reason then do you denounce his death as cowardly? If upon his death-bed he renounced the opinions he had published, the business of defaming him should be done by Infidels, not by Christians.

I ask you if it is honest to throw away the testimony of his friends—the evidence of fair and honorable men—and take the putrid words of avowed and malignant enemies?

When Thomas Paine was dying, he was infested by fanatics—by the snaky spies of bigotry. In the shadows of death were the unclean birds of prey waiting to tear with beak and claw the corpse of him who wrote the "Rights of Man." And there lurking and crouching in the darkness were the jackals and hyenas of superstition ready to violate his grave.

These birds of prey—these unclean beasts are the witnesses produced and relied upon by you.

One by one the instruments of torture have been wrenched from the cruel clutch of the church, until within the armory of orthodoxy there remains but one weapon—Slander.

Against the witnesses that I have produced you can bring just two—Mary Roscoe and Mary Hinsdale. The first is referred to in the memoir of Stephen Grellet. She had once been a servant in his house. Grellet tells what happened between this girl and Paine. According to this account Paine asked her if she had ever read any of his writings, and on being told that she had read very *little* of them, he inquired what she thought of them, adding that from such an one as she he expected a correct answer.

Let us examine this falsehood. Why would Paine expect a correct answer about his writings from one who had read very little of them? Does not such a statement devour itself? This young lady further said that the "Age of Reason" was put in her hands and that the more she read in it the more dark and distressed she felt, and that she threw the book into the fire. Whereupon Mr. Paine remarked, "I wish all had done as you did, for if the devil ever had any agency in any work, he had it in my writing that book."

The next is Mary Hinsdale. She was a servant in the family of Willet Hicks. She, like Mary Roscoe, was sent to carry some delicacy to Mr. Paine. To this young lady Paine, according to her account, said precisely the same that he did to Mary Roscoe, and she said the same thing to Mr. Paine.

My own opinion is that Mary Roscoe and Mary Hinsdale are one and the same person, or the same story has been by mistake put in the mouth of both.

It is not possible that the same conversation should have taken place between Paine and Mary Roscoe, and between him and Mary Hinsdale.

Mary Hinsdale lived with Willet Hicks and he pronounced her story a pious fraud and fabrication. He said that Thomas Paine never said any such thing to Mary Hinsdale. (See Vale's *Life of Paine*.)

Another thing about this witness. A woman by the name of Mary Lockwood, a Hicksite Quaker, died. Mary Hinsdale met her brother about that time and told him that his sister had recanted, and wanted her to say so at her funeral. This turned out to be false.

It has been claimed that Mary Hinsdale made her statement to Charles Collins. Long after the alleged occurrence Gilbert Vale, one of the biographers of Paine, had a conversation with Collins concerning Mary Hinsdale. Vale asked him what he thought of her. He replied that some of the Friends believed that she used opiates, and that they did not give credit to her statements. He also said that he believed what the Friends said, but thought that when a young woman, she *might* have told the truth.

In 1818 William Cobbett came to New York. He began collecting materials for a life of Thomas Paine. In this he became acquainted with Mary Hinsdale and Charles Collins. Mr. Cobbett gave a full account of what happened in a letter addressed to the Norwich *Mercury* in 1819. From this account it seems that Charles Collins told Cobbett that Paine had recanted. Cobbett called for the testimony, and told Mr. Collins that he must give time, place, and the circumstances. He finally brought a statement that he stated had been made by Mary Hinsdale. Armed with this document Cobbett, in October of that year, called upon the said Mary Hinsdale, at No. 10 Anthony street, New York, and showed her the statement. Upon being questioned by Mr. Cobbett she said, "That it was so long ago that she could not speak positively to any part of the matter—that she would not say that any part of the paper was true—that she had never seen the paper—and that she had never given Charles Collins authority to say anything about the matter in her name." And so in the month of October, in the year of grace 1818, in the mist and fog of forgetfulness disappeared forever one Mary Hinsdale—the last and only witness against the intellectual honesty of Thomas Paine.

Did Thomas Paine live the life of a drunken beast, and did he die a drunken, cowardly and beastly death?

Upon you rests the burden of substantiating these infamous charges.

You have, I suppose, produced the best evidence in your possession, and that evidence I will now proceed to examine. Your first witness is Grant Thorburn. He makes three charges against Thomas Paine. 1st. That his wife obtained a divorce from him in England for cruelty and neglect. 2d. That he was a defaulter and fled from England to America. 3d. That he was a drunkard.

These three charges stand upon the same evidence—the word of Grant Thorburn. If they are not all true Mr. Thorburn stands impeached.

The charge that Mrs. Paine obtained a divorce on account of the cruelty and neglect of her husband is utterly false. There is no such record in the world, and never was. Paine and his wife separated by mutual consent. Each respected the other. They remained friends. This charge is without any foundation in fact. I challenge the Christian world to produce the record of this decree of divorce. According to Mr. Thorburn it was granted in England. In that country public records are kept of all such decrees. Have the kindness to produce this decree showing that it was given on account of cruelty or admit that Mr. Thorburn was mistaken.

Thomas Paine was a just man. Although separated from his wife, he always spoke of her with tenderness and respect, and frequently sent her money without letting her know the source from whence it came. Was this the conduct of a drunken beast?

The second charge, that Paine was a defaulter in England and fled to America, is equally false. He did not flee from England. He came to America, not as a fugitive, but as a free man. He came with a letter of introduction signed by another Infidel, Benjamin Franklin. He came as a soldier of Freedom—an apostle of Liberty.

In this second charge there is not one word of truth.

He held a small office in England. If he was a defaulter the records of that country will show that fact.

Mr. Thorburn, unless the record can be produced to substantiate him, stands convicted of at least two mistakes.

Now, as to the third: He says that in 1802 Paine was an "old remnant of mortality, drunk, bloated and half asleep."

Can any one believe this to be a true account of the personal appearance of Mr. Paine in 1802? He had just returned from France. He had been welcomed home by Thomas Jefferson, who had said that he was entitled to the hospitality of every American.

In 1802 Mr. Paine was honored with a public dinner in the city of New York. He was called upon and treated with kindness and respect by such men as DeWitt Clinton.

In 1806 Mr. Paine wrote a letter to Andrew A. Dean upon the subject of religion. Read that letter and then say that the writer of it was an " old remnant of mortality, drunk, bloated and half asleep." Search the files of the *New York Observer* from the first issue to the last, and you will find nothing superior to this letter.

In 1803 Mr. Paine wrote a letter of considerable length, and of great force, to his friend Samuel Adams. Such letters are not written by drunken beasts, nor by remnants of old mortality, nor by drunkards. It was about the same time that he wrote his " Remarks on Robert Hall's Sermons."

These " Remarks " were not written by a drunken beast, but by a clear-headed and thoughtful man.

In 1804 he published an essay on the invasion of England, and a treatise on gunboats, full of valuable maritime information :—in 1805, a treatise on yellow fever, suggesting modes of prevention. In short, he was an industrious and thoughtful man. He sympathized with the poor and oppressed of all lands. He looked upon monarchy as a species of physical slavery. He had the goodness to attack that form of government. He regarded the religion of his day as a kind of mental slavery. He had the courage to give his reasons for his opinion. His reasons filled the churches with hatred. Instead of answering his arguments they attacked him. Men who were not fit to blacken his shoes, blackened his character.

There is too much religious cant in the statement of Mr. Thorburn. He exhibited too much anxiety to tell what Grant Thorburn said to Thomas Paine. He names Thomas Jefferson as one of the disreputable men who welcomed Paine with open arms. The testimony of a man who regarded Thomas Jefferson as a disreputable person, as to the character of anybody, is utterly without value. In my judgment, the testimony of Mr. Thorburn should be thrown aside as wholly unworthy of belief.

Your next witness is the Rev. J. D. Wickham, D. D., who tells what an elder in his church said. This elder said that Paine passed his last days on his farm at New Rochelle with a solitary female attendant. This is not true. He did not pass his last days at New Rochelle. Consequently this pious elder did not see him during his last days at that place. Upon this elder we prove an alibi. Mr. Paine passed his last days in the city of New York, in a house upon

Columbia street. The story of the Rev. J. D. Wickham, D.D., is simply false.

The next competent false witness is the Rev. Charles Hawley, D.D., who proceeds to state that the story of the Rev. J. D. Wickham, D.D., is corroborated by older citizens of New Rochelle. The names of these ancient residents are withheld. According to these unknown witnesses, the account given by the deceased elder was entirely correct. But as the particulars of Mr. Paine's conduct "were too loathsome to be described in print," we are left entirely in the dark as to what he really did.

While at New Rochelle Mr. Paine lived with Mr. Purdy—with Mr. Dean—with Captain Pelton, and with Mr. Staple. It is worthy of note that all of these gentlemen give the lie direct to the statements of "older residents" and ancient citizens spoken of by the Rev. Charles Hawley, D.D., and leave him with his "loathsome particulars" existing only in his own mind.

The next gentleman you bring upon the stand is W. H. Ladd, who quotes from the memoirs of Stephen Grellet. This gentleman also has the misfortune to be dead. According to his account, Mr. Paine made his recantation to a servant girl of his by the name of Mary Roscoe. To this girl, according to the account, Mr. Paine uttered the wish that all who read his book had burned it. I believe there is a mistake in the name of this girl. Her name was probably Mary Hinsdale, as it was once claimed that Paine made the same remark to her, but this point I shall notice hereafter. These are your witnesses, and the only ones you bring forward, to support your charge that Thomas Paine lived a drunken and beastly life and died a drunken, cowardly and beastly death. All these calumnies are found in a life of Paine by a Mr. Cheetham, the convicted libeler already referred to. Mr. Cheetham was an enemy of the man whose life he pretended to write.

In order to show you the estimation in which Mr. Cheetham was held by Mr. Paine, I will give you a copy of a letter that throws light upon this point:

October 28, 1807.

"MR. CHEETHAM: Unless you make a public apology for the abuse and falsehood in your paper of Tuesday, October 27th, respecting me, I will prosecute you for lying." THOMAS PAINE.

In another letter, speaking of this same man, Mr. Paine says: "If an unprincipled bully cannot be reformed, he can be punished." "Cheetham has been so long in the habit of giving false information, that truth is to him like a foreign language."

Mr. Cheetham wrote the life of Paine to gratify his malice and to support religion. He was prosecuted for libel—was convicted and fined.

Yet the life of Paine written by this man is referred to by the Christian world as the highest authority.

As to the personal habits of Mr. Paine, we have the testimony of William Carver, with whom he lived; of Mr. Jarvis, the artist, with whom he lived; of Mr. Staple, with whom he lived; of Mr. Purdy, who was a tenant of Paine's; of Mr. Burger, with whom he was intimate; of Thomas Nixon and Captain Daniel Pelton, both of whom knew him well; of Amasa Woodsworth, who was with him when he died; of John Fellows, who boarded at the same house; of James Wilburn, with whom he boarded; of B. F. Haskin, a lawyer, who was well acquainted with him and called upon him during his last illness; of Walter Morton, a friend; of Clio Rickman, who had known him for many years; of Willet and Elias Hicks, Quakers, who knew him intimately and well; of Judge Herttell, H. Margary, Elihu Palmer, and many others. All these testified to the fact that Mr. Paine was a temperate man. In those days nearly everybody used spirituous liquors. Paine was not an exception; but he did not drink to excess. Mr. Lovett, who kept the City Hotel where

Paine stopped, in a note to Caleb Bingham, declared that Paine drank less than any boarder he had.

Against all this evidence you produce the story of Grant Thorburn—the story of the Rev. J. D. Wickham that an elder in his church told him that Paine was a drunkard, corroborated by the Rev. Charles Hawley, and an extract from Lossing's history to the same effect. The evidence is overwhelmingly against you. Will you have the fairness to admit it? Your witnesses are merely the repeaters of the falsehoods of James Cheetham, the convicted libeler.

After all, drinking is not as bad as lying. An honest drunkard is better than a calumniator of the dead. "A remnant of old mortality, drunk, bloated and half asleep" is better than a perfectly sober defender of human slavery.

To become drunk is a virtue compared with stealing a babe from the breast of its mother.

Drunkenness is one of the beatitudes, compared with editing a religious paper devoted to the defence of slavery upon the ground that it is a divine institution.

Do you really think that Paine was a drunken beast when he wrote "Common Sense"—a pamphlet that aroused three millions of people, as people were never aroused by a pamphlet before? Was he a drunken beast when he wrote the "Crisis"? Was it to a drunken beast that the following letter was addressed:

ROCKY HILL, September 10, 1783.

"I have learned since I have been at this place, that you are at Bordentown.—Whether for the sake of retirement or economy I know not. Be it for either or both, or whatever it may, if you will come to this place and partake with me I shall be exceedingly happy to see you at it. Your presence may remind Congress of your past services to this country; and if it is in my power to impress them, command my best exertions with freedom, as they will be rendered cheerfully by one who entertains a lively sense of the importance of your works, and who with much pleasure subscribes himself,"

Your Sincere Friend,

GEORGE WASHINGTON.

Did any of your ancestors ever receive a letter like that?

Do you think that Paine was a drunken beast when the following letter was received by him?

"You express a wish in your letter to return to America in a national ship; Mr. Dawson, who brings over the treaty, and who will present you with this letter, is charged with orders to the captain of the

Maryland to receive and accommodate you back, if you can be ready to depart at such a short warning. You will in general find us returned to sentiments worthy of former times; *in these it will be your glory to have steadily labored and with as much effect as any man living.* That you may live long to continue your useful labors, and reap the reward in the *thankfulness of nations*, is my sincere prayer. Accept the assurances of my high esteem and affectionate attachment."

THOMAS JEFFERSON.

Did any of your ancestors ever receive a letter like that?

"It has been very generally propagated through the continent that I wrote the pamphlet 'Common Sense.' I could not have written anything in so manly and striking a style."—JOHN ADAMS.

"A few more such *flaming* arguments as were exhibited at Falmouth and Norfolk, added to the sound doctrine and unanswerable reasoning contained in the pamphlet 'Common Sense,' will not leave numbers at a loss to decide on the propriety of a separation."—GEORGE WASHINGTON.

"It is not necessary for me to tell you how much all your countrymen—I speak of the great mass of the people—are interested in your welfare.

They have not forgotten the history of their own Revolution and the difficult scenes through which they passed; nor do they review its several stages without reviving in their bosoms a due sensibility of the merits of those who served them in that great and arduous conflict. The crime of ingratitude has not yet stained, and I trust never will stain, our national character. You are considered by them as not only having rendered important services in our own Revolution, but as being on a more extensive scale the friend of human rights, and a distinguished and able defender of public liberty. To the welfare of Thomas Paine the Americans are not, nor can they be indifferent." . . JAMES MONROE.

Did any of your ancestors ever receive a letter like that?

"No writer has exceeded Paine in ease and familiarity of style, in perspicuity of expression, happiness of elucidation, and in simple and unassuming language."—THOMAS JEFFERSON.

Was ever a letter like that written about an editor of the *New York Observer?*

Was it in consideration of the services of a drunken beast that the Legislature of Pennsylvania presented Thomas Paine with five hundred pounds sterling?

Did the State of New York feel indebted to a drunken beast, and confer upon Thomas Paine an estate of several hundred acres?

"I believe in the equality of man, and I believe that religious duties consist in doing justice, loving mercy, and endeavoring to make our fellow-creatures happy."

"My own mind is my own church."

"It is necessary to the happiness of man that he be mentally faithful to himself."

"Any system of religion that shocks the mind of a child cannot be a true system."

"The Word of God is the creation which we behold."

"The age of ignorance commenced with the Christian system."

"It is with a pious fraud as with a bad action—it begets a calamitous necessity of going on."

"To read the Bible without horror, we must undo everything that is tender, sympathizing and benevolent in the heart of man."

"The man does not exist who can say I have persecuted him, or that I have in any case returned evil for evil."

"Of all tyrannies that afflict mankind, tyranny in religion is the worst."

"My own opinion is, that those whose lives have been spent in doing good and endeavoring to make their fellow-mortals happy, will be happy hereafter."

"The belief in a cruel god makes a cruel man."

"The intellectual part of religion is a private affair between every man and his Maker, and in which no third party has any right to interfere. The practical part consists in our doing good to each other."

"No man ought to make a living by religion. One person cannot act religion for another—every person must perform it for himself."

"One good schoolmaster is of more use than a hundred priests."

"Let us propagate morality unfettered by superstition."

"God is the power, or first cause, Nature is the law, and matter is the subject acted upon."

"I believe in one God and no more, and I hope for happiness beyond this life."

"The key of heaven is not in the keeping of any sect nor ought the road to it to be obstructed by any."

"My religion, and the whole of it, is the fear and love of the Deity and universal philanthropy."

"I have yet, I believe, some years in store, for I have a good state of health and a happy mind. I take care of both, by nourishing the first with *temperance* and the latter with abundance."

"He lives immured within the Bastile of a word."

How perfectly that sentence describes you! The Bastile in which you are immured is the word "Calvinism."

"Man has no property in man."

What a splendid motto that would have made for the *New York Observer* in the olden time!

"The world is my country; to do good, my religion."

I ask you again whether these splendid utterances came from the lips of a drunken beast?

Did Thomas Paine die in destitution and want?

The charge has been made, over and over again, that Thomas Paine died in want and destitution—that he was an abandoned pauper—an outcast without friends and without money. This charge is just as false as the rest.

Upon his return to this country in 1802, he was worth $30,000, according to his own statement made at that time in the following letter addressed to Clio Rickman:

"My Dear Friend: Mr. Monroe, who is appointed minister extraordinary to France, takes charge of this, to be delivered to Mr. Este, banker in Paris, to be forwarded to you.

"I arrived at Baltimore the 30th of October, and you can have no idea of the agitation which my arrival occasioned. From New Hampshire to Georgia (an extent of 1,500 miles) every newspaper was filled with applause or abuse.

"My property in this country has been taken care of by my friends, and is now worth six thousand pounds sterling; which put in the funds will bring me £400 sterling a year.

"Remember me in affection and friendship to your wife and family, and in the circle of your friends."

THOMAS PAINE.

A man in those days worth thirty thousand dollars was not a pauper. That amount would bring an income of at least two thousand dollars per annum. Two thousand dollars then would be fully equal to five thousand dollars now.

On the 12th of July, 1809, the year in which he died, Mr. Paine made his will. From this instrument we learn that he was the owner of a valuable farm within twenty miles of New York. He also was the owner of thirty shares in the New York Phœnix Insurance Company, worth upwards of fifteen hundred dollars. Besides this, some personal property and ready money. By his will he gave to Walter Morton, and Thomas Addis Emmett, brother of Robert Emmett, two hundred dollars each, and one hundred to the widow of Elihu Palmer.

Is it possible that this will was made by a pauper—by a destitute outcast—by a man who suffered for the ordinary necessaries of life?

But suppose, for the sake of the argument, that he was poor and that he died a beggar, does that tend to show that the Bible is an inspired book and that Calvin did not burn Servetus? Do you really regard poverty as a crime? If Paine had died a millionaire, would you have accepted his religious opinions? If Paine had drank nothing but cold water would you have repudiated the five cardinal points of Calvinism? Does an argument depend for its force upon the pecuniary condition of the person making it? As a matter of fact, most reformers—most men and women of genius, have been acquainted with poverty. Beneath a covering of rags have been found some of the tenderest and bravest hearts.

Owing to the attitude of the churches for the last fifteen hundred years, truth-telling has not been a very lucrative business. As a rule, hypocrisy has worn the robes, and honesty the rags. That day is passing away. You cannot now answer the arguments of a man by pointing at holes in his coat. Thomas Paine attacked the church when it was powerful—when it had what was called honors to bestow—when it was the keeper of the public conscience—when it was strong and cruel. The church waited till he was dead then attacked his reputation and his clothes.

Once upon a time a donkey kicked a lion. The lion was dead.

Conclusion.

From the persistence with which the orthodox have charged for the last sixty-eight years that Thomas Paine recanted, and that when dying he was filled with remorse and fear; from the malignity of the attacks upon his personal character, I had concluded that there must be some evidence of some kind to support these charges. Even with my ideas of the average honor of believers in superstition—the disciples of fear—I did not quite believe that all these infamies rested solely upon poorly attested lies. I had charity enough to suppose that something had been said or done by Thomas Paine capable of being tortured into a foundation for these calumnies. And I was foolish enough to think that even you would be willing to fairly examine the pretended evidence said to sustain these charges, and give your honest conclusion to the world. I supposed that you, being acquainted with the history of your country, felt under a certain obligation to Thomas Paine for the splendid services rendered by him in the darkest days of the Revolution. It was only reasonable to suppose that you were aware that in the midnight of Valley Forge the "Crisis," by Thomas Paine, was the first star that glittered in the wide horizon of despair. I took it for granted that you knew of the bold stand taken and the brave words spoken by Thomas Paine, in the French Convention, against the death of the king. I thought it probable that you, being an editor, had read the "Rights of Man;" that you knew that Thomas Paine was a champion of human liberty; that he was one of the founders and fathers of this Republic; that he was one of the foremost men of his age; that he had never written a word in favor of injustice; that he was a despiser of slavery; that he abhorred tyranny in all its forms; that he was in the widest and highest sense a friend of his race; that his head was as clear as his heart was good, and that he had the courage to speak his honest thought. Under these circumstances I had hoped that you would for the moment forget your religious prejudices and submit to the enlightened judgment of the world the evidence you had, or could obtain, affecting in any way the character of so great and so generous a man. This you have refused to do. In my judgment, you have mistaken the temper of even your own readers. A large majority of the religious people of this country have, to a considerable extent, outgrown the prejudices of their fathers. They are willing to know the truth and the whole truth, about the life and death of Thomas Paine. They will not thank you for having presented them the moss-covered, the maimed and distorted traditions of ignorance, prejudice, and credulity. By this course you will convince them not of the wickedness of Paine, but of your own unfairness.

What crime had Thomas Paine committed that he should have feared to die? The only answer you can give is, that he denied the inspiration of the Scriptures. If this is a crime, the civilized world is filled with criminals. The pioneers of human thought —the intellectual leaders of the world—the foremost men in every science—the kings of literature and art—those who stand in the front rank of investigation—the men who are civilizing, elevating, instructing, and refining mankind, are to-day unbelievers in the dogma of inspiration. Upon this question, the intellect of Christendom agrees with the conclusions reached by the genius of Thomas Paine. Centuries ago a noise was made for the purpose of frightening mankind. Orthodoxy is the echo of that noise.

The man who now regards the Old Testament as in any sense a sacred or inspired book is, in my judgment, an intellectual and moral deformity. There is in it so much that is cruel, ignorant, and ferocious that it is to me a matter of amazement that it was ever thought to be the work of a most merciful deity.

Upon the question of inspiration Thomas Paine gave his honest opinion. Can it be that to give an honest opinion causes one to die in terror and despair? Have you in your writings been actuated by the fear of such a consequence? Why should it be taken for granted that Thomas Paine, who devoted his life to the sacred cause of freedom, should have been hissed at in the hour of death by the snakes of conscience, while editors of Presbyterian papers who defended slavery as a divine institution, and cheerfully justified the stealing of babes from the breasts of mothers, are supposed to have passed smilingly from earth to the embraces of angels? Why should you think that the heroic author of the "Rights of Man" should shudderingly dread to leave this "bank and shoal of time," while Calvin, dripping with the blood of Servetus, was anxious to be judged of God? Is it possible that the persecutors—the instigators of the massacre of St. Bartholomew—the inventors and users of thumb-screws, and iron boots, and racks—the burners and tearers of human flesh—the stealers, whippers and enslavers of men—the buyers and beaters of babes and mothers—the founders of inquisitions—the makers of chains, the builders of dungeons, the slanderers of the living and the calumniators of the dead, all died in the odor of sanctity, with white, forgiven hands folded upon the breasts of peace, while the destroyers of prejudice—the apostles of humanity—the soldiers of liberty—the breakers of fetters—the creators of light—died surrounded with the fierce fiends of fear?

In your attempt to destroy the character of Thomas Paine you have failed, and have succeeded only in leaving a stain upon your own. You have written words as cruel, bitter and heartless as the creed of Calvin. Hereafter you will stand in the pillory of history as a defamer—a calumniator of the dead. You will be known as the man who said that Thomas Paine, the "Author Hero," lived a drunken, cowardly and beastly life, and died a drunken and beastly death. These infamous words will be branded upon the forehead of your reputation. They will be remembered against you when all else you may have uttered shall have passed from the memory of men.

ROBERT G. INGERSOLL.

THE OBSERVER'S SECOND ATTACK.*

TOM PAINE AGAIN.

In the *Observer* of September 27th, in response to numerous calls from different parts of the country for information, and in fulfillment of a promise, we presented a mass of testimony, chiefly from persons with whom we had been personally acquainted, establishing the truth of our assertions in regard to the dissolute life and miserable end of Paine. It was not a pleasing subject for discussion, and an apology, or at least an explanation, is due to our readers for resuming it, and for occupying so much space, or any space, in exhibiting the truth and the proofs in regard to the character of a man who had become so debased by his intemperance, and so vile in his habits, as to be excluded, for many years before and up to the time of his death, from all decent society.

Our reasons for taking up the subject at all, and for presenting at this time so much additional testimony in regard to the facts of the case, are these: At different periods for the last fifty years, efforts

* From the *N. Y. Observer* of Nov. 1, 1877.

have been made by Infidels to revive and honor the memory of one whose friends would honor him most by suffering his name to sink into oblivion, if that were possible. About two years since, Rev. O. B. Frothingham, of this city, came to their aid, and undertook a sort of championship of Paine, making in a public discourse this statement: "No private character has been more foully calumniated in the name of God than that of Thomas Paine." (Mr. Frothingham, it will be remembered, is the one who recently, in a public discourse, announced the downfall of Christianity, although he very kindly made the allowance that, "it may be a thousand years before its decay will be visible to all eyes." It is our private opinion that it will be at least a thousand and one.) Rev. John W. Chadwick, a minister of the same order of unbelief, who signs himself, "Minister of the Second Unitarian Society in Brooklyn," has devoted two discourses to the same end, eulogizing Paine. In one of these, which we have before us in a handsomely printed pamphlet, entitled, "Method and Value of his (Paine's) Religious Teachings," he says: "Christian usage has determined that an Infidel means one who does not believe in Christianity as a supernatural religion; in the Bible as a supernatural book; in Jesus as a supernatural person. And in this sense Paine was an Infidel, and so, thank God, am I." It is proper to add that Unitarians generally decline all responsibility for the utterances of both of these men, and that they compose a denomination, or rather two denominations, of their own.

There is also a certain class of Infidels who are not quite prepared to meet the odium that attaches to the name; they call themselves Christians, but their sympathies are all with the enemies of Christianity, and they are not always able to conceal it. They have not the courage of their opinions, like Mr. Frothingham and Mr. Chadwick, and they work only sideways toward the same end. We have been no little amused since our last article on this subject appeared, to read some of the articles that have been written on the other side, though professedly on no side, and to observe how sincerely these men deprecate the discussion of the character of Paine, as an unprofitable topic. It never appeared to them unprofitable when the discussion was on the other side.

Then, too, we have for months past been receiving letters from different parts of the country, asking authentic information on the subject and stating that the followers of Paine are making extraordinary efforts to circulate his writings against the Christian religion, and in order to give currency to these writings they are endeavoring to rescue his name from the disgrace into which it sank during the latter years of his life. Paine spent several of his last years in furnishing a commentary upon his Infidel principles. This commentary was contained in his besotted, degraded life and miserable end, but his friends do not wish the commentary to go out in connection with his writings. They prefer to have them read without the comments by their author. Hence this anxiety to free the great apostle of Infidelity from the obloquy which his life brought upon his name; to represent him as a pure, noble, virtuous man, and to make it appear that he died a peaceful, happy death, just like a philosopher.

But what makes the publication of the facts in the case still more imperative at this time is the wholesale accusation brought against the Christian public by the friends and admirers of Paine. Christian ministers as a class, and Christian journals are expressly accused of falsifying history, of defaming "the mighty dead!" (meaning Paine,) &c., &c. In the face of all these accusations it cannot be out of place to state the facts and to fortify the statement by satisfactory evidence, as we are abundantly able to do.

The two points on which we proposed to produce the testimony are, the character of Paine's life (referring of course to his last residence in this country, for no one has intimated that he had sunk into such besotted drunkenness until about the time of his return to the United States in 1802), and the real character of his death as consistent with such a life, and as marked further by the cowardliness, which has been often exhibited by Infidels in the same circumstances.

It is nothing at all to the purpose to show, as his friends are fond of doing, that Paine rendered important service to the cause of American Independence. This is not the point under discussion and is not denied. No one ever called in question the valuable service that Benedict Arnold rendered to the country in the early part of the Revolutionary war; but this, with true Americans, does not suffice to cast a shade of loveliness or even to spread a mantle of charity over his subsequent career. Whatever share Paine had in the personal friendship of the fathers of the Revolution he forfeited by his subsequent life of beastly drunkenness and degradation, and on this account as well as on account of his blasphemy he was shunned by all decent people.

We wish to make one or two corrections of misstatements by Paine's advocates, on which a vast amount of argument has been simply wasted. We have never stated in any form, nor have we ever supposed, that Paine actually renounced his Infidelity. The accounts agree in stating that he died a blaspheming Infidel, and his horrible death we regard as one of the fruits, the fitting complement of his Infidelity. We have never seen anything that encouraged the hope that he was not abandoned of God in his last hours. But we have no doubt, on the other hand, that having become a wreck in body and mind through his intemperance, abandoned of God, deserted by his Infidel companions, and dependent upon Christian charity for the attentions he received, miserable beyond description in his condition, and seeing nothing to hope for in the future, he was afraid to die, and was ready to call upon God and upon Christ for mercy, and ready perhaps in the next minute to blaspheme. This is what we referred to in speaking of Paine's death as cowardly. It is shown in the testimony we have produced, and still more fully in that which we now present. The most wicked men are ready to call upon God in seasons of great peril, and sometimes ask for Christian ministrations when in extreme illness; but they are often ready on any alleviation of distress to turn to their wickedness again, in the expressive language of Scripture, "as the sow that was washed to her wallowing in the mire."

We have never stated or intimated, nor, so far as we are aware, has any one of our correspondents stated, that Paine died in poverty. It has been frequently and truthfully stated that Paine was dependent on Christian charity for the attentions he received in his last days, and so he was. His Infidel companions forsook him and Christian hearts and hands ministered to his wants, notwithstanding the blasphemies of his death-bed.

Nor has one of our correspondents stated, as alleged, that Paine died at New Rochelle. The Rev. Dr. Wickham, who was a resident of that place nearly fifty years ago, and who was perfectly familiar with the facts of his life, wrote that Paine spent "his latter days" on the farm presented to him by the State of New York, which was strictly true, but made no reference to it as the place of his death.

Such misrepresentations serve to show how much the advocates of Paine admire "truth."

With these explanations we produce further evidence in regard to the manner of Paine's life and the character of his death, both of which we have already characterized in appropriate terms, as the following testimony will show.

In regard to Paine's "personal habits," even before his return to this country, and particularly his aversion to soap and water, Elkana Watson, a gentleman of the highest social position, who resided in France during a part of the Revolutionary war, and who was the personal friend of Washington, Franklin, and other patriots of the period, makes some incidental statements in his "Men and Times of the Revolution." Though eulogizing Paine's efforts in behalf of American Independence, he describes him as "coarse and uncouth in his manners, loathsome in his appearance, and a disgusting egotist." On Paine's arrival at Nantes, the Mayor and other distinguished citizens called upon him to pay their respects to the American patriot. Mr. Watson says: "He was soon rid of his respectable visitors, who left the room with marks of astonishment and disgust." Mr. W., after much entreaty, and only by promising him a bundle of newspapers to read while undergoing the operation, succeeded in prevailing on Paine to "stew, for an hour, in a hot bath." Mr. W. accompanied Paine to the bath, and "instructed the keeper, in French, (which Paine did not understand,) gradually to increase the heat of the water until '*le Monsieur serait bien bouillé*' (until the gentleman shall be well boiled;) and adds that "he became so much absorbed in his reading that he was nearly parboiled before leaving the bath, much to his improvement and my satisfaction."

William Carver has been cited as a witness in behalf of Paine, and particularly as to his "personal habits." In a letter to Paine, dated December 2, 1776, he bears the following testimony:

"A respectable gentlemen from New Rochelle called to see me a few days back, and said that everybody was tired of you there, and no one would undertake to board and lodge you. I thought this was the case, as I found you at a tavern in a most miserable situation. You appeared as if you had not been shaved for a fortnight, and as to a shirt, it could not be said that you had one on. It was only the remains of one, and this, likewise, appeared not to have been off your back for a fortnight, and was nearly the color of tanned leather; and you had the most disagreeable smell possible; just like that of our poor beggars in England. Do you remember the pains I took to clean you? that I got a tub of warm water and soap and washed you from head to foot, and this I had to do three times before I could get you clean." (And then follow more disgusting details.)

"You say, also, that you found your own liquors during the time you boarded with me; but you should have said, 'I found only a small part of the liquor I drank during my stay with you; this part I purchased of John Fellows, which was a demijohn of brandy containing four gallons, and this did not serve me three weeks.' This can be proved, and I mean not to say anything that I cannot prove; for I hold truth as a precious jewel. It is a well-known fact, that you drank one quart of brandy per day, at my expense, during the different times that you have boarded with me, the demijohn above mentioned excepted, and the last fourteen weeks you were sick. Is not this a supply of liquor for dinner and supper?"

This chosen witness in behalf of Paine, closes his letter, which is full of loathsome descriptions of Paine's manner of life, as follows:

"Now, sir, I think I have drawn a complete portrait of your character; yet to enter upon every minutiæ would be to give a history of your life, and to develop the fallacious mask of hypocrisy and deception under which you have acted in your political as well as moral capacity of life."

(Signed) "WILLIAM CARVER."

Carver had the same opinion of Paine to his dying day. When an old man, and an Infidel of the Paine type and habits, he was visited by the Rev. E. F. Hatfield, D.D., of this city, who writes to us of his interview with Carver, under date of Sept. 27, 1877:

"I conversed with him nearly an hour. I took special pains to learn from him all that I could about Paine, whose landlord he had been for eighteen months. He spoke of him as a base and shameless drunkard, utterly destitute of moral principle. His denunciations of the man were perfectly fearful, and fully confirmed, in my apprehension, all that had been written of Paine's immorality and repulsiveness."

Cheetham's Life of Paine, which was published the year that he died, and which has passed through several editions (we have three of them now before us) describes a man lost to all moral sensibility and to all sense of decency, a habitual drunkard, and it is simply incredible that a book should have appeared so soon after the death of its subject and should have been so frequently republished without being at once refuted, if the testimony were not substantially true. Many years later, when it was found necessary to bolster up the reputation of Paine, Cheetham's Memoirs were called a pack of lies. If only one-tenth part of what he publishes circumstantially in his volume, as facts in regard to Paine, were true, all that has been written against him in later years does not begin to set forth the degraded character of the man's life. And with all that has been written on the subject we see no good reason to doubt the substantial accuracy of Cheetham's portrait of the man whom he knew so well.

Dr. J. W. Francis, well-known as an eminent physician, of this city, in his Reminiscences of New York, says of Paine:

"He who, in his early days, had been associated with, and had received counsel from Franklin, was, in his old age, deserted by the humblest menial; he, whose pen has proved a very sword among nations, had shaken empires, and made kings tremble, now yielded up the mastery to the most treacherous of tyrants, King Alcohol."

The physician who attended Paine during his last illness was Dr. James R. Manley, a gentleman of the highest character. A letter of his, written in October of the year that Paine died, fully corroborates the account of his state as recorded by Stephen Grellet in his Memoirs, which we have already printed. He writes:

"New York, October 2, 1809: I was called upon by accident to visit Mr. Paine, on the 25th of February last, and found him indisposed with fever, and very apprehensive of an attack of apoplexy, as he stated that he had that disease before, and at this time felt a great degree of vertigo, and was unable to help himself as he had hitherto done, on account of an intense pain above the eyes. On inquiry of the attendants I was told that three or four days previously he had concluded to dispense with his usual quantity of accustomed stimulus and that he had on that day resumed it. To the want of his usual drink they attributed his illness, and it is highly probable that the usual quantity operating upon a state of system more excited from the above privations, was the cause of the symptoms of which he then complained. . . . And here let me be permitted to observe (lest blame might attach to those whose business it was to pay any particular attention to his cleanliness of person) that it was absolutely impossible to effect that purpose. Cleanliness appeared to make no part of his comfort; he seemed to have a singular aversion to soap and water; he would never ask to be washed, and when he was he would always make objections; and it was not unusual to wash and to dress him clean very much against his inclinations. In this deplorable state, with confirmed dropsy, attended with frequent cough, vomiting and hiccough, he continued growing from bad to worse till the morning of the 8th of June, when he died. Though I may remark that during the last three weeks of his life his situation was such that his decease was confidently expected every day, his ulcers having assumed a gangrenous appearance, being excessively fetid, and discolored blisters having taken place on the soles of his feet without any ostensible cause, which baffled the usual attempts to arrest their progress; and when we consider his former habits, his advanced age, the feebleness of his constitution, his constant habit of using ardent spirits *ad libitum* till the commencement of his last illness, so far from wondering that he died so soon, we are constrained to ask, How did he live so long? Concerning his conduct during his disease I have not much to remark, though the little I have may be somewhat interesting. Mr. Paine professed to be above the fear of death, and a great part of his conversation was principally directed to give the impression that he was perfectly willing to leave this world, and yet some parts of his conduct were with difficulty reconcilable with his belief. In the first stages of his illness he was satisfied to be left alone during the day, but he required some person to be with him at night, urging as his reason that he was afraid that he should die when unattended, and at this period his deportment and his principle seemed to be consistent; so much so that a stranger would judge from some of the remarks he would make that he was an Infidel. I recollect being with him at night, watching; he was very apprehensive of a speedy dissolution, and suffered great distress of body, and perhaps of mind (for he was waiting the event of an application to the Society of Friends for permission that his corpse might be deposited in their grave-ground, and had reason to believe that the request might be refused), when he remarked in these words, 'I think I can say what *they* made Jesus Christ to say—"My God, my God! why hast thou forsaken me?" He went on to observe on the want of that respect which he conceived he merited, when I observed to him that I thought his corpse should be matter of least concern to him; that those whom he would leave behind him would see that he was properly interred, and, further, that it would be of little consequence to *me* where I was deposited provided I was buried; upon which he answered that he had nothing else to talk about, and that he would as lief talk of his death as of anything, but that he was not so indifferent about his corpse as I appeared to be.

" During the latter part of his life, though his conversation was equivocal, his conduct was singular; he could not be left alone night or day; he not only required to have some person with him, but he must see that he or she was there, and would not allow his curtain to be closed at any time; and if, as it would sometimes unavoidably happen, he was left alone, he would scream and halloo until some person came to him. When relief from pain would admit, he seemed thoughtful and contemplative, his eyes being generally closed, and his hands folded upon his breast, although he never slept without the assistance of an anodyne. There was something remarkable in his conduct about this period (which comprises about two weeks immediately preceding his death), particularly when we reflect that Thomas Paine was the author of the 'Age of Reason.' He would call out during his paroxysms of distress, without intermission, 'O Lord help me! God help me! Jesus Christ help me! Lord help me!' etc., repeating the same expressions without the least variation, in a tone of voice that would alarm the house. It was this conduct which induced me to think that he had abandoned his former opinions, and I was more inclined to that belief when I understood from his nurse (who is a very serious and, I believe, pious woman), that he would occasionally inquire, when he saw her engaged with a book, what she was reading, and, being answered, and at the same time asked whether she should read aloud, he assented, and would appear to give particular attention.

"I took occasion during the nights of the fifth and sixth of June to test the strength of his opinions respecting revelation. I purposely made him a very late visit; it was a time which seemed to suit exactly with my errand; it was midnight, he was in great distress, constantly exclaiming in the words above mentioned, when, after a considerable preface, I addressed him in the following manner, the nurse being present: 'Mr. Paine, your opinions, by a large portion of the community, have been treated with deference, you have never been in the habit of mixing in your conversation words of coarse meaning; you have never indulged in the practice of profane swearing; you must be sensible that we are acquainted with your religious opinions as they are given to the world. What must we think of your present conduct? Why do you call upon Jesus Christ to help you? Do you believe that he can help you? Do you believe in the divinity of Jesus Christ? Come, now, answer me honestly. I want an answer from the lips of a dying man, for I verily believe that you will not live twenty-four hours.' I waited some time at the end of every question; he did not answer, but ceased to exclaim in the above manner. Again I addressed him; 'Mr. Paine, you have not answered my questions; will you answer them? Allow me to ask again, do you believe? or let me qualify the question, do you wish to believe that Jesus Christ is the Son of God?' After a pause of some minutes, he answered, 'I have no wish to believe on that subject.' I then left him, and knew not whether he afterward spoke to any person on any subject, though he lived, as I before observed, till the morning of the 8th. Such conduct, under usual circumstances, I conceive absolutely unaccountable, though, with diffidence, I would remark, not so much so in the present instance; for though the first necessary and general result of conviction be a sincere wish to atone for evil committed, yet it may be a question worthy of able consideration whether excessive pride of opinion, consummate vanity, and inordinate self-love might not prevent or retard that otherwise natural consequence. For my own part, I believe that had not Thomas Paine been such a distinguished Infidel he would have left less equivocal evidences of a change of opinion. Concerning the persons who visited Mr. Paine in his distress as his personal friends, I heard very little, though I may observe that their number was small, and of that number there were not wanting those who endeavored to support him in his deistical opinions, and to encourage him to 'die like a man,' to 'hold fast his integrity,' lest Christians, or, as they were pleased to term them, hypocrites, might take advantage of his weakness, and furnish themselves with a weapon by which they might hope to destroy their glorious system of morals. Numbers visited him from motives of benevolence and Christian charity, endeavoring to effect a change of mind in respect to his religious sentiments. The labor of such was apparently lost, and they pretty generally received such treatment from him as none but good men would risk a second time, though some of those persons called frequently."

The following testimony will be new to most of our readers. It is from a letter written by Bishop Fenwick (Roman Catholic Bishop of Boston), containing a full account of a visit which he paid to Paine in his last illness. It was printed in the *United States Catholic Magazine* for 1846; in the *Catholic Herald* of Philadelphia, October 15, 1846; in a supplement to the *Hartford Courant*, October 23, 1847; and in *Littell's Living Age* for January 22, 1848, from which we copy. Bishop Fenwick writes:

" A short time before Paine died I was sent for by him. He was prompted to this by a poor Catholic woman who went to see him in his sickness, and who told him, among other things, that in his wretched condition if anybody could do him any good it would be a Roman Catholic priest. This woman was an American convert (formerly a Shaking Quakeress) whom I had received into the church but a few weeks before. She was the bearer of this message to me from Paine. I stated this circumstance to F. Kohlmann, at breakfast, and requested him to accompany me. After some solicitation on my part he agreed to do so, at which I was greatly rejoiced, because I was at the time quite young and inexperienced in the ministry, and was glad to have his assistance, as I knew, from the great reputation of Paine, that I should have to do with one of the most impious as well as infamous of men. We shortly after set out for the house at Greenwich where Paine lodged, and on the way agreed on a mode of proceeding with him.

"We arrived at the house; a decent-looking elderly woman (probably his housekeeper,) came to the door and inquired whether we were the Catholic priests, for said she, 'Mr. Paine has been so much annoyed of late by other denominations calling upon him that he has left express orders with me to admit no one to-day but the clergymen of the Catholic Church. Upon assuring her that we were Catholic clergymen she opened the door and showed us into the parlor. She then left the room and shortly after returned to inform us that Paine was asleep, and, at the same time, expressed a wish that we would not disturb him, 'for,' said she, 'he is always in a bad humor when roused out of his sleep. It is better we wait a little till he be awake.' We accordingly sat down and resolved to await a more favorable moment. 'Gentlemen,' said the lady, after having taken her seat also, 'I really wish you may succeed with Mr. Paine, for he is laboring under great distress of mind ever since he was informed by his physicians that he cannot possibly live and must die shortly. He sent for you to-day because he was told that if any one could do him good you might. Possibly he may think you know of some remedy which his physicians are ignorant of. He is truly to be pitied. His cries when he is left alone are heart-rending. 'O Lord help me!' he will exclaim during his paroxysms of distress—'God help me—Jesus Christ help me!' repeating the same expressions without the least variation, in a tone of voice that would alarm the house. Sometimes he will say, 'O God, what have I done to suffer so much!' then, shortly after, 'But there is no God,' and again a little after, 'Yet if there should be, what would become of me hereafter.'

Thus he will continue for some time, when on a sudden he will scream, as if in terror and agony, and call out for me by name. On one of these occasions, which are very frequent, I went to him and inquired what he wanted. 'Stay with me,' he replied, 'for God's sake, for I cannot bear to be left alone.' I then observed that I could not always be with him, as I had much to attend to in the house. 'Then,' said he, 'send even a child to stay with me, for it is a hell to be alone.' 'I never saw,' she concluded, 'a more unhappy, a more forsaken man. It seems he cannot reconcile himself to die.'

"Such was the conversation of the woman who had received us, and who probably had been employed to nurse and take care of him during his illness. She was a Protestant, yet seemed very desirous that we should afford him some relief in his state of abandonment, bordering on complete despair. Having remained thus some time in the parlor, we at length heard a noise in the adjoining passage-way, which induced us to believe that Mr. Paine, who was sick in that room, had awoke. We accordingly proposed to proceed thither, which was assented to by the woman, and she opened the door for us. On entering, we found him just getting out of his slumber. A more wretched being in appearance I never beheld. He was lying in a bed sufficiently decent of itself, but at present besmeared with filth; his look was that of a man greatly tortured in mind; his eyes haggard, his countenance forbidding, and his whole appearance that of one whose better days had been one continued scene of debauch. His only nourishment at this time, as we were informed, was nothing more than milk punch, in which he indulged to the full extent of his weak state. He had partaken, undoubtedly, but very recently of it, as the sides and corners of his mouth exhibited very unequivocal traces of it, as well as of blood, which had also followed in the track and left its mark on the pillow. His face, to a certain extent, had also been besmeared with it."

Immediately upon their making known the object of their visit, Paine interrupted the speaker by saying: "That's enough, sir; that's enough," and again interrupting him, "I see what you would be about. I wish to hear no more from you, sir. My mind is made up on that subject. I look upon the whole of the Christian scheme to be a tissue of absurdities and lies, and Jesus Christ to be nothing more than a cunning knave and impostor." He drove them out of the room, exclaiming: "Away with you and your God, too; leave the room instantly; all that you have uttered are lies—filthy lies; and if I had a little more time I would prove it, as I did about your impostor, Jesus Christ."

This, we think, will suffice. We have a mass of letters containing statements confirmatory of what we have published in regard to the life and death of Paine, but nothing more can be required.

INGERSOLL'S SECOND REPLY.

PEORIA, Nov. 2d, 1877.

To the Editor of the New York Observer:

You ought to have honesty enough to admit that you did, in your paper of July 19th, offer to prove that the absurd story that Thomas Paine died in terror and agony on account of the religious opinions he had expressed, was true. You ought to have fairness enough to admit that you called upon me to deposit one thousand dollars with an honest man, that you might, by proving that Thomas Paine did die in terror, obtain the money.

You ought to have honor enough to admit that you challenged me and that you commenced the controversy concerning Thomas Paine.

You ought to have goodness enough to admit that you were mistaken in the charges you made.

You ought to have manhood enough to do what you falsely asserted that Thomas Paine did:—you ought to recant. You ought to admit publicly that you slandered the dead; that you falsified history; that you defamed the defenceless; that you deliberately denied what you had published in your own paper. There is an old saying to the effect that open confession is good for the soul. To you is presented a splendid opportunity of testing the truth of this saying.

Nothing has astonished me more than your lack of common honesty exhibited in this controversy. In your last, you quote from Dr. J. W. Francis. Why did you leave out that portion in which Dr. Francis says *that Cheetham with settled malignity wrote the life of Paine?* Why did you leave out that part in which Dr. Francis says that Cheetham in the same way *slandered Alexander Hamilton and De Witt Clinton?* Is it your business to suppress the truth? Why did you not publish the entire letter of Bishop Fenwick? Was it because it proved beyond all cavil that Thomas Paine did not recant? Was it because in the light of that letter Mary Roscoe, Mary Hinsdale and Grant Thorburn appeared unworthy of belief? Dr. J. W. Francis says in the same article from which you quoted, "*Paine clung to his Infidelity until the last moment of his life.*" Why did you not publish that? It was the first line immediately above what you did quote. You must have seen it. Why did you suppress it? A lawyer, doing a thing of this character, is denominated a shyster. I do not know the appropriate word to designate a theologian guilty of such an act.

You brought forward three witnesses, pretending to have personal knowledge about the life and death of Thomas Paine: Grant Thorburn, Mary Roscoe and Mary Hinsdale. In my reply I took the ground that Mary Roscoe and Mary Hinsdale must have been the same person. I thought it impossible that Paine should have had a conversation with Mary Roscoe, and then one *precisely* like it with Mary Hinsdale. Acting upon this conviction, I proceeded to show that the conversation never could have happened, that it was absurdly false to say that Paine asked the opinion of a girl as to his works who had never read but little of them. I then showed by the testimony of William Cobbett, that he visited Mary Hinsdale in 1819, taking with him a statement concerning the recantation of Paine, given him by Mr. Collins, and that upon being shown this statement she said that " it was so long ago that she could not speak positively to any part of the matter—that she would not say any part of the paper was true." At that time she knew nothing, and remembered nothing. I also showed that she was a kind of standing witness to prove that others recanted. Willett Hicks denounced her as unworthy of belief.

To-day the following from the New York *World* was received, showing that I was right in my conjecture:

TOM PAINE'S DEATH-BED.

To the Editor of the World:

SIR: I see by your paper that Bob Ingersoll discredits Mary Hinsdale's story of the scenes which occurred at the death-bed of Thomas Paine. No one who knew that good lady would for one moment doubt her veracity or question her testimony. Both she and her husband were Quaker preachers, and well known and respected inhabitants of New York City. *Ingersoll is right in his conjecture that Mary Roscoe and Mary Hinsdale was the same person.* Her maiden name was Roscoe, and she married Henry Hinsdale. My mother was a Roscoe, a niece of Mary Roscoe, and lived with her for some time. I have heard her relate the story of Tom Paine's dying remorse, as told her by her aunt, who was a witness to it. She says (in a letter I have just received from her), " he (Tom Paine) suffered fearfully from remorse, and renounced his Infidel principles, calling on God to forgive him, and wishing his pamphlets and books to be burned, saying he could not die in peace until it was done."   (REV.) A. W. CORNELL.

Harpersville, New York.

You will notice that the testimony of Mary Hinsdale has been drawing interest since 1809, and has materially increased. If Paine "suffered fearfully from remorse, renounced his Infidel opinions and called on God to forgive him," it is hardly generous for the Christian world to fasten the fangs of malice in the flesh of his reputation.

So Mary Roscoe was Mary Hinsdale, and as Mary Hinsdale has been shown by her own admission to Mr. Cobbett to have known nothing of the matter; and as Mary Hinsdale was not, according to Willet Hicks, worthy of belief—as she told a falsehood of the same kind about Mary Lockwood, and was, according to Mr. Collins, addicted to the use of opium—this disposes of her and her testimony.

There remains upon the stand Grant Thorburn. Concerning this witness, I received, yesterday, from the eminent biographer and essayist, James Parton, the following epistle:

NEWBURYPORT, MASS.

Col. R. G. Ingersoll:

Touching Grant Thorburn, I personally know him to have been a dishonest man. At the age of ninety-two he copied, with trembling hand, a piece from a newspaper and brought it to the office of the *Home Journal, as his own.* It was I who received it and detected the deliberate forgery. If you are ever going to continue this subject, I will give you the exact facts.

Fervently yours,

JAMES PARTON.

After this, you are welcome to what remains of Grant Thorburn.

There is one thing that I have noticed during this controversy regarding Thomas Paine. In no instance that I now call to mind has any Christian writer spoken respectfully of Mr. Paine. All have taken particular pains to call him "Tom" Paine. Is it not a little strange that religion should make men so coarse and ill-mannered?

I have often wondered what these same gentlemen would say if I should speak of the men eminent in the annals of Christianity in the same way. What would they say if I should write about "Tim" Dwight, old "Ad" Clark, "Tom" Scott, "Jim" McKnight, "Bill" Hamilton, "Dick" Whately, "Bill" Paley, and "Jack" Calvin?

They would *say* of me then, just what I *think* of them now.

Even if we have religion, do not let us try to get along without good manners. Rudeness is exceedingly unbecoming, even in a saint. Persons who forgive their enemies ought, to say the least, **to** treat with politeness those who have never injured them.

It is exceedingly gratifying to me that I have compelled you to say that "Paine died a blaspheming Infidel." Hereafter it is to be hoped nothing will be heard about his having recanted. As an answer to such slander his friends can confidently quote the following from the *New York Observer* of November 1st, 1877:

"WE HAVE NEVER STATED IN ANY FORM, NOR HAVE WE EVER SUPPOSED THAT PAINE ACTUALLY RENOUNCED HIS INFIDELITY. THE ACCOUNTS AGREE IN STATING THAT HE DIED A BLASPHEMING INFIDEL."

This for all coming time will refute the slanders of the churches yet to be.

Right here allow me to ask: If you never supposed that Paine renounced his Infidelity, why did you try to prove by Mary Hinsdale that which you believed to be untrue?

From the bottom of my heart I thank myself for having compelled you to admit that Thomas Paine did not recant.

For the purpose of verifying your own admission concerning the death of Mr. Paine, permit me to call your attention to the following affidavit:

WABASH, INDIANA, October 27, 1877.
Col. R. G. Ingersoll:

DEAR SIR: The following statement of facts is at your disposal. In the year 1833 Willet Hicks made a visit to Indiana and stayed over night at my father's house, four miles east of Richmond. In the morning at breakfast my mother asked Willet Hicks the following questions:

"Was thee with Thomas Paine during his last sickness?"

Mr. Hicks said: "I was with him every day during the latter part of his last sickness."

"Did he express any regret in regard to writing the 'Age of Reason,' as the published accounts say he did—those accounts that have the credit of emanating from his Catholic housekeeper?"

Mr. Hicks replied: "He did not in any way by word or action."

"Did he call on God or Jesus Christ, asking either of them to forgive his sins, or did he curse them or either of them?"

Mr. Hicks answered: "He did not. He died as easy as any one I ever saw die, and I have seen many die in my time."

WILLIAM B. BARNES.

Subscribed and sworn to before me Oct. 27, 1877.

WARREN BIGLER, Notary Public.

You say in your last that "Thomas Paine was abandoned of God." So far as this controversy is concerned, it seems to me that in that sentence you have most graphically described your own condition.

Wishing you success in all honest undertakings, I remain,

Yours truly,

Robert G. Ingersoll.

CPSIA information can be obtained at www.ICGtesting.com
Printed in the USA
LVOW010235051012

301608LV00003B/13/P